SOCIOLOGICAL PERSPECTIVES

Understanding Human Society

Merrill Sociology Series

Under the editorship of
Richard L. Simpson
University of North Carolina, Chapel Hill
and
Paul E. Mott

SOCIOLOGICAL PERSPECTIVES

Understanding Human Society

Edited by

PAUL E. MOTT
HOWARD M. KAPLAN
GEORGE J. YELAGOTES
DONALD B. PITTENGER
MARC RIEDEL

Charles E. Merrill Publishing Company
A Bell & Howell Company
Columbus, Ohio

301.08
S678

Published by
CHARLES E. MERRILL PUBLISHING CO.
A Bell & Howell Co.
Columbus, Ohio 43216

ISBN: 0-675-09044-X

Library of Congress Catalog Card Number: 72-87428

1 2 3 4 5 6 7 8 / 77 76 75 74 73

74-960

Printed in the United States of America

THE EDITORS

Howard M. Kaplan is assistant professor of sociology and research associate in Institute for Social Research, Florida State University, Tallahassee, Florida.

George J. Yelagotes is assistant professor of sociology, Millersville State College, Millersville, Pennsylvania.

Donald B. Pittenger is associate demographer, Data and Systems Bureau, New York State Office of Planning Services, Albany, New York.

Marc Riedel is lecturer, School of Social Work, University of Pennsylvania, Philadelphia, Pennsylvania.

CONTENTS

vii

III SYMBOLS, CULTURE, AND SOCIALIZATION 113

IV THE ORGANIZATION OF PEOPLE 167

PREFACE

Developing a series of readers for undergraduate sociology courses can be a very personal act. Every instructor has his own notions about what is valuable in his field and for his teaching. Some prefer the feisty stuff of so-called "pop" sociology; others want case examples of specific social problems. Classic-contemporary, functionalist-systemic, high brow-middle brow (no one will admit to less) are some of the more common forks in sociological highways.

The editors of these volumes are no exceptions. Generally dissatisfied with the readers that were available for introductory sociology, we tried to gather our own collection of articles for our introductory courses and make them available in the library. It was cumbersome and inconvenient. We sought an alternative approach. The readers in this series are the result.

Reflected in them are our values of what is useful and important in undergraduate sociology, recognizing that these values are neither better nor worse than many others. Whenever possible we wanted to publish the whole article or the continuous book segment. The snippets of articles and patchwork abridgments of book excerpts found in many readers rob the student of a full understanding of how the author thought and worked. The figure of the idea presented is separated from its ground. Of course, we violated our intention sometimes when the article or the chapter was unusually long.

We feel that there are many old "standards" that still are key works in the field; still alive with their imaginative ideas. We included many of these. Our mix of old and new acknowledges that there is much useful sociology to be found in newspapers, magazines, and governmental reports. As the "popular" written media these sources may be viewed as barometers of contemporary concern. We borrowed liberally from them. But we also confess to a bias concerning the importance of history to our field, embracing C. Wright Mills's charge to us to infuse our ideas and theories with the perspectives of history. We included a large dollop of historical materials in these readers. We hope that they demonstrate, however modestly, history's contribution to an understanding of the present. Finally, we aimed for the serious teacher and student, driving to the central ideas and concerns of the field.

Even the report on the "body ritual" practiced by the Nacirema carries a sociologically serious message. It appears in this volume's third part, "Symbols, Culture, and Socialization." With tongue in cheek, Horace Miner gives us a glimpse at a distinctly human process: only humans can create symbols, the basic units of culture; only humans can communicate the meanings of and impute significance to these symbols. The power of such shared interpretations of reality to limit, control, and even direct behavior is awesome. Consider, for example, Leslie White's comment in the first selection of this part: "[Only] man . . . uses amulets, confesses sins, makes laws, observes codes of etiquette, explains his dreams, classifies his relatives in designated categories. . . ."

Man frequently has developed belief systems founded on little more than myth, superstition, and prejudice. Why? From another perspective we often suspect that our activities and interactions have been organized in ways which work against our achieving the goals we had set out to reach. How could man-the-rational-animal be a party to such goings on? Sociological analyses can provide insights into these processes.

Awareness of *cultural* forces and the processes by which individuals come to respond to and elaborate them — this is one contribution of a sociological perspective. Awareness of *social* forces — how patterns of interaction can help shape behavior — is a second. Thus, as people are organized under different sets of rules, this volume's final section suggests, different modes of behavior can be observed. People confronted by disaster act differently than those same people do under conditions of routine activities or gradual change. We are familiar, for example, with newspaper reports of disasters which constantly play upon the "humanitarianism" and "concern for fellow citizens" demonstrated by people who normally are uninvolved or impersonal in their behavior toward others.

How do sociologists come to focus on one set of facts rather than another in their diverse attempts to render human behavior meaningful? Part II, "Sociological Perspectives," speaks to this question directly. Levels of analysis, we are told, comprise major crossroads. Are the primary variables to be cultural, socio-cultural, social, or socio-psychological? Each approach carries with it certain assumptions and limitations. In this section's concluding article, John Horton suggests that even this choice reflects an underlying perspective. Is the search for facts governed by a consensual view of the healthy society? Or is conflict the "natural condition"? Sociology students and professionals alike would do well not to underestimate the significance of this issue, a sin commited all too frequently in analyses of human situations.

Part I, "The Crisis Society," reminds the reader that these situations are best understood in the broadest context: they are timeless. Violence, drug abuse, and urban blight, for example, are societal issues today. They also created problems for nineteenth-century America and ancient Rome. These crises *are* different today; yet they also must reflect some processes common to the human condition. Our ability to understand human society depends on our ability to distinguish the specific and the generic and to build on what is significant in each. Sociological perspectives are the vehicles which can carry us forward in this continuing quest.

No preface is complete without an acknowledgment of intellectual and interpersonal debts. This is particularly true for the preface to introductory readers. Most obvious is our appreciation to the authors and publishers whose works appear here. Their permission to reprint the fruits of their scholarship gives substance to our otherwise abstract notions of what the field should offer to undergraduate sociology students. Less obvious, but no less important, is our continuing obligation to the students who have passed through our introductory sociology courses. Their demands for stimulating readings moved us to make this effort. Finally, we acknowledge the debt shared by all authors and editors fortunate enough to have concerned families and thank them for their forbearance, assistance, and encouragement throughout this effort.

PEM
HMK
GJY
DBP
MR

PART I

The
Crisis
Society

A FEELING OF CRISIS PERVADES AMERICAN SOCIETY. IT
began building in the late 1950s when black Americans
started their search for social and political equality at lunch
counters and on buses in Southern cities. In the early 1960s a
new dimension was added when Americans learned that fully
twenty percent of their population—more than thirty million
people—lived in poverty. For every black who was poor there
were three white Americans in similar straits. Furthermore,
social data revealed that this stratum of poverty had existed
for generations and confirmed that the problem was chronic.

As the 1960s continued, new problems emerged. Youth
movements of great variety appeared which despite their
variousness shared a common concern. The young people
were reacting negatively to their parents' values and to the
directions in which the society was moving. Sit-ins and strikes
at colleges and universities, protests against the war in
Vietnam, or involvement in the black protest movements were
among the more active expressions of these concerns. Withdrawal from an offensive society whether through the drug

1

culture or living in a commune, or both, were frequently chosen options.

If many of the youth cultures seemed symbolic of new forms of deviance from the traditional American norms, some of the older forms of deviance were assuming alarming proportions. The rates of serious crimes—murder, rape and robbery—were rising precipitously, particularly in the cities where people began to feel that their lives and property were increasingly threatened.

These threats were yet another reason for escaping from the city. Although the concern for the environment did not achieve popular currency until the early 1970s, urban residents had long been aware that their air was polluted, their water "tasted bad," and their rivers were no longer safe for swimming. Much of the century old move to the suburbs has been a rush to fresh air, space, and "a good place for kids." But now the problem of pollution has won overt, collective attention and the litany of environmental and human damage daily grows longer, again adding to the psychology of crisis that touches the remotest parts of our society.

The present crises seem new because we Americans never have shown much interest in our social history nor in the histories of other industrial societies. If we had, we would have found that the social problems that concern us so greatly are not new nor even of very recent vintage. Our purpose here is not to downgrade the significance of the present crises, but rather to add new dimensions in order to achieve a better understanding of human society.

Air and water pollution and the attendant problems of plague and death have been partners in human life as long as men have lived in cities. Pollution plagued the ancient Sumerians over four thousand years ago and reached monumental proportions in ancient Rome. In a selection in this section Lewis Mumford describes the pollution, poverty, tenements, and slum landlords which were entrenched features of the urban scene in ancient Rome.

Pollution increased in the Western world with the onset of the industrial revolution. Pittsburgh was shrouded with smog before 1815 and the air and rivers around Chicago were polluted before the Civil War.

This society has always had a drug problem. Before 1917 there was no national legislation forbidding the sale of addicting drugs without prescriptions. Belladonna and opium were taken routinely for ailments ranging from headaches and colds to pneumonia and tuberculosis with the result that many people unwittingly became addicted. But others—no one knows how many—deliberately took drugs to relieve the rigors of their lives: the dawn to dusk, six day work week in miserable conditions; low wages; the emptiness of family life; and the barrenness of their personal worlds. Drugs were readily available and whiskey was cheap, 25 cents a gallon in 1850 for the legally distilled variety. It was not uncommon for parents to give opium derivatives to their children to keep them quiet. More evidence that the drug problem is not new is found in a selection from O'Donnell and Ball's book on narcotic addiction.

Nor are the problems of prevalent crime and violence new. In its report the National Commission on the Causes and Prevention of Violence showed that although we are now at a relatively high peak of violence, there have been other, equally serious periods of violence in our history. Fear for personal safety was widespread in American cities in the late 1700s and resulted in the development of police forces during the next fifty years. In the second volume in this series the historian, Richard Wade, describes this and other growing pains of early American frontier cities.

This recital could be continued at length and documented in detail, but the point is that if the American society is a crisis society today, then it has been one for at least 150 years.

If this is so, then our perspective changes and new questions emerge. Why do these problems exist and why have they resisted solution? Why has our society been less successful at coping with them than some other Western nations?

The Violence Commission starts us in the direction of answering these questions. When it looked for the sources of violence, it looked to the social structure and the wheeling social forces within it. In effect, the Commission said the ways in which we organize ourselves into factories and nuclear families, into cities and social classes, give rise to our problems. This idea that the way human beings routinely relate to each other can provoke unexpected problems is illustrated in William F. Whyte's study of restaurants. He shows that changes in the organization of restaurants can cause problems and that one pattern of relationships between waitresses and cooks caused the waitresses tension and upset. This relationship between social structure and human behavior and social problems is a part of the core concerns of sociology.

The Violence Commission suggests that some American values and beliefs are at the root of the problem. It also notes that people's rising expectations are a source of violence. The first points to our culture, the second to changing attitudes. These concerns—culture and the social-psychology of individuals—along with the already mentioned concern about social structure form the base of sociology. In the next section we will spell out in more detail how these concepts are used by sociologists.

Violence
in
America

I. THE COMMONALITY OF COLLECTIVE VIOLENCE IN THE WESTERN TRADITION

Future historians may marvel at the ostensible "rediscovery" of violence that has both fascinated and bemused contemporary observers. That the recent resurgence of collective nonmilitary violence in Western society is widely regarded as anomalous probably reflects both a cultural and a contemporary bias. We have tended to assume, perhaps unconsciously, that such violence was an uncivilized practice of more primitive societies that the civilized and affluent West had largely outgrown. Our historians have themselves been guilty of contributing to this popular illusion; while they have retained their fascination for military exploits, they have tended either to ignore the persistence of domestic turmoil except when it reached revolutionary proportions, or to minimize its significance by viewing it from the perspective of established authority. When viewed from the top down, violence was understandably regarded as an abnormal and undesirable breach of the public order.

On the contrary, Tilly concludes, "collective violence is normal."

Historically, collective violence has flowed regularly out of the central, political processes of western countries. Men seeking to seize, hold, or realign the levers of power have continually engaged in collective violence as part of their struggles. The oppressed have struck in the name of justice, the privileged in the name of order, those in between in the name of fear.

In Tilly's analysis, collective violence in the European experience was fundamentally transformed but not foredoomed by the processes of in-

Reprinted from United States National Commission on the Causes and Prevention of Violence, *Violence in America: Historical and Comparative Perspectives,* Report of the Task Force on Historical and Comparative Perspectives, Hugh Davis Graham and Ted Robert Gurr, Codirectors (Washington, D.C.: United States Government Printing Office, 1969): 621-35.

dustrialization and urbanization. The old "primitive" forms of violence in feudal Europe—such as communal feuds and religious persecutions—were characterized by small scale, local scope, communal group participation, and inexplicit and unpolitical objectives. The subsequent evolution of the nation-state prompted such "reactionary" disturbances as food riots, Luddite destruction, tax revolts, and anticonscription rebellions. Although industrialization and urbanization muted such disorders by disrupting their cohesive communal base, the metropolitan society these forces forged gave rise to "modern" forms of protest—such as demonstrations and strikes—which involved relatively large and specialized associations with relatively well-defined and "forward-looking" objectives and which were explicitly organized for political or economic action.

Tilly's model suggests that modern collective protest, owing to its broader associational base, is more likely to occur on a large scale. But modern protest is less likely to become violent because the associational form gives the group a surer control over its own actions, and thus permits shows of force without concomitant damage or bloodshed. Moreover, the historic shift from communal to associational bases for collective protest brought into being a number of modern nonviolent mechanisms for the regulation of conflicts: the strike, the demonstration, the parliament, and the political campaign. Collective violence, then, historically belongs to political life, and changes in its form tell us that something important is happening to the political system itself.

What is happening to the political system in contemporary America? Preliminary to such an inquiry is the historical task of surveying the patterns of group violence that have accompanied the development of the United States. Brown has traced an overview of American collective violence, and his organizational categories of "negative" and "positive" violence in some ways parallel Tilly's analytical distinctions between reactionary disturbances, which center on rights once enjoyed but now threatened, and modern disturbances, which center on rights not yet enjoyed but now within reach. It might be more appropriate in this conclusion to discuss the American historical legacy of violence in relation to the contemporary relevance of the various categories Brown employed. Brown catalogued as "negative" forms of American violence that associated with feuds, lynching, political assassination, free-lance multiple murder, crime, ethnic and racial prejudice, and urban rioting. "Positive" forms were associated with the American Revolution and Civil War, agrarian uprisings, labor protests, vigilantism, Indian wars, and police violence.

Perhaps the historically violent episode that is least relevant to our contemporary concerns is the family feud. The famous and colorful clan feuding seems to have been triggered by the Civil War in border areas where loyalties were sharply divided and where the large extended family of the 19th century provided both a locus for intense loyalties and a ready instrument of aggression. But this tradition has waned with the fading of the circumstances that conditioned its birth. It is arguable, however, that the brutalizing traditions associated with the Indian wars have left their callous imprint on our national character long after the estimated 850,000 American Indians had been ruthlessly reduced by 1950 to 400,000. Similarly, the violence associated with the American Revolution, the Civil War, and Reconstruction has surely reinforced the ancient notion that the ends justify the means, and clearly the defeat of the Confederacy and the failure of Reconstruction has convinced generations of white Southerners that Negro political participation and Federal efforts at reform are irrevocably linked with corruption and subversion.

Whether the long association with violence of agrarian uprisings and the labor movement has permanently faded with changing modern circumstances is fervently to be hoped, but by no means certain. Employer acceptance of unions during and after the New Deal suggests that that long and bloody conflict is largely behind us. But the stubborn persistence of rural poverty constitutes a latent invitation to a resurgence of latter-day populism.

Two other sordid American traditions that have largely waned but that recently have shown some signs of revival are vigilantism and lynching. Although vigilantism is associated in the popular mind with such frontier and rural practices as antirustler and antihorsethief popular "justice" in areas largely devoid of regular enforcement agencies, the largest local American vigilance committee was organized in San Francisco in 1856. If vigilantism is defined more broadly to include regional and even national movements as well as local organizations, then America's preeminent vigilante movement has been the Ku Klux Klan—or rather, the Ku Klux Klans, for there have essentially been three of them. The original Klan arose in the South in response to radical Reconstruction, and through terror and intimidation was instrumental in the "redemption" of the Southern state governments by white conservatives. The second Klan, by far the largest, was resurrected in Atlanta in 1915 and boomed nationally in the 1920's. Strong in the Midwest and Far West as well as the South, and making inroads even in the cities, the Klan of the 1920's—despite its traditional racist and xenophobic rhetoric—focused its chastisement less upon Negroes, Catholics, and Jews than upon local white Protestants who were adjudged guilty of violating smalltown America's Victorian moral code. The third Klan represented a proliferation of competing Klans in the South in response to the civil rights movement of the 1950's. Generally lacking the prestige and organizational strength of the earlier Klans, these groups engaged in a period of unrestrained terrorism in the rural and smalltown Black Belt South in the 1950's and early 1960's, but have belatedly been brought under greater control.

Lynching, vigilantism's supreme instrument of terror and summary "justice," has been widely practiced in America certainly since the Revolutionary era, when miscreant Tories were tarred and feathered, and worse. Although lynching is popularly associated with racial mob murder, this pattern is a relatively recent one, for prior to the late 19 century, white Americans perforce lynched one another—Negro slaves being far too valuable to squander at the stake. But lynching became predominantly racial from 1882 to 1903, when 1,985 Negroes were murdered in the tragic but successful effort of those years to forge a rigid system of biracial caste, most brutal and explicit in the South but generally reflective of national attitudes. Once the point—that this was a white man's country—was made, lynching gradually declined. Its recent resurgence in response to the civil rights movement is notorious, but it nowhere approximates its scale at the turn of the century.

The contemporary relevance of political assassination and freelance multiple murder needs no documentation to a nation that has so recently witnessed the murders of John and Robert Kennedy, Dr. Martin Luther King, and, on television, Lee Harvey Oswald—in addition to the chilling mass slaughtering sprees of Charles Whitman in Austin, Texas, and Richard Speck in Chicago. Historically, political assassination has become a recurrent feature of the political system only in the South during (the first) Reconstruction and in New Mexico Territory. Although four American Presidents have been assassinated since 1865, prominent politicans and civil servants occupying the myriad lesser levels of government have been largely immune. Whether the current spate of public murder is an endemic symptom of a new social malaise is a crucial question that history cannot yet answer, other than to observe that precedents in our past are minimal.

Similarly, historical precedents are few regarding massive student and anti-war protests. American students have historically succumbed to the annual spring throes of the panty-raid syndrome, but the current wave of campus confrontations is essentially an unprecedented phenomenon—as is the massive and prolonged opposition to the war in Vietnam. As Professor Brooks has observed, "unfortunately the past does not have much to tell us; we will have to make our own history along uncharted and frightening ways."

But the past has much to tell us about the rioting and crime that have gripped our cities. Urban mobs are as old as the city itself. Colonial seaports frequently were rocked for days by roving mobs—groups of unruly and often drunken men whose energies were shrewdly put to political purpose as Liberty Boys in the American Revolution. Indeed, our two principal instruments of physical control evolved directly in response to 19th-century urban turmoil. The professional city police system replaced the inadequate constabulary and watch-and-ward in response to the rioting of the 1840's and 1850's, largely in the Northeast. Similarly, the national guard was organized in order to control the labor violence—or more appropriately, the antilabor violence—of the 1880's and 1890's.

Probably all nations are given to a kind of historical amnesia or selective recollection that masks unpleasant traumas of the past. Certainly Americans since the Puritans have historically regarded themselves as a latter-day "Chosen People" sent on a holy errand to the wilderness, there to create a New Jerusalem. One beneficent side effect of our current turmoil may be to force a harder and more candid look at our past and at our behavior in comparison with other peoples and nations.

II. CONTEMPORARY AMERICAN VIOLENCE IN HISTORICAL PERSPECTIVE

Our current eruption of violence must appear paradoxical to a generation of Americans who witnessed the successful emergence from depression to unparalleled affluence of a nation they regarded as the world's moral leader in defense of freedom. Only a decade ago America's historians were celebrating the emergence of a unique society, sustained by a burgeoning prosperity and solidly grounded on a broad political consensus. We were told—and the implications were reassuring—that our uniqueness was derived from at least half a dozen historical sources which, mutually reinforcing one another, had joined to propel us toward a manifestly benevolent destiny. We were a nation of immigrants, culturally enriched by the variety of mankind. Sons of the frontier, our national character has grown to reflect the democratic individualism and pragmatic ingenuity that had conquered the wilderness. Our new nation was born in anticolonial revolution and in its crucible was forged a democratic republic of unparalleled vitality and longevity. Lacking a feudal past, our political spectrum was so truncated about the consensual liberal center that, unlike Europe, divisive radicalism of the left or right had found no sizable constituency. Finally, we had both created and survived the great transformation from agrarian frontier to industrial metropolis, to become the richest nation of all time.

It was a justly proud legacy, one which seemed to make sense in the relatively tranquil 1950's. But with the 1960's came shock and frustration. It was a decade against itself: the students of affluence were marching in the streets; middle-class matrons were besieging the Pentagon; and Negro Americans were responding to victories in civil rights and to their collectively unprecedented prosperity with a paradoxical venting of outrage. In a fundamental sense, history—the ancient human encounter

with poverty, defeat, and guilt as well as with affluence, victory, and innocence—had finally caught up with America. Or at least it had caught up
with white America.

Historical analysis of our national experience and character would
suggest that the seeds of our contemporary discontent were to a large
extent deeply embedded in those same ostensibly benevolent forces which
contributed to our uniqueness. First, we are a nation of immigrants, but
one in which the original dominant immigrant group, the so-called Anglo-
Saxons, effectively preempted the crucial levers of economic and political
power in government, commerce, and the professions. This elite group has
tenaciously resisted the upward strivings of successive "ethnic" immigrant
waves. The resultant competitive hierarchy of immigrants has always been
highly conducive to violence, but this violence has taken different forms.
The Anglo-Americans have used their access to the levers of power to
maintain their dominance, using legal force surrounded by an aura of
legitimacy for such ends as economic exploitation; the restriction of
immigration by a national-origin quota system which clearly branded later
immigrants as culturally undesirable; the confinement of the original
Indian immigrants largely to barren reservations; and the restriction of
blacks to a degraded caste. But the system was also conducive to violence
among the latter groups themselves—when, for instance, Irish-Americans
rioted against Afro-American "scabs." Given America's unprecedented
ethnic pluralism, simply being born American conferred no automatic and
equal citizenship in the eyes of the larger society. In the face of such
reservations, ethnic minorities had constantly to affirm their Americanism
through a kind of patriotic ritual which intensified the ethnic competition
for status. As a fragment culture based on bourgeois-liberal values, as
Hartz has observed, yet one populated by an unprecedented variety of
immigrant stock, America's tightened consensus on what properly constituted "Americanism" prompted status rivalries among the ethnic
minorities which, when combined with economic rivalries, invited severe
and abiding conflict.

Most distinctive among the immigrant minorities was the Negro. The
eternal exception in American history, Afro-Americans were among the
first to arrive and the last to emerge. To them, America meant slavery, and
manumission meant elevation to the cast of black pariah. Comer has seen
in the psychological legacy of slavery and caste a psychically crippling
Negro dependency and even self-hatred which is largely immune to mere
economic advance. The contemporary black awareness of this tenacious
legacy of racial shame is abundantly reflected in the radical rhetoric of
black power and "Black-is-Beautiful," and goes far toward resolving the
paradox of black rebellion against a backdrop of general—albeit uneven,
as Davies suggests—economic improvement. Meier and Rudwick have

charted the transformation of racial violence from white pogrom to black aggression—or, in the analysis of Janowitz, from "communal" to "commodity" rioting. While emphasizing that the transformation has led to violent black assault less against white persons than against white property, and while Janowitz speculates that the summer of 1968 may have been yet another turning point, we are reminded that history, even very recent history, is an imperfect guide to the future.

The second major formative historical experience was America's uniquely prolonged encounter with the frontier. While the frontier experience indubitably strengthened the mettle of the American character, it witnessed the brutal and brutalizing ousting of the Indians and the forceful incorporation of Mexican and other original inhabitants, as Frantz has so graphically portrayed. Further, it concomitantly created an environment in which, owing to the paucity of law enforcement agencies, a tradition of vigilante "justice" was legitimized. The longevity of the Ku Klux Klan and the vitality both of contemporary urban rioting and of the stiffening resistance to it owe much to this tradition. As Brown has observed, vigilantism has persisted as a socially malleable instrument long after the disappearance of the frontier environment that gave it birth, and it has proved quite congenial to an urban setting.

Similarly, the revolutionary doctrine that our Declaration of Independence proudly proclaims stands as a tempting model of legitimate violence to be emulated by contemporary groups, such as militant Negroes and radical students who confront a system of both public and private government that they regard as contemptuous of their consent. Entranced by the resurgence of revolution in the underdeveloped world and of international university unrest, radical students and blacks naturally seize upon our historically sacrosanct doctrine of the inherent right of revolution and self-determination to justify their rebellion. That their analogies are fatefully problematical in no way dilutes the majesty of our own proud Declaration.

The fourth historic legacy, our consensual political philosophy of Lockean-Jeffersonian liberalism, was premised upon a pervasive fear of governmental power and has reinforced the tendency to define freedom negatively as freedom *from*. As a consequence, conservatives have been able paradoxically to invoke the doctrines of Jefferson in resistance to legislative reforms, and the Sumnerian imperative that "stateways cannot change folkways" has historically enjoyed a wide and not altogether unjustified allegiance in the public eye (witness the debacle of the first Reconstruction, and the dilemma of our contemporary second attempt). Its implicit corollary has been that forceful and, if necessary, violent local and state resistance to unpopular federal stateways is a legitimate response; both Calhoun and Wallace could confidently repair to a strict construction of the same document invoked by Lincoln and the Warren court.

A fifth historic source both of our modern society and our current plight is our industrial revolution and the great internal migration from the countryside to the city. Yet the process occurred with such astonishing rapidity that it produced widespread socioeconomic dislocation in an environment in which the internal controls of the American social structure were loose and the external controls were weak. Urban historian Richard Wade has observed that—

> The cities inherited no system of police control adequate to the numbers or to the rapid increase of the urban centers. The modern police force is the creation of the 20th century; the establishment of genuinely professional systems is historically a very recent thing. Throughout the 18th and 19th century, the force was small, untrained, poorly paid, and part of the political system. In case of any sizeable disorder, it was hopelessly inadequate; and rioters sometimes routed the constabulary in the first confrontation.

Organized labor's protracted and bloody battles for recognition and power occurred during these years of minimal control and maximal social upheaval. The violence of workers' confrontations with their employers, Taft and Ross concluded, was partly the result of a lack of consensus on the legitimacy of workers' protests, partly the result of the lack of means of social control. Workers used force to press their grievances, employers organized violent resistance, and repeatedly state or federal troops had to be summoned to restore order.

The final distinctive characteristic—in many ways perhaps our most distinctive—has been our unmatched prosperity; we have been, in the words of David Potter, most characteristically a "people of plenty." Ranked celestially with life and liberty in the sacrosanct Lockean trilogy, property has generated a quest and prompted a devotion in the American character that has matched our devotion to equality and, in a fundamental sense, has transformed it from the radical leveling of the European democratic tradition into a typically American insistence upon equality of opportunity. In an acquisitive society of individuals with unequal talents and groups with unequal advantages, this had resulted in an unequal distribution of the rapid accumulation of abundance that, especially since World War II, has promised widespread participation in the affluent society to a degree unprecedented in history. Central to the notion of "revolutions of rising expectations," and to Davies' J-curve hypothesis as well, is the assumption that improved economic rewards can coincide with and often obscure a degree of relative deprivation that generates frustration and can prompt men toward violent protest despite measurable gains.

Our historical evolution, then, has given our national character a dual nature: we strive, paradoxically, for both liberty and equality, which can be and often in practice are quite contradictory goals. This is not to suggest that American society is grounded in a fatal contradiction. For all the conflict inherent in a simultaneous quest for liberty and equality, American history is replete with dramatic instances of the successful adjustment of "the system" to the demands of disparate protesting groups. An historical appraisal of these genuine achievements should give pause to contemporary Cassandras who bemoan in selfflagellation how hopelessly wretched we all are. These radically disillusioned social critics can find abundant evil in our historical legacy: centuries of Negro slavery, the cultural deracination and near extinction of the Indians, our initiation of atomic destruction—ad infinitum. Much as the contemporary literary Jeremiahs have, in Lynn's view, libeled the American character by extrapolating violence from its literary context, these social critics in their overcompensations have distorted the American experience in much the same fashion, although in an opposite direction, as have the more familiar superpatriotic celebrants of American virtuosity. While a careful and honest historical appraisal should remind us that violence has been far more intrinsic to our past than we should like to think—Brooks reminds us, for example, that the New York Draft Riot of 1863 vastly exceeded the destruction of Watts—our assessment of the origins and dimensions of contemporary American violence must embrace the experience of other societies.

III. COMPARISONS OF PROTEST AND VIOLENCE

Whether the United States is now a "violent society" can be answered not in the abstract but only by comparison, either with the American past or with other nations. The historical evidence, above, suggests that we were somewhat more violent toward one another in this decade than we have been in most others, but probably less violent in total magnitude of civil strife than in the latter 19th century, when the turmoil of Reconstruction was followed by massive racial and labor violence. Even so, in contemporary comparison with other nations, acts of collective violence by private citizens in the United States in the last 20 years have been extraordinarily numerous, and this is true also of peaceful demonstrations. In numbers of political assassinations, riots, politically relevant armed group attacks, and demonstrations, the United States since 1948 has been among the half-dozen most tumultuous nations in the world. When such events are evaluated in terms of their relative severity, however, the rank of the United States is somewhat lower. The Feierabends and Nesvold have used ranking scales to weigh the severity and numbers of such events during the years from 1948 to 1965, rating peaceful demonstrations as having the least serious impact, civil wars the most serious impact on political systems. In a comparison that gives greatest weight to the frequency of violent events, the United States ranks 14th among 84 nations. In another comparison, based mainly on the severity of all manifestations of political instability, violent or not, the United States stands below the midpoint, 46th among 84 nations. In other words, the United States up to 1965 had much political violence by comparison with other nations but relative stability of its political institutions in spite of it. Paradoxically, we have been a turbulent people but a relatively stable republic.

Some more detailed comparisons are provided by a study of the characteristics of civil strife in 114 nations and colonies in the 1960's. The information on "civil strife" includes all reported acts of collective violence involving 100 or more people; organized private attacks on political targets, whatever the number of participants; and antigovernment demonstrations involving 100 or more people. Three general kinds of civil strife are distinguished: (1) *Turmoil* is relatively spontaneous, partially organized or unorganized strife with substantial popular participation and limited objectives. (2) *Conspiracy* is intensively organized strife with limited participation but with terroristic or revolutionary objectives. (3) *Internal war* is intensively organized strife with widespread participation, always accompanied by extensive and intensive violence and usually directed at the overthrow of political regimes.

The comparisons of the strife study are proportional to population rather than absolute, on grounds that a demonstration by 10,000 of Portugal's 9 million citizens, for example, is more consequential for that nation than a demonstration by the same number of the United States' 200 million citizens is for ours. About 11 of every 1,000 Americans took part in civil strife, almost all of it turmoil, between mid-1963 and mid-1968, compared with an average of 7 per thousand in 17 other Western democracies during the 1961-65 period. Six of these 17 had higher rates of participation than the United States, including Belgium, France, and Italy. About 9,500 reported casualties resulted from American strife, most of them the result of police action. This is a rate of 48 per million population, compared with an average of 12 per million in other Western nations, but American casualties are almost certain to be overreported by comparison with casualties elsewhere. Strife was also of longer duration in the United States than in all but a handful of countries in the world. In total magnitude of strife, taking these three factors into account, the United States ranks first among the 17 Western democracies.

Despite its frequency, civil strife in the United States has taken much less disruptive forms than in many non-Western and some Western countries. More than a million citizens participated in 370 reported civil-rights demonstrations and marches in the 5-year period; almost all of them were peacefully organized and conducted. Of 170 reported antiwar demonstrations, which involved a total of about 700,000 people, the participants initiated violence in about 20: The most extensive violence occurred in 239 recorded hostile outbreaks by Negroes, which resulted in more than 8,000 casualties and 191 deaths. Yet the nation has experienced no internal wars since the Civil War and almost none of the chronic revolutionary conspiracy and terrorism that plague dozens of other nations. The most consequential conspiratorial violence has been white terrorism against blacks and civil-rights workers, which caused some 20 deaths between 1963 and 1968, and black terrorism against whites, mostly the police, which began in 1968.

Although about 220 Americans died in violent civil strife in the 5 years before mid-1968, the rate of 1.1 per million population was infinitesimal compared with the average of all nations of 238 deaths per million, and less than the European average of 2.4 per million. These differences reflect the comparative evidence that, from a worldwide perspective, Americans have seldom organized for violence. Most demonstrators and rioters are protesting, not rebelling. If there were many serious revolutionaries in the United States, or effective revolutionary organizations, levels of violence would be much higher than they have been.

These comparisons afford little comfort when the tumult of the United States is contrasted with the relative domestic tranquillity of developed democratic nations like Sweden, Great Britain, and Australia, or with the comparable current tranquillity of nations as diverse as Yugoslavia, Turkey, Jamaica, or Malaysia. In total magnitude of strife, the United States ranks 24th among the 114 larger nations and colonies of the world. In magnitude of turmoil alone, it ranks sixth.

Though greater in magnitude, civil strife in the United States is about the same in kind as strife in other Western nations. The antigovernment demonstration and riot, violent clashes of political or ethnic groups, and student protests are pervasive forms of conflict in modern democracies. Some such public protest has occurred in every Western nation in the past decade. People in non-Western countries also resort to these limited forms of public protest, but they are much more likely to organize serious conspiratorial and revolutionary movements as well. Strife in the United States and other European countries is quite likely to mobilize members of both the working class and middle classes, but rarely members of the political establishment such as military officers, civil servants, and disaffected political leaders, who so often organize conspiracies and internal wars in non-European nations. Strife also is likely to occur within or on the periphery of the normal political process in Western nations, rather than being organized by clandestine revolutionary movements or cells of plotters. If some overt strife is an inevitable accompaniment of organized social existence, as all our comparative evidence suggests it is, it seems socially preferable that it take the form of open political protest, even violent protest, rather than concerted, intensively violent attempts to seize political power.

One evident characteristic of civil strife in the United States in recent years is the extent to which it is an outgrowth of ethnic tensions. Much of the civil protest and collective violence in the United States has been directly related to the nation's racial problems. Comparative studies show evidence of parallel though not identical situations in other developed, European, and democratic nations. The unsatisfied demands of regional, ethnic, and linguistic groups for greater rights and socioeconomic benefits are more common sources of civil strife in Western nations than in almost any other group of countries. These problems have persisted long after the resolution of fundamental questions about the nature of the state, the terms of political power and who should hold it, and economic development. It seems ironical that nations that have been missionaries of technology and political organization to the rest of the world apparently have failed to provide satisfactory conditions of life for all the groups within their midst.

IV. THE SOURCES OF VIOLENCE

Is man violent by nature or by circumstance? In the Hobbesian view, the inescapable legacy of human nature is a "life of man solitary, poor, nasty, brutish, and short." This ancient pessimistic view is given recent credence by the ethologists, whose study of animals in their natural habitats had led them to conclude that the aggressive drive in animals is innate, ranking with the instinctive trilogy of hunger, sex, and fear or flight. But most psychologists and social scientists do not regard aggression as fundamentally spontaneous or instinctive, nor does the weight of their evidence support such a view. Rather they regard most aggression, including violence, as sometimes an emotional response to socially induced frustrations, and sometimes a dispassionate, learned response evoked by specific situations. This assumption underlies almost all the studies in this volume: nature provides us only with the capacity for violence; it is social circumstance that determines whether and how we exercise that capacity.

Man's cultural diversity offers concrete evidence that this essentially optimistic view of human nature is justified. Man can through his intelligence so construct his cultural traditions and institutions as to minimize violence and encourage the realization of his humanistic goals. Cultural anthropologists have identified societies, such as four contiguous language groups in the remote Eastern Highlands of New Guinea, in which the rhythms of life were focused on a deadly and institutionally permanent game of rape and cannibalism. But they have also studied such gentle societies as those of the Arapesh of New Guinea, the Lepchas of Sikkim, and the pygmies of the Congo rain forest, cultures in which an appetite for aggression has been replaced by an "enormous gusto for concrete physical pleasures—eating, drinking, sex, and laughter." Revealingly, these gentle societies generally lack the cultural model of brave, aggressive masculinity, a pervasive model that seems so conducive to violence. Evidence that culture is a powerful if not omnipotent determinant of man's propensity for violence is the melancholy contemporary fact that Manhattan Island (population 1.7 million) has more murders per year than all of England and Wales (population 49 million). We need not resolve the interminable hen-and-egg debate over the primacy of nature versus nurture to conclude that man has the cultural capacity to minimize his recourse to violence.

One general approach to the explanation of the nature and extent of collective violence, supported by considerable evidence in this report, begins with the assumption that men's frustration over some of the material and social circumstances of their lives is a necessary precondition of group protest and collective violence. The more intense and widespread frustration-induced discontent is among a people, the more intense and widespread collective violence is likely to be. Several general attitudinal and social conditions determine the extent and form of consequent violence. People are most strongly disposed to act violently on their discontent if they believe that violence is justifiable and likely of success; they are likely to take violent political action to the extent that they regard their government as illegitimate and responsible for their frustrations. The extent, intensity, and organization of civil strife is finally determined by characteristics of the social system: the degree and consistency of social control, and the extent to which institutions afford peaceful alternatives to violent protest.

If discontent is a root cause of violence within the political community, what kinds of conditions give rise to the widespread discontents that lead to collective violence? All societies generate some discontent because organized social life by its very nature frustrates all human beings, by inhibiting some of their natural impulses. Socialized inhibitions and outlets for such discontents are provided by every society, though their relative effectiveness is certainly an underlying factor in national differences in rates of aggressive crimes. Another fundamental factor may be the ecological one. Carstairs summarizes evidence that overcrowding of human populations may lead to aggressiveness. On the other hand, Tilly shows that high rates of immigration to French cities in the 18th and 19th centuries was, if anything, associated with civil peace rather than rising disorder. Lane also finds that increasing urbanization in 19th-century Massachusetts was accompanied by a decline in violent crime rates. Neither culture stress nor population concentrations per se seem to be consequential causes of upsurges in collective violence, though they probably contribute to the "background noise" of violence common to almost all cultures. Probably the most important cause of major increases in group violence is the widespread frustration of socially deprived expectations about the goods and conditions of life men believe theirs by right. These frustratable expectations relate not only to material well-being but to more intangible conditions such as security, status, freedom to manage one's own affairs, and satisfying personal relations with others. Men's rightful expectations have many sources, among them their past experience of gain or loss, ideologies of scarcity or abundance, and the condition of groups with which they identify. In any case, men feel satisfactions and frustrations with reference to what they think they ought to have, not according to some absolute standard.

New expectations and new frustrations are more likely to be generated in times of social change than social stasis. The quantitative comparisons of the Feierabends and Nesvold suggest, for example, that nations undergoing the most rapid socioeconomic change also are likely to experience the highest levels of collective violence. Large-scale socioeconomic change is ordinarily accompanied by changes in peoples' values, by institutional dislocations that affect people on top as much as people "on the way up," and even by the temporary breakdown of some social institutions. Rapid social change is thus likely to add to the discontents of many groups at the same time that it improves the conditions of some. In addition, it may contribute to the partial breakdown of systems of normative control, to the collapse of old institutions through which some groups were once able to satisfy their expectations, and to the creation of new organizations of the discontented. Under these conditions the motivational and institutional potential for collective violence is high.

Some specific patterns of social change are directly indicted as causes of collective violence. One is a pattern of rising expectations among people so situated that lack of opportunity or the obdurate resistance of others precludes their attainment of those expectations. American society is especially vulnerable to the frustration of disappointed expectations, for we have proclaimed ourselves the harbinger of a New Jerusalem and invited millions of destitute immigrants to our shores to partake of its fulfillment. "Progressive" demands by such groups that have felt themselves unjustifiably excluded from a fair share of the social, economic, and political privileges of the majority have repeatedly provided motivation and justification for group conflict in our past, as they have in the history of Western Europe. Demands of workers for economic recognition and political participation were pervasive and chronic sources of turmoil in the United States and Europe. The aspirations of the Irish, Italians, Slavs, and—far most consequentially—Negroes have also provided repeated occasion for violence in America. Demands for an end to discriminatory privilege have not been confined to minorities or ethnic strata either. The struggle for women's suffrage in the United States was not peaceful, and America has not heard the last of women's claims for effective socioeconomic equality with men. Although the current resurgence of protest by many groups testifies to the continued inequity in the distribution of rewards, it also reflects the self-sustaining nature of social adjustment in this most pluralistic of nations. The same process through which Americans have made successive accommodations to demands for equity encourages the regeneration of new demands.

Protective resistance to undesirable change has been a more common source of collective violence in America than "revolutions of rising expectations," however. For example, most ethnic and religious violence in American history has been retaliatory violence by groups farther up the socioeconomic ladder who felt threatened by the prospect of the "new immigrant" and the Negro getting both "too big" and "too close." As Taft and Ross have demonstrated, most labor violence in American history was not a deliberate tactic of workingclass organization but a result of forceful employer resistance to worker organization and demands. Companies repeatedly resorted to coercive and sometimes terroristic activities against union organizers and to violent strikebreaking tactics. The violence of employers often provided both model and impetus to counterviolence by workers, leading in many situations to an escalating spiral of violent conflict to the point of military intervention or mutual exhaustion.

Aggressive vigilantism has been a recurrent response of middle- and working-class Americans to perceived threats by outsiders or lesser classes to their status, security, and cultural integrity. The most widely known manifestations have been the frontier tradition of citizens' enforcement of the law and Ku Klux Klan efforts to maintain class lines and the moral code by taking their version of the law into their own hands. Brown has traced the emergence of such vigilante groups as the "Regulators" of pre-Revolutionary South Carolina and the Bald Knobbers of the Missouri Ozarks in the late 1800's. There are many other manifestations of aggressive vigilantism as well; no regions and few historical eras have been free of it, including the present. A contemporary one is the sporadic harassment of "hippie" and "peacenik" settlements in rural and smalltown America, and the neovigilante organizations of urban Americans, white and black, for "group defense" that often have aggressive overtones. There also is a vigilantism of a somewhat different sort, an aggressive and active suppression of deviancy within an otherwise-cohesive group. An historical example was the White Cap movement of the 1880's and 1890's, a spontaneous movement for the moral regulation of the poor whites and ne'er-do-wells of rural America. Such vigilantism also is apparent in the internecine strife of defensive black organizations, which have occasionally used violence to rid themselves of innovative "traitors" like Malcolm X.

Agrarian protests and uprisings have characterized both frontier and settled regions of the United States since before the Revolution. They have reflected both progressive and protective sentiments, including demands for land reform, defense against more powerful economic interests, and relief from onerous political restrictions. Among them have been Shays' Rebellion in Massachusetts, 1786-87; Fries' Rebellion in eastern Pennsylvania, 1799; some of the activities of the Grangers, Greenbackers, and Farmers' Alliance after the Civil War; and the "Green Corn Rebellion" of Oklahoma farmers during World War I.

Antiwar protest in American history also has a predominantly protective quality. The nation's 19th-century wars, especially the Civil War, led often to violent resistance to military conscription and the economic impositions of war. The 20th century has seen the development of a strong, indigenous strain of pacifism in the United States. The goals of those who have promoted the cause of peace, during both the First World War and the Vietnam war, have been protective in this sense: they adhere to a set of humanitarian values that are embodied in the basic social contract of American life, and see that contract threatened by those who regard force as the solution to American and foreign problems. The evidence of American history and comparative studies suggests no exact relationship between the occurrence of war and domestic protest against it, however. In the United States it appears to be the pervasive sense that a particular war and its demands are unjust or illegitimate that leads to protest and, occasionally, to violent resistance.

Davies identifies a third general pattern of change that is frequently associated with the outbreak of rebellion and revolution: the occurrence of a short period of sharp relative decline in socioeconomic or political conditions after a prolonged period of improving conditions. A period of steady progress generates expectations that progress will continue. If it does not continue, a pervasive sense of frustration develops which, if focused on the government, is likely to lead to widespread political violence. It is not only economic reversal in this pattern that leads to violence. People whose dignity, career expectations, or political ambitions are so frustrated are as likely to rebel as those whose pocketbooks are being emptied.

This specific pattern is identified in Davies' studies of socioeconomic and political changes affecting various groups before the outbreak of the French Revolution, the American Civil War, and the Nazi revolution. It may also be present in data on relative rates of white and Negro socioeconomic progress in the United States during the last several decades. From 1940 to 1952, nonwhite family income relative to educational attainment appears to have increased steadily and substantially in comparison with white income. In 1940 the average Negro with a high school education was likely to receive 55 percent of the earnings of a white worker with comparable education. This figure increased to 85 percent in 1952—but then declined to a low of 74 percent by 1962. These data call into question simplistic notions to the effect that unsatisfied expectations of black Americans increased to the point of violence simply because of "agitation" or because of unfulfilled promises. Rather it may have been real progress, judged by the firsthand experience of the 1940's and early 1950's, and probably also by reference to the rise of the black bourgeoisie, which generated expectations that were substantially frustrated by events of the late 1950's and early 1960's.

Discontent is only the initial condition of collective violence, which raises the question of the extent to which the actualization of violence is determined by popular attitudes and institutional patterns. A cross-national study by Gurr was designed to provide preliminary answers to this question, by relating differences among nations in economic and political discontent, apparent justifications for violence, and institutional strength to differences in magnitudes and forms of civil strife. The results are that more than a third of the differences among contemporary nations in magnitudes of strife are accounted for by differences in the extent and intensity of their citizens' discontent, even though measured imprecisely. Attitudes about politics and violence are almost as important. Nations whose political systems have low legitimacy are likely to have extensive strife; nations with a violent past—and, by implication, popular attitudes that support violence—are likely to have a violent present, and future. Institutional patterns can meliorate or magnify these dispositions to violence. If physical controls are weak, and especially if they are inconsistent in application, strife is likely to be high. Similarly the weakness of conventional institutions, and the availability of material and organizational support for rebellion, lead to high levels of strife, particularly in its most intensive and violent forms.

The experience of the United States is consistent with this general pattern. For all our rhetoric, we have never been a very law-abiding nation, and illegal violence has sometimes been abundantly rewarded. Hence there have developed broad normative sanctions for the expression or acting out of discontent, somewhat limited inhibitions, and—owing to Jeffersonian liberalism's legacy of fear of central public authority—very circumscribed physical controls. Public sympathy has often been with the lawbreaker—sometimes with the nightrider who punished the transgressor of community mores, sometimes with the integrationists who refused to obey racial segregation laws. Lack of full respect for law and support for violence in one's own interest have both contributed to the justifications for private violence, justifications that in turn have helped make the United States historically and at present a tumultuous society.

On the other hand, the United States also has the characteristics that in other countries appear to minimize intense revolutionary conspiracies and internal wars. Thus far in our history the American political system has maintained a relatively high degree of legitimacy in the eyes of most of its citizens. American political and economic institutions are generally strong. They are not pervasive enough to provide adequate opportunities for some regional and minority groups to satisfy their expectations, but sufficiently pervasive and egalitarian that the most ambitious and talented men—if not women—can pursue the "American dream" with some chance of success. These are conditions that minimize the prospects of revolutionary movements: a majoritarian consensus on the legitimacy of government, and provision of opportunity for men of talent who, if intensely alienated, might otherwise provide revolutionary cadres. But if such a system is open to the majority yet partly closed to a minority, or legitimate for the majority but illegitimate for a minority, the minority is likely to create chronic tumult even though it cannot organize effective revolutionary movements.

JOHN A. O'DONNELL
JOHN C. BALL

Narcotic
Addiction

Opium has been used for a variety of medical purposes through recorded history, and probably earlier. Some physicians in medieval Europe regarded it as a panacea and it is likely that many of their patients became addicted. Opium use was first regarded as a social problem in China in the eighteenth century, when the introduction of opium smoking and the commercial exploitation of opium by the East India Company led to edicts against importation, and to the Opium War in 1840. One of the results of that war was a growing moral concern over the abuse of opium.

Opium preparations were used medicinally in the United States from colonial days, but there was a large increase in consumption in the latter half of the nineteenth century. This increase has been attributed to a number of factors. The science of medicine was undeveloped, and there were few specific treatments for disease. Opiates were prescribed for the relief of symptoms caused by a variety of disorders, especially diarrheas and gynecologic conditions. Patent medicines, including soothing syrups for infants, contained opium and later morphine, codeine, and even heroin. When the original disease was gone the patient often found himself addicted to opiates.

Morphine had been isolated in 1812, and the hypodermic syringe and needle were invented only a few years before the Civil War. Many ill or wounded soldiers became addicted and addiction for some years was known as the "soldier's disease." These veterans and the "medical addicts" produced by physicians or by self-medication are not known to have differed much from the general population; they were not necessarily antisocial or criminal, and they included respectable citizens of all social classes.

Reprinted and abridged with the permission of the publisher and the authors from *Narcotic Addiction*, ed. John A. O'Donnell and John C. Ball (New York: Harper and Row, 1966), pp 1-2. Copyright ©1966 by John A. O'Donnell and John C. Ball.

Opium smoking was introduced to the United States by Chinese laborers imported to work on railroad construction, taken up by gamblers and criminals on the West Coast, and rapidly spread to delinquent individuals all over the country. By the 1870s people began to connect the use of opium with criminal behavior, and to regard the former as the cause of the latter.

Heroin was first produced in 1898, and was originally thought to be nonaddicting and a "cure" for the opium habit. By 1910 the medical profession, over-reacting to its original excessive regard for heroin, was perceiving it as worse than morphine. Heroin was widely used as a snuff, as was cocaine, which was introduced to the underworld at about the same time. Both are white powders, and it is likely that the bizarre and often dangerous behavior of the cocaine user was attributed to the heroin user. Isbell suggests that the term "dope fiend" originated to describe cocaine users, but later came to be applied to narcotic addicts because of a confusion between the drugs.[1]

By the beginning of the twentieth century, the nature of narcotic addiction was beginning to be understood. Many of its evils were recognized and other evils were wrongly attributed to it. Simultaneously, the United States was assuming leadership in international efforts to suppress opium traffic in the Far East. One of the major reasons for passage of the Harrison Narcotic Act in 1914—the basic law for domestic regulation of narcotics—was to honor obligations assumed by adhering to the principles of the Hague Convention of 1912.

Narcotic addiction has not been studied as intensively in other countries as it has in the United States. Available data show that it never became the problem in Europe that it has been in this country. In Europe, the number of addicts is small, and most of them are middle-class medical addicts, physicians, or other health professionals. In the Near and Far East, opium smoking was widespread until recent years, when it has been largely replaced by the use of heroin. The rate of narcotic addiction in Hong Kong, Singapore, Thailand, and Iran is much higher than in the United States.

NOTES

1. Harris Isbell, "Historical Development of Attitudes Toward Opiate Addiction in the United States," in *Conflict and Creativity,* Seymour M. Farber and Roger H. L. Wilson (eds.). New York: McGraw-Hill Book Company, 1963, pp. 154-170.

LEWIS MUMFORD

Living Conditions
in
Ancient Rome

So far we have dealt with those aspects of the Roman town that the Romans derived mainly from the peoples they conquered and crushed; for up to 751 B.C., when according to Cicero Rome was founded, the Romans themselves had been only villagers. Even the "New Towns" policy was not an innovation: what was it indeed but the Ionic practice of growth by colonization, more systematically carried out, yet more jealously restricted.

In the smaller towns of Gaul, just because of their modest scale, towns like Marseille, Narbonne, or Orange in southern France, with their independent foundations in Hellenic culture dating back many centuries, the Greek tradition must have dominated both politically and architecturally. The special Roman contribution to planning was chiefly a matter of sturdy engineering and flatulent exhibitionism: the taste of *nouveaux riches,* proud of their pillaged bric-a-brac, their numerous statues and obelisks, stolen or meticulously copied, their imitative acquisitions, their expensive newly commissioned decorations. But in the Greek provinces, whether in Gaul or Sicily, the Greek refinements of taste and style would not be lacking. Certainly the famous Maison Carée at Nîmes, beloved of Thomas Jefferson, is as exquisite a production as Attic art could have encouraged in its best period. Even when fresh this building must have seemed fragile, just as today, in its fragility, it seems curiously fresh.

But it is not by its derivative works, or by its pompous inflation of the classic orders, that Rome left its impress on urbanism. To find what Rome stood for, at both its physical best and its human worst, one must center attention on the city of Rome itself. Here is where the new scale was established: here is where the soldier and the engineer joined forces, not

Reprinted from *The City in History,* ©1961, by Lewis Mumford, pp. 213-21. Reprinted with the permission of Harcourt Brace Jovanovich, Inc. and Martin Secker & Warburg Limited.

just to create walls and moats, but embankments and reservoirs, on a cyclopean scale. Here is where, in its great public structures, Rome attempted, not merely to cope with the large quantities of people it had brought together, but to give to its otherwise degraded mass culture an appropriate urban guise, reflecting imperial magnificence.

To investigate this contribution one must fortify oneself for an ordeal: to enjoy it, one must keep one's eyes open, but learn to close one's nose to the stench, one's ears to the screams of anguish and terror, one's gullet to the retching of one's own stomach. Above all, one must keep one's heart on ice and check any impulse to tenderness and pity, with a truly Roman stolidity. All the magnitudes will be stretched in Rome: not least the magnitude of debasement and evil. Only one symbol can do justice to the contents of that life: an open sewer. And it is with the sewer that we shall begin.

Surely it is no accident that the oldest monument of Roman engineering is the Cloaca Maxima, the great sewer, constructed in the sixth century on a scale so gigantic that either its builders must have clairvoyantly seen, at the earliest moment, that this heap of villages would become a metropolis of a million inhabitants, or else they must have taken for granted that the chief business and ultimate end of life is the physiological process of evacuation. So sound was the stone construction, so ample the dimensions, that this sewer is still in use today. With its record of continuous service for more than twenty-five hundred years, that structure proves that in the planning of cities low first costs do not necessarily denote economy; for if the utility needed has been soundly conceived and built, the final costs, extended over its whole prospective lifetime, are what really matter. On these terms, the Cloaca Maxima has turned out to be one of the cheapest pieces of engineering on record, though it is rivalled by some of the later viaducts and bridges that are still in use, not least by the magnificent Pont du Gard in Provence.

The Greek geographer Strabo remarked that while the Greeks attended chiefly to beauty and fortification, to harbors and to fertile soil, in planning their cities, the Romans were conspicuous for the pavement of streets, the water supply, and the sewers. This trait was fully established, then, by the first century A.D. Dionysius of Halicarnassus confirms this observation in almost the same words, and that consensus has lasted. Rome's capital achievements in more than one department might be summed up with words once used by a great scientist about a flatulent architectural interpretation of his highly revolutionary concepts of space and time: "Poorly digested but splendidly evacuated."

The Cloaca Maxima antedated the piping of water from distant springs and streams, perhaps because the local water supply from wells remained adequate till 109 A.D., when the Trajan aqueduct brought water for the first time to the right bank of the Tiber to satisfy the thirst of a growing population. Street paving came in even before the water mains; but it was applied to the roads outside the city before it was used on any scale within the city itself, for Rome was still wallowing in mud, on its marshy lowland soil, when, in 312 B.C., Appius Claudius constructed the first veritable Roman road, the Via Appia. The satires of Juvenal show, indeed, that paving could not have been universal in Rome, even in the time of the Empire, though there is no doubt that it was widely used, like many other innovations in whose employment Rome herself lagged, in the newer, smaller cities. The pedestrian had even an elevated sidewalk and stepping-stones across the traffic thoroughfare in Pompeii.

In all three examples, sewers, water mains, and paved roads, royal engineering innovations not unknown in more ancient towns and regions were converted into great collective forms, serving the urban masses. But as frequently happens in the vulgar applications of engineering, the physical benefits were limited by a certain poverty of imagination in carrying them through. The superabundant engineering was inadequate because—as in so much imposing American highway construction today—the human end in view was too dimly perceived or too reluctantly accepted as a final guide. Thus just as our expressways are not articulated with the local street system, so the great sewers of Rome were not connected with water-closets above the first floor. Even worse, they were not connected to the crowded tenements at all.

In short where the need was greatest, the mechanical facilities were least. Though the mass of the population might by day patronize at a small fee the public toilets in the neighborhood, they deposited their domestic ordure in covered cisterns at the bottom of the stair wells of their crowded tenements, from which it would be periodically removed by the dung-farmers and scavengers. Even punctual nightly removal would hardly lessen the foul odor that must have pervaded the buildings. (Urine, collected in special jars, was used by fullers in working up cloth.) In contrast with water removal, this dung-farming had the advantage of replenishing the soil of the surrounding farms with valuable nitrogenous compost, for then as now, flush toilets both wasted potential fertilizer and polluted the streams. But the load of excrement from this vast slum population must have been greater than the nearby land could bear; for there are records of open sewers and cess trenches in residential quarters, which were finally covered over, though not removed, at a later day.

The same uneconomic combination of refined technical devices and primitive social planning applied to the water supply. The public sources of water were ample, so much so that the vast volumes used for the baths apparently did not overtax it. But the private bath was a luxury of the rich; and the buildings exhumed in Rome show no pipes that would indicate the use of water above the first floor, though such a convenience sometimes existed in a little provincial town like Pompeii. Water and slops, in other words, had to be transported by hand, the first upwards, the second downwards, in the high tenements of Rome, just as they were transported in the equally high tenements of seventeenth-century Edinburgh. In this respect, Rome, for all its engineering skill and wealth, failed miserably in the rudiments of municipal hygiene. As a result, the danger of having a chamberpot emptied on one's head was as great, again, as in Edinburgh (Gardy-lo!), though the Roman courts exercised themselves to detect and punish the culprits in such cases as were brought to their attention by the municipal police.

In sum, in the great feats of engineering where Rome stood supreme, in the aqueducts, the underground sewers, and the paved ways, their total application was absurdly spotty and inefficient. By its very bigness and its rapacity, Rome defeated itself and never caught up with its own needs. There seems little doubt that the smaller provincial cities were better managed in these departments, just because they had not overpassed the human measure.

One cannot leave the subject of sewage disposal without noting another feature that casts serious doubt on the intelligence and competence of the municipal officials of Rome, for it records a low point in sanitation and hygiene that more primitive communities never descended to. The most elementary precautions against disease were lacking in the disposal of the great mass of refuse and garbage that accumulates in a big city; and Rome, in the heyday of the empire, must have numbered around a million human beings, give or take a few hundred thousand. If the disposal of fecal matter in carts and in open trenches was a hygienic misdemeanor, what shall one say of the disposal of other forms of offal and ordure in open pits? Not least, the indiscriminate dumping of human corpses into such noisome holes, scattered on the outskirts of the city, forming as it were a *cordon malsanitaire.*

Even without this invitation to typhoid, typhus, and cholera, the prevalence of malaria had made Rome and the surrounding campagna one of the most unhealthy areas in the world, right through the nineteenth century, as the readers of Henry James' "Daisy Miller" still have reason to know. To make up for lack of health-department statistics, a large number of altars and shrines dedicated to the Goddess of Fever testify to the chronic threat of malarial infection; while the repeated onslaught of plagues, virulent and devastating, is on the record, with thousands dying in a single day. Is it any wonder that Rome, even in the palmiest days of imperial glory, was visited by a succession of desolating plagues—23 B.C. and A.D. 65, 79 and 162?

As an emergency measure to meet such mass inhumations, there might have been some justification for these pits; but as a matter of everyday practice they testify to Rome's chronic contempt for life. The quantity of dead matter that was thus dumped every day might indeed have frightened an even better technical organization than the Romans ever developed; for when the great gladiatorial spectacles were put on, as many as five thousand animals, including creatures as large as the elephant and the water buffalo, might be slaughtered in a single day, to say nothing of the hundreds of human beings who were likewise done to death in the arena. So incredible is the evidence that I prefer to quote directly one of the scholars who examined it first hand, the archaeologist, Rodolfo Lanciani.

"It is hard," says Lanciani, "to conceive the idea of a Roman carnarium, an assemblage of pits into which men and beasts, bodies and carcasses, and any kind of unmentionable refuse, were thrown in disorder. Imagine what must have been the conditions of these dreadful districts in times of plague, when the pits (puticuli) were kept open by night and day. And when the pits became filled, up to the mouth, the moat which skirted the wall of Servius Tullius, between the Colline and the Esquiline gates, was filled with corpses, thrown in as if they were carrion, until the level of the adjacent streets was reached."

In his excavations, Lanciani found about seventy-five pits or vaults, twelve feet square, thirty deep, filled with a "uniform mass of black, viscid, unctuous matter," and he remembered that on the day of finding the third pit, he was "obliged to relieve my gang of workmen from time to time, because the stench from that putrid mound, turned up after a lapse of twenty centuries, was unbearable, even for men inured to every kind of hardship, as were my excavators."

Under the provident Augustus, at the beginning of the Empire, a partial reform, which resulted in the substitution of cremation for inhumation—one could scarcely call it decent burial—took place. But this did not solve the other serious problem, that of garbage disposal.

If the sewage and water supply of the city of Rome, however grand the superficial impression of their engineering, do not stand up well under close inspection, the same applies also to the street system, which, over great areas, bore the traces of primitive footways and cartways, never sufficiently widened to accommodate wheeled traffic. Again, it was only in the small provincial and colonial cities that Roman order truly prevailed. There one discovers generous sidewalks for pedestrians, a convenience which, though known in Rome, never became common in every part of the city, for shops kept on spilling into the public ways of minor thoroughfares. Under the republic, according to Jerome Carcopino, only two streets could claim the name of "viae," that is, streets wide enough for two carts to pass—the Via Sacra, which was a processional way, and the Via Nova, whose very name indicates that it was an innovation. One of them crossed, the other flanked, the Forum Romanum. Roman roads varied from twelve to as much as twenty-four feet wide on parts of the great trunk highways; but about fifteen feet was the standard width. In other words, the two great avenues of Rome were no more than a prolongation of the great highroads; and the same system did not penetrate into the rest of the city.

As soon as the increase of population created a demand for wheeled traffic in Rome, the congestion became intolerable. One of Julius Caesar's first acts on seizing power was to ban wheeled traffic from the center of Rome during the day. The effect of this, of course, was to create such a noise at night, with wood or iron-shod cartwheels rumbling over the stone paving blocks, that the racket tormented sleep: at a much later date, it drove the poet Juvenal into insomnia. Just as motor car congestion now affects small towns as well as big ones, so the increase of animal-drawn vehicles impeded circulation everywhere. Hence Claudius extended Caesar's prohibition to the municipalities of Italy; and Marcus Aurelius, still later, applied it without regard to their municipal status to every town in the Empire; while, to complete the picture, Hadrian (A.D. 117-138) limited the number of the teams and loads of carts permitted to enter the city—cutting down even the night-time traffic at source. In a century and a half, traffic congestion had gone from bad to worse.

The fact that these regulations applied even in new cities, with their relatively commodious straight streets, indicates that it was in the nature of this new urban order to generate more traffic than the street network could cope with. And the reason for this disability was precisely the same reason that makes present-day traffic regulations, with the widening and multiplication of traffic arteries, so futile and inept: namely, no attempt was made to control the congestion of the land itself, or to reduce the density of population housed in its buildings. Absurdly, the factors that generate traffic remained outside the scheme of control. As if high building densities were not enough, poverty and lack of rentable space, according to Martial (A.D. 92), caused many streets to be cluttered with the stands and stalls of butchers, publicans, barbers, and tradesmen.

So far from arriving at a just proportion between roadways and buildings, between traffic densities and housing densities, Rome did just the opposite. The municipality permitted, indeed by its continued neglect it even encouraged, the housing of the vast mass of its population in overcrowded tenements, forming huge blocks called insulae or islands. These insulae contend with Rome's refuse pits as classic examples of vile municipal housekeeping.

Rome shows in diagrammatic contrast the relation of an exploiting ruling class to a depressed proletariat, and, as Petronius Arbiter well put it in the "Satyricon," "The little people came off badly; for the jaws of the upper classes are always keeping carnival." While a handful of patricians, about eighteen hundred families, occupied large private mansions, often with ample gardens and houses big enough to contain a whole retinue of free servants and slaves, many of the houses veritable palaces, the members of the middle classes, including officials, merchants, small industrial employers, probably lived in apartment houses such as those that have been excavated at the neighboring seaport of Ostia. These quarters were decent, perhaps, but the occupants paid a rent in Caesar's time, according to Ludwig Friedländer, about four times that of other towns in Italy. The great mass of the proletariat, in dire contrast, lived in some forty-six thousand tenement houses, which must have contained, on the average, close to two hundred people each.

These tenement houses bore the same relation to the spacious palaces and baths of the city as the open cess trenches did to the Cloaca Maxima. The building of these insulae, like the building of the tenements of New York, was a speculative enterprise in which the greatest profits were made by both the dishonest contractors, putting together flimsy structures that would barely hold up, and profiteering landlords, who learned how to subdivide old quarters into even narrower cells to accommodate even poorer artisans at a higher return of rent per unit. (One notes, not without a cynical smile, that the one kind of wheeled traffic permitted by day in Rome was that of the building contractors.)

Crassus, who made a fabulous fortune in tenement house properties, boasted that he never spent money in building: it was more profitable to buy partly damaged old properties at fire sales and rent them with meager repairs. Such systematic slum clearance projects as Nero's great fire naturally increased the housing shortage and tightened the hold of the rapacious landlords. Thus the traditional slave's diet, the meagerest ration that would keep his body alive, was matched by the equally depressing slave's shelter—crowded, ramshackle, noisome. Such were the accommodations provided for the "free citizens" of Rome.

Even in the crudest neolithic village, the house was always more than mere shelter for the physical body: it was the meeting place of a household; its hearth was a center of religious ceremony as well as an aid to cooking; it was the home of the household god and the locus of a family's being, a repository of moral values not measurable in money. All these associations and traditions were stripped away from the Roman insula: to squeeze maximum profit out of shoddy building and congested space, bare shelter sufficed; and to have recognized any other values would have been to diminish the possibilities of extortion. All the pious household usages, all the sentimental values attached to the family itself by writers like Cicero, applied only to the households of patricians. No one pretended that the denizens of Rome's slums had such favoring guardian spirits or could participate in ceremonial meals and family rites. Well did Tiberius Gracchus say, according to Plutarch: "The beasts of the field and the birds of the air have their holes and their hiding places, but the men who fight and die for Italy enjoy but the blessings of light and air." Under the Empire, even light and air were lacking in Rome. The floors were piled on top of each other, as they had never, in historic record, been piled before. Juvenal, writing in the second century A.D., exclaimed:

> Behold the mansion's towering size
> Where floors on floors to the tenth story rise.

The houses of the patricians, spacious, airy, sanitary, equipped with bathrooms and water closets, heated in winter by hypocausts, which carried hot air through chambers in the floors, were perhaps the most commodious and comfortable houses built for a temperate climate anywhere until the twentieth century: a triumph of domestic architecture. But the tenements of Rome easily take the prize for being the most crowded and insanitary buildings produced in Western Europe until the sixteenth century, when site over-filling and room over-crowding became common, from Naples to Edinburgh, and even Elizabethan London for a while succumbed to the same speculative misdemeanors. Not only were these buildings unheated, unprovided with waste pipes or water closets, unadapted to cooking; not merely did they contain an undue number of airless rooms, indecently over-crowded: though poor in all the facilities that make for decent daily living, they were in addition so badly built and so high that they offered no means of safe exit from the frequent fires that occurred. And if their tenants escaped typhoid, typhus, fire, they might easily meet their death in the collapse of the whole structure. Such accidents were all too frequent. So badly were the insulae clapped together that, in Juvenal's words, they "shook with every gust of wind that blew." That was hardly a poetic exaggeration.

These buildings and their people constituted the core of imperial Rome, and that core was rotten. As Rome grew and its system of exploitation turned more and more parasitic, the rot ate into ever larger masses of urban tissue. The main population of the city that boasted its world conquests lived in cramped, noisy, airless, foul-smelling, infected quarters, paying extortionate rents to merciless landlords, undergoing daily indignities and terrors that coarsened and brutalized them, and in turn demanded compensatory outlets. These outlets carried the brutalization even further, in a continuous carnival of sadism and death.

But before examining the chief recreations of the proletariat, by which they relieved their own sufferings by lasciviously gloating on people made to endure even worse tortures and degradations, let us behold Rome at its best. For Rome had more human attributes; and to the masses it exploited, it presented, even in its worst moments, astonishing glimpses of civic beauty and order, seemingly untainted by violence and greed.

PART II

Sociological
Perspectives

T<small>HE</small> <small>BASIC CONCERNS OF SOCIOLOGY ARE QUITE</small>
diverse and their diversity is sometimes confusing to the
beginning student. In this section we hope to convey some of
the diversity, but hopefully without the confusion.

To start, we have a selection by Marvin Olsen on the major
approaches taken to the study of human life. He distinguishes
among organic, psychological, social, and cultural analyses
and then shows the ways in which these different types of
analyses are related to each other. The central focus of
sociology is on the social level with its concern for relationships among people, but very often sociologists will link social
concepts with concepts from other levels of analysis. They
may link social values (cultural) with group memberships
(social) and attitudes (psychological) as Newcomb did in his
Bennington study which appears in this section. Or they may
show how certain kinship patterns (social) are related to
particular religious beliefs (cultural). Or they may study the
differential prevalence of ulcers (organic) among managers,
foremen and nonsupervisory workers in factories (social).

To Olsen's basic outline of the field C. Wright Mills would add one additional requirement. He argued that our analyses of social phenomena should be grounded in historical perspective. For him, as for many other social scientists, the perspective of history gives new dimensions to any social situation or problem. Viewing the current crisis in American society this way becomes an analysis of the problems accompanying the emergence of modern industrial society, problems that have been solved with more or less effectiveness in different parts of the world. This view guided the selections made in the different volumes in this series.

The dynamic character of the social level of analysis is demonstrated by Sudnow's study of the role of the public defender (an increasingly common feature of the American court system), the constraints on his behavior, and his relationships with his clients and other people in the court system.

The combination of the social and psychological is illustrated in the next two sections by Newcomb and Bettelheim. Like the Mills article they are regarded as classic statements which did much to shape the directions of social science. Newcomb's study was done during his tenure at Bennington College, a women's college in Vermont. He observed that the political culture at Bennington was liberal and Democratic, oriented to the values of President Franklin Roosevelt's New Deal, yet the girls themselves usually came from conservative, Republican, upper-middle-class or upper-class families. He documented the girls' shift from conservatism to liberalism as they progressed through their four years at college and traced the reasons for the shift to the structure and processes of group life among the students.

The terrifying conditions surrounding Bettelheim's participant observation make his study one no student of human behavior would wish to replicate. A Jew living in Nazi Germany, Bettelheim was arrested and shipped via boxcar to a concentration camp. To preserve his sanity, he chose to study the effects of the camp experience on the behavior and attitudes of the inmates. No study gives more powerful testimony to the capacity of social organizations to affect people in them in the most fundamental and, in this instance, saddening ways. In a brief space of time mature, adult human beings were made to regress to infantile behavior and finally, to identify so closely with the guards that many altered their prison uniforms to look like those of their captors. In their different ways both Newcomb and Bettelheim illustrate a fundamental sociological hypothesis that the very structure and functioning of human groups can have profound effects on the attitudes and behaviors of their members.

In this section's final article, John Horton reminds us that even the knowledge with which we work is a function of the cultural and social circumstances under which it is gathered. Thus, he suggests, contrasting ideological assumptions underlie "order" and "conflict" theories of social problems and deviant behavior. Should the status quo be conserved or upset? The data sought, and the solutions called for, follow directly and are markedly different. Horton makes this explicit when he utilizes each model to analyze sociological approaches to the "Negro question." Some anti-sociologists among our nation's politicians will be surprised at his conclusion: most sociologists are merely liberal variants of the order theorist.

MARVIN E. OLSEN

Levels of Analysis
in
Sociology

Students of the social sciences are sometimes confused by the fact that the same term—social organization—is used to designate both the process by which social relationships become ordered and also the specific outcomes or products of this process. "Social organization," in other words, may refer either to actions and processes, or to objects and entities. Thus we might first describe the process of organizing a new business and then refer to this business as a type of organization. There is a crucial semantic reason for this double meaning of "social organization." The entities that we call "social organizations" are always results or outcomes of the underlying process of social organization; they are specific forms of an ongoing process. Furthermore, the social entities that emerge from this process are themselves constantly changing. Use of the term "social organization" as both process and entity should remind us that social reality, no matter how it may be structured at any given instant, is forever undergoing a process of becoming.

LEVELS OF ANALYSIS

To be aware that social organization occurs is one thing; to study and comprehend this process is quite another task. As a point of departure, we note that human life can be analyzed from several different perspectives. All of human existence must ultimately be conceptualized as a single, unified whole, since all aspects of the ongoing process of reality are to some extent interrelated. Because of the extreme complexity of human life, however, our minds most ordinarily view it from one perspective at a time. Four distinct and basic outlooks on human life are commonly used by all of us: organic, psychological, social, and cultural perspectives.

Adapted by the author and reprinted with the permission of the publisher and the author from Marvin E. Olsen, *The Process of Social Organization,* Chapter One, "The Phenomenon of Social Organization" (New York: Holt, Rinehart and Winston, 1968), pp. 2-8. Copyright© 1968 by Holt, Rinehart and Winston, Inc.

With an *organic perspective* one focuses on the biological features of human life, so that *the individual is viewed primarily as an organism.* Medical practice is perhaps the clearest example of this perspective; part of a physician's training involves learning to treat a body solely as a biological organism, not as a unique person. An organic perspective may also prevail in sexual attraction, or when we study such things as the process of heredity or man's ability to survive in space.

With a *psychological perspective* one focuses on the mental characteristics of human life, so that *the individual is viewed primarily as a self-conscious mind or personality.* This perspective predominates in such problems as teaching a child to read, administering psychotherapy to a mentally ill person, becoming acquainted with a new friend, or testing an employee's aptitude for promotion to a supervisory job.

With a *social perspective* one focuses on the interpersonal aspects of human life, so that *the individual is viewed primarily as a member of some social relationship.* Activities such as maintaining a marriage, implementing a community recreation program, operating a business, or running a government are appropriately viewed from this perspective.

With a *cultural perspective* one focuses on the symbolic meanings in human life, so that *the individual is viewed primarily as a carrier of shared cultural ideas.* This perspective comes into play, for instance, when we observe people criticizing the literary qualities of a book, expounding religious beliefs, perpetuating the myth of Santa Claus, or attempting to increase scientific knowledge.

All four of these perspectives on human life are fabrications, in the sense that they are intellectual abstractions imposed upon ongoing processes of reality by human observers. Nonetheless, the distinctions between them are not entirely arbitrary. The simple observation that these four perspectives on human life have been used by mankind throughout history should suggest that each of them has some basis in reality. If this is so, then they should also provide foundations for different types of analysis of human life. That is, the use of each perspective suggests a different set of questions to be asked, problems to be investigated, and theoretical explanations to be formulated.

These four types of analysis have been developed as scientists concerned with studying man have divided human life into a number of specialized disciplines, each of which focuses primarily on one basic perspective. As a result, there are four fundamentally different ways of studying, analyzing, and explaining human life. Some disciplines associated with each type of analysis are listed in Table 1. This chart is incomplete in that it ignores the tendency of each discipline to "spill over" into other types of analysis. Psychology, for example, takes account of physiological and social influences on the personality. We have also ignored the many interdisciplinary fields that attempt to bridge adjacent types of analyses,

TABLE I   Types of Analysis of Human Life and Associated
Academic Disciplines

Type of Analysis	Academic Disciplines
Cultural	Philosophy, linguistics, ethnology, law, literature
Social	Sociology, economics, political science, social anthropology
Personality	Psychology, psychoanalysis
Organic	Biology, medicine, physical anthropology

such as physiological psychology, social psychology, and sociocultural studies of art, religion, knowledge. Finally, history cannot be identified with any particular level of analysis, since it is not so much a separate discipline as a special type of inquiry—essentially a concern with describing specific past events—which may be applied to any substantive area, from philosophy to politics to personalities.

The chart nevertheless clearly emphasizes one important point about the social sciences. All of these disciplines—sociology, economics, political science, social anthropology, as well as related interdisciplinary fields—share a single analytic perspective. All of them are concerned with describing and explaining ordered social relationships, whatever their particular substantive concerns. In fact sociologists, economists, and political scientists are finding it increasingly difficult to distinguish one field from another as their disciplines become more sophisticated, and the major difference now between sociologists and social anthropologists is that the latter normally restrict themselves to studying nonliterate or "premodern" societies.

Thus far we have sought only to distinguish among the organic, psychological, social, and cultural perspectives on human life. Let us now observe that these four types of analysis represent increasing degrees of separation or independence from the physical world. It is not that social or cultural perspectives are necessarily more complex or conceptually abstract than are organic and psychological perspectives. The point is that social and cultural life are somewhat less directly related to, and constrained by, physical existence than are organic and psychological phenomena. To reflect this ordered sequence we shall refer to these perspectives as "levels" of analysis.

To the extent that the four levels of analysis are grounded in reality, and thus represent different kinds of real phenomena, they are interrelated in three ways: by emergence, independence, and interpenetration.

The concept of *emergence* refers to the observation that *each succeedingly higher level of phenomena develops out of the level immediately preceding it, and is always dependent to some extent on all lower levels.* More specifically: (a) personalities develop only in conjunction with organic life, and cannot survive if the organism dies; (b) social relationships occur only when two or more personalities interact, and cease to exist when all of their members withdraw either psychologically or physically; and (c) cultures are outgrowths of social activities, and become mere relics when the social entities that created them or the individuals who carry them disappear.

The concept of *independence* refers to the observation that *each level of phenomena, although emergent from those below it, nevertheless, possesses some degree of autonomy.* Phenomena at each level have characteristics uniquely their own that are not fully determined by the lower levels. It is impossible to explain any given level solely in terms of those below it; the properties of the prior phenomena do not sufficiently explain the emergent phenomena. A personality is something more than just an acting organism, a group is something more than just several interacting personalities, and a culture is something more than just a symbolic reflection of its society.

The concept of *interpenetration* refers to the observation that *each succeedingly higher level, by virtue of its partial independence, can and frequently does influence the lower levels from which it emerged, even though it could not exist without them.* In other words, influences between levels of phenomena are always reciprocal. Personality tensions cause stomach ulcers, while poor health often affects one's personality. Communities exercise many constraints upon the actions of their members, as well as providing for their biological welfare, while at the same time the sustenance needs and personality characteristics of individuals continually affect the nature and scope of community activities. And at the cultural level, beliefs and ideas can shape societies, change personalities, and even produce martyrs, while concurrently such cultural phenomena always reflect the social life, personality structures, and organic characteristics of their proponents.

Although social life emerges from the organic and personality levels, we have argued that it has characteristics of its own that cannot be explained by biological or psychological principles. The social sciences—economics, political science, social anthropology, and sociology—are all expressly concerned with the study of social processes as real phenomena. All of them seek to discover uniquely social principles that will help us understand, explain, and predict social life in all its various manifestations. But if these different social sciences all focus on the social level of analysis, what is distinctive about sociology? How might we describe this discipline and distinguish it from the other social sciences?

To some extent sociology has tended to become the residual category of the social sciences, absorbing whatever substantive areas were not already claimed by the older disciplines of economics and political science. Thus we find sociologists studying such diverse phenomena as the family, communities, voluntary associations, race relations, social stratification, crime, bureaucracies, and mass communications.

One traditional way of giving sociology some intellectual unity is to take a "social-problems" approach. Sociology is then seen primarily as seeking solutions to the social problems besetting contemporary societies—from juvenile delinquency to international tensions. And in fact the findings of sociology, as well as those of all the other social sciences, may be applied to practical affairs whenever they are relevant. But to define sociology solely in such terms is to forget that it is a pure science, concerned with increasing our knowledge about human social life. It is not itself a form of applied social engineering.

Another way of imposing coherence upon sociology is to conceive of it as virtually synonymous with social psychology. Sociology is then described as the study of individual social behavior or of interpersonal interaction. Such areas of study are perfectly legitimate and very important, but they ignore the whole realm of social organization. The name we give to the discipline that studies social organization is irrelevant, and it might just as well be "organology" as "sociology," except for the weight of tradition. To all of the founders of this field—Auguste Comte, Herbert Spencer, Émile Durkheim, and Max Weber, to mention a few—the fundamental and unique concern of sociology was with social organization. Actions of individuals were incidental except insofar as they contributed to broader social processes.

Contemporary sociologists are increasingly realizing that their discipline has a unique scientific task—one that cuts across all the specialized subfields of sociology as well as all the other social sciences, that goes far beyond the social-problems approach in intellectual depth, and that clearly distinguishes sociology from social psychology. This unique task of sociology is to describe empirically and to explain theoretically the process of social organization wherever and whenever it occurs. Sociology thus becomes the fundamental source of concepts and theories for whatever substantive phenomena social scientists choose to study. From this viewpoint, sociology can be described as the scientific study of the process and forms of social organization.

C. WRIGHT MILLS

Sociology
and
History

Nowadays men often feel that their private lives are a series of traps. They sense that within their everyday worlds, they cannot overcome their troubles, and in this feeling, they are often quite correct: What ordinary men are directly aware of and what they try to do are bounded by the private orbits in which they live; their visions and their powers are limited to the close-up scenes of job, family, neighborhood; in other milieux, they move vicariously and remain spectators. And the more aware they become, however vaguely, of ambitions and of threats which transcend their immediate locales, the more trapped they seem to feel.

Underlying this sense of being trapped are seemingly impersonal changes in the very structure of continent-wide societies. The facts of contemporary history are also facts about the success and the failure of individual men and women. When a society is industrialized, a peasant becomes a worker; a feudal lord is liquidated or becomes a businessman. When classes rise or fall, a man is employed or unemployed; when the rate of investment goes up or down, a man takes new heart or goes broke. When wars happen, an insurance salesman becomes a rocket launcher; a store clerk, a radar man; a wife lives alone; a child grows up without a father. Neither the life of an individual nor the history of a society can be understood without understanding both.

Yet men do not usually define the troubles they endure in terms of historical change and institutional contradiction. The well-being they enjoy, they do not usually impute to the big ups and downs of the societies in which they live. Seldom aware of the intricate connection between the patterns of their own lives and the course of world history, ordinary men do not usually know what this connection means for the kinds of men they are becoming and for the kinds of history-making in which they might take part. They do not possess the quality of mind essential to grasp the interplay of man and society, of biography and history, of self and world. They cannot cope with their personal troubles in such ways as to control the structural transformations that usually lie behind them.

Surely it is no wonder. In what period have so many men been so totally exposed at so fast a pace to such earthquakes of change? That Americans have not known such catastrophic changes as have the men and women of other societies is due to historical facts that are now quickly becoming "merely history." The history that now affects every man is world history. Within this scene and this period, in the course of a single generation, one sixth of mankind is transformed from all that is feudal and backward into all that is modern, advanced, and fearful. Political colonies are freed; new and less visible forms of imperialism installed. Revolutions occur; men feel the intimate grip of new kinds of authority. Totalitarian societies rise, and are smashed to bits—or succeed fabulously. After two centuries of ascendancy, capitalism is shown up as only one way to make society into an industrial apparatus. After two centuries of hope, even formal democracy is restricted to a quite small portion of mankind. Everywhere in the underdeveloped world, ancient ways of life are broken up and vague expectations become urgent demands. Everywhere in the overdeveloped world, the means of authority and of violence become total in scope and bureaucratic in form. Humanity itself now lies before us, the super-nation at either pole concentrating its most co-ordinated and massive efforts upon the preparation of World War Three.

The very shaping of history now outpaces the ability of men to orient themselves in accordance with cherished values. And which values? Even when they do not panic, men often sense that older ways of feeling and thinking have collapsed and that newer beginnings are ambiguous to the point of moral stasis. Is it any wonder that ordinary men feel they cannot cope with the larger worlds with which they are so suddenly confronted? That they cannot understand the meaning of their epoch for their own lives? That—in defense of selfhood—they become morally insensible, trying to remain altogether private men? Is it any wonder that they come to be possessed by a sense of the trap?

It is not only information that they need—in this Age of Fact, information often dominates their attention and overwhelms their capacities to assimilate it. It is not only the skills of reason that they need—although their struggles to acquire these often exhaust their limited moral energy.

What they need, and what they feel they need, is a quality of mind that will help them to use information and to develop reason in order to achieve lucid summations of what is going on in the world and of what may be happening within themselves. It is this quality, I am going to contend, that journalists and scholars, artists and publics, scientists and editors are coming to expect of what may be called the sociological imagination.

1

The sociological imagination enables its possessor to understand the larger historical scene in terms of its meaning for the inner life and the external career of a variety of individuals. It enables him to take into account how individuals, in the welter of their daily experience, often become falsely conscious of their social positions. Within that welter, the framework of modern society is sought, and within that framework the psychologies of a variety of men and women are formulated. By such means the personal uneasiness of individuals is focused upon explicit troubles and the indifference of publics is transformed into involvement with public issues.

The first fruit of this imagination—and the first lesson of the social science that embodies it—is the idea that the individual can understand his own experience and gauge his own fate only by locating himself within his period, that he can know his own chances in life only by becoming aware of those of all individuals in his circumstances. In many ways it is a terrible lesson; in many ways a magnificent one. We do not know the limits of man's capacities for supreme effort or willing degradation, for agony or glee, for pleasurable brutality or the sweetness of reason. But in our time we have come to know that the limits of "human nature" are frighteningly broad. We have come to know that every individual lives, from one generation to the next, in some society; that he lives out a biography, and that he lives it out within some historical sequence. By the fact of his living he contributes, however minutely, to the shaping of this society and to the course of its history, even as he is made by society and by its historical push and shove.

The sociological imagination enables us to grasp history and biography and the relations between the two within society. That is its task and its promise. To recognize this task and this promise is the mark of the classic social analyst. It is characteristic of Herbert Spencer—turgid, polysyllabic, comprehensive; of E. A. Ross—graceful, muckraking, upright; of Auguste Comte and Émile Durkheim; of the intricate and subtle Karl Mannheim. It is the quality of all that is intellectually excellent in Karl Marx; it is the clue to Thorstein Veblen's brilliant and ironic insight, to Joseph Schumpeter's many-sided constructions of reality; it is the basis of the psychological sweep of W. E. H. Lecky no less than of the profundity and clarity of Max Weber. And it is the signal of what is best in contemporary studies of man and society.

No social study that does not come back to the problems of biography, of history and of their intersections within a society has completed its intellectual journey. Whatever the specific problems of the classic social analysts, however limited or however broad the features of social reality they have examined, those who have been imaginatively aware of the promise of their work have consistently asked three sorts of questions:

(1) What is the structure of this particular society as a whole? What are its essential components, and how are they related to one another? How does it differ from other varieties of social order? Within it, what is the meaning of any particular feature for its continuance and for its change?

(2) Where does this society stand in human history? What are the mechanics by which it is changing? What is its place within and its meaning for the development of humanity as a whole? How does any particular feature we are examining affect, and how is it affected by, the historical period in which it moves? And this period—what are its essential features? How does it differ from other periods? What are its characteristic ways of history-making?

(3) What varieties of men and women now prevail in this society and in this period? And what varieties are coming to prevail? In what ways are they selected and formed, liberated and repressed, made sensitive and blunted? What kinds of "human nature" are revealed in the conduct and character we observe in this society in this period? And what is the meaning for "human nature" of each and every feature of the society we are examining?

Whether the point of interest is a great power state or a minor literary mood, a family, a prison, a creed—these are the kinds of questions the best social analysts have asked. They are the intellectual pivots of classic studies of man in society—and they are the questions inevitably raised by any mind possessing the sociological imagination. For that imagination is the capacity to shift from one perspective to another—from the political to the psychological; from examination of a single family to comparative assessment of the national budgets of the world; from the theological school to the military establishment; from considerations of an oil industry to studies of contemporary poetry. It is the capacity to range from the most impersonal and remote transformations to the most intimate features of the human self—and to see the relations between the two. Back of its use there is always the urge to know the social and historical meaning of the individual in the society and in the period in which he has his quality and his being.

That, in brief, is why it is by means of the sociological imagination that men now hope to grasp what is going on in the world, and to understand what is happening in themselves as minute points of the intersections of biography and history within society. In large part, contemporary man's self-conscious view of himself as at least an outsider, if not a permanent stranger, rests upon an absorbed realization of social relativity and of the transformative power of history. The sociological imagination is the most fruitful form of this self-consciousness. By its use men whose mentalities have swept only a series of limited orbits often come to feel as if suddenly awakened in a house with which they had only supposed themselves to be familiar. Correctly or incorrectly, they often come to feel that they can now provide themselves with adequate summations, cohesive assessments, comprehensive orientations. Older decisions that once appeared sound now seem to them products of a mind unaccountably dense. Their capacity for astonishment is made lively again. They acquire a new way of thinking, they experience a transvaluation of values: in a word, by their reflection and by their sensibility, they realize the cultural meaning of the social sciences.

2

Perhaps the most fruitful distinction with which the sociological imagination works is between "the personal troubles of milieu" and "the public issues of social structure." This distinction is an essential tool of the sociological imagination and a feature of all classic work in social science.

Troubles occur within the character of the individual and within the range of his immediate relations with others; they have to do with his self and with those limited areas of social life of which he is directly and personally aware. Accordingly, the statement and the resolution of troubles properly lie within the individual as a biographical entity and within the scope of his immediate milieu—the social setting that is directly open to his personal experience and to some extent his willful activity. A trouble is a private matter: values cherished by an individual are felt by him to be threatened.

Issues have to do with matters that transcend these local environments of the individual and the range of his inner life. They have to do with the organization of many such milieux into the institutions of an historical society as a whole, with the ways in which various milieux overlap and interpenetrate to form the larger structure of social and historical life. An issue is a public matter: some value cherished by publics is felt to be threatened. Often there is a debate about what that value really is and about what it is that really threatens it. This debate is often without focus if only because it is the very nature of an issue, unlike even widespread trouble, that it cannot very well be defined in terms of the immediate and everyday environments of ordinary men. An issue, in fact, often involves a crisis in institutional arrangements, and often too it involves what Marxists call "contradictions" or "antagonisms."

In these terms, consider unemployment. When, in a city of 100,000, only one man is unemployed, that is his personal trouble, and for its relief we properly look to the character of the man, his skills, and his immediate opportunities. But when in a nation of 50 million employees, 15 million men are unemployed, that is an issue, and we may not hope to find its solution within the range of opportunities open to any one individual. The very structure of opportunities has collapsed. Both the correct statement of the problem and the range of possible solutions require us to consider the economic and political institutions of the society, and not merely the personal situation and character of a scatter of individuals.

Consider war. The personal problem of war, when it occurs, may be how to survive it or how to die in it with honor; how to make money out of it; how to climb into the higher safety of the military apparatus; or how to contribute to the war's termination. In short, according to one's values, to find a set of milieux and within it to survive the war or make one's death in it meaningful. But the structural issues of war have to do with its causes; with what types of men it throws up into command; with its effects upon economic and political, family and religious institutions, with the unorganized irresponsibility of a world of nation-states.

Consider marriage. Inside a marriage a man and a woman may experience personal troubles, but when the divorce rate during the first four years of marriage is 250 out of every 1,000 attempts, this is an indication of a structural issue having to do with the institutions of marriage and the family and other institutions that bear upon them.

Or consider the metropolis—the horrible, beautiful, ugly, magnificent sprawl of the great city. For many upper-class people, the personal solution to "the problem of the city" is to have an apartment with private garage under it in the heart of the city, and forty miles out, a house by Henry Hill, garden by Garrett Eckbo, on a hundred acres of private land. In these two controlled environments—with a small staff at each end and a private helicopter connection—most people could solve many of the problems of personal milieux caused by the facts of the city. But all this, however splendid, does not solve the public issues that the structural fact of the city poses. What should be done with this wonderful monstrosity? Break it all up into scattered units, combining residence and work? Refurbish it as it stands? Or, after evacuation, dynamite it and build new cities according to new plans in new places? What should those plans be? And who is to decide and to accomplish whatever choice is made? These are structural issues; to confront them and to solve them requires us to consider political and economic issues that affect innumerable milieux.

In so far as an economy is so arranged that slumps occur, the problem of unemployment becomes incapable of personal solution. In so far as war is inherent in the nation-state system and in the uneven industrialization of the world, the ordinary individual in his restricted milieu will be powerless—with or without psychiatric aid—to solve the troubles this system or lack of system imposes upon him. In so far as the family as an institution turns women into darling little slaves and men into their chief providers and unweaned dependents, the problem of a satisfactory marriage remains incapable of purely private solution. In so far as the overdeveloped megalopolis and the overdeveloped automobile are built-in features of the overdeveloped society, the issues of urban living will not be solved by personal ingenuity and private wealth.

What we experience in various and specific milieux, I have noted, is often caused by structural changes. Accordingly, to understand the changes of many personal milieux we are required to look beyond them. And the number and variety of such structural changes increase as the institutions within which we live become more embracing and more intricately connected with one another. To be aware of the idea of social structure and to use it with sensibility is to be capable of tracing such linkages among a great variety of milieux. To be able to do that is to possess the sociological imagination.

3

What are the major issues for publics and the key troubles of private individuals in our time? To formulate issues and troubles, we must ask what values are cherished yet threatened, and what values are cherished and supported, by the characterizing trends of our period. In the case both of threat and of support we must ask what salient contradictions of structure may be involved.

When people cherish some set of values and do not feel any threat to them, they experience *well-being*. When they cherish values but *do* feel them to be threatened, they experience a crisis—either as a personal trouble or as a public issue. And if all their values seem involved, they feel the total threat of panic.

But suppose people are neither aware of any cherished values nor experience any threat? That is the experience of *indifference*, which, if it seems to involve all their values, becomes apathy. Suppose, finally, they are unaware of any cherished values, but still are very much aware of a threat? That is the experience of *uneasiness*, of anxiety, which, if it is total enough, becomes a deadly unspecified malaise.

Ours is a time of uneasiness and indifference—not yet formulated in such ways as to permit the work of reason and the play of sensibility. Instead of troubles—defined in terms of values and threats—there is often the misery of vague uneasiness; instead of explicit issues there is often merely the beat feeling that all is somehow not right. Neither the values threatened nor whatever threatens them has been stated; in short, they have not been carried to the point of decision. Much less have they been formulated as problems of social science.

In the 'thirties there was little doubt—except among certain deluded business circles that there was an economic issue which was also a pack of personal troubles. In these arguments about "the crisis of capitalism," the formulations of Marx and the many unacknowledged re-formulations of his work probably set the leading terms of the issue, and some men came to understand their personal troubles in these terms. The values threatened were plain to see and cherished by all; the structural contradictions that threatened them also seemed plain. Both were widely and deeply experienced. It was a political age.

But the values threatened in the era after World War Two are often neither widely acknowledged as values nor widely felt to be threatened. Much private uneasiness goes unformulated; much public malaise and many decisions of enormous structural relevance never become public issues. For those who accept such inherited values as reason and freedom, it is the uneasiness itself that is the trouble; it is the indifference itself that is the issue. And it is this condition, of uneasiness and indifference, that is the signal feature of our period.

All this is so striking that it is often interpreted by observers as a shift in the very kinds of problems that need now to be formulated. We are frequently told that the problems of our decade, or even the crises of our period, have shifted from the external realm of economics and now have to do with the quality of individual life—in fact with the question of whether there is soon going to be anything that can properly be called individual life. Not child labor but comic books, not poverty but mass leisure, are at the center of concern. Many great public issues as well as many private troubles are described in terms of "the psychiatric"—often, it seems, in a pathetic attempt to avoid the large issues and problems of modern society. Often this statement seems to rest upon a provincial narrowing of interest to the Western societies, or even to the United States—thus ignoring two-thirds of mankind; often, too, it arbitrarily divorces the individual life from the larger institutions within which that life is enacted, and which on occasion bear upon it more grievously than do the intimate environments of childhood.

Problems of leisure, for example, cannot even be stated without considering problems of work. Family troubles over comic books cannot be formulated as problems without considering the plight of the contemporary family in its new relations with the newer institutions of the social structure. Neither leisure nor its debilitating uses can be understood as problems without recognition of the extent to which malaise and indifference now form the social and personal climate of contemporary American society. In this climate, no problems of "the private life" can be stated and solved without recognition of the crisis of ambition that is part of the very career of men at work in the incorporated economy.

It is true, as psychoanalysts continually point out, that people do often have "the increasing sense of being moved by obscure forces within themselves which they are unable to define." But it is *not* true, as Ernest Jones asserted, that "man's chief enemy and danger is his own unruly nature and the dark forces pent up within him." On the contrary: "Man's chief danger" today lies in the unruly forces of contemporary society itself, with its alienating methods of production, its enveloping techniques of political domination, its international anarchy—in a word, its pervasive transformations of the very "nature" of man and the conditions and aims of his life.

It is now the social scientist's foremost political and intellectual task—for here the two coincide—to make clear the elements of contemporary uneasiness and indifference. It is the central demand made upon him by other cultural workmen—by physical scientists and artists, by the intellectual community in general. It is because of this task and these demands, I believe, that the social sciences are becoming the common denominator of our cultural period, and the sociological imagination our most needed quality of mind.

DAVID SUDNOW

Normal Crimes:
Sociological Features of the Penal Code in
a Public Defender Office

CONCLUSIONS

An examination of the use of the penal code by actually practicing attorneys has revealed that categories of crime, rather than being "unsuited" to sociological analysis, are so employed as to make their analysis crucial to empirical understanding. What categories of crime are, i.e., who is assembled under this one or that, what constitute the behaviors inspected for deciding such matters, what "etiologically significant" matters are incorporated within their scope, is not, the present findings indicate, to be decided on the basis of an *a priori* inspection of their formally available definitions. The sociologist who regards the category "theft" with penal code in hand and proposes necessary, "theoretically relevant" revisions, is constructing an imagined use of the penal code as the basis for his criticism. For in their actual use, categories of crime, as we have reiterated continuously above, are, at least for this legal establishment, the shorthand reference terms for that knowledge of the social structure and its criminal events upon which the task of practically organizing the work of "representation" is premised. That knowledge includes, embodied within what burglary, petty theft, narcotics violations, child molestation and the rest *actually stand for*, knowledge of modes of criminal activity, ecological characteristics of the community, patterns of daily slum life, psychological and social biographies of offenders, criminal histories and futures; in sum, practically tested criminological wisdom. The operations of the Public Defender system, and it is clear that upon comparative analysis with other legal "firms" it would be somewhat distinctive in character, are routinely maintained via the proper use of categories of crime for everyday decision making. The proprieties of that use are not described in the state criminal code, nor are the operations of reduction, detailed above.

Abridged with the permission of the author and publisher from *Social Problems* 12 (Winter 1965): 255-76.

A cautionary word is required. It will appear as obvious that the system of providing "defense" to indigent persons described above is not representative of criminal defense work generally. How the penal code is employed, i.e., how behaviors are scrutinized under its jurisdiction and dispensations made via operations performed on its categories, in other kinds of legal establishments, has not been investigated here. The present case, albeit apparently specialized, was chosen as an example only. It may well be that, in certain forms of legal work, the penal code as a statutory document is accorded a much different and more "rigorous" scrutiny. The legalistic character of some criminal prosecutions leads one to suspect that the "letter of the law" might constitute a key reference point in preparing for a criminal defense, aiming for acquittal, or changing a statutory regulation.

PUBLIC "DEFENSE"

Recently, in many communities, the burden of securing counsel has been taken from the defendant.[1] As the accused is, by law, entitled to the aid of counsel, and as his pocketbook is often empty, numerous cities have felt obliged to establish a public defender system. There has been little resistance to this development by private attorneys among whom it is widely felt that the less time they need spend in the criminal courts, where practice is least prestigeful and lucrative, the better.[2]

Whatever the reasons for its development, we now find, in many urban places, a public defender occupying a place alongside judge and prosecutor as a regular court employee. In the county studied, the P.D. mans a daily station, like the public prosecutor, and "defends" all who come before him. He appears in court when court begins and his "clientele," composed without regard for his preferences, consists of that residual category of persons who cannot afford to bring their own spokesmen to court. In this county, the "residual" category approximates 65 per cent of the total number of criminal cases. In a given year, the twelve attorneys who comprise the P.D. Office "represent" about 3,000 defendants in the municipal and superior courts of the county.

While the courtroom encounters of private attorneys are brief, businesslike and circumscribed, interactionally and temporally, by the particular cases that bring them there, the P.D. attends to the courtroom as his regular work place and conveys in his demeanor his place as a member of its core personnel.

While private attorneys come and leave court with their clients (who are generally "on bail"), the P.D. arrives in court each morning at nine, takes his station at the defense table, and deposits there the batch of files that he will refer to during the day. When, during morning "calendar,"[3] a private attorney's case is called, the P.D. steps back from the defense table, leaving his belongings in place there, and temporarily relinquishes his station. No private attorney has enough defendants in a given court on a given day to claim a right to make a desk of the defense table. If the P.D. needs some information from his central office, he uses the clerk's telephone, a privilege that few private lawyers feel at home enough to take. In the course of calendar work, a lawyer will often have occasion to request a delay or "continuance" of several days until the next stage of his client's proceedings. The private attorney addresses the prosecutor via the judge to request such an alteration; the P.D. walks directly over to the D.A.:

> Private attorney: "If the prosecutor finds it convenient your Honor, my client would prefer to have his preliminary hearing on Monday, the 24th."
> Judge: "Is that date suitable to the district attorney?"
> Prosecutor: "Yes, your honor."
> Private attorney: "Thank you, your Honor."
>
> Public Defender: "Bob (D.A.), how about moving Smith's prelim up to the 16th?"
> Prosecutor: "Well, Jim, we've got Jones on that afternoon."
> Public Defender: "Let's see, how's the 22nd?"
> Prosecutor: "That's fine, Jim, the 22nd."

If, during the course of a proceeding, the P.D. has some minor matter to tend to with the D.A., he uses the time when a private attorney is addressing the bench to walk over to the prosecutor's table and whisper his requests, suggestions or questions. The P.D. uses the prosecutor's master calendar to check on an upcoming court date; so does the D.A. with the P.D.'s. The D.A. and P.D. are on a first name basis and throughout the course of a routine day interact as a team of co-workers.

While the central focus of the private attorney's attention is his client, the courtroom and affairs of court constitute the locus of involvements for the P.D. The public defender and public prosecutor, each representatives of their respective offices, jointly handle the greatest bulk of the court's daily activity.

The P.D. office, rather than assign its attorneys to clients, employs the arrangement of stationing attorneys in different courts to "represent" all those who come before that station. As defendants are moved about from courtroom to courtroom throughout the course of their proceedings (both from municipal to superior courtrooms for felony cases, and from one municipal courtroom to another when there is a specialization of courts, e.g., jury, non-jury, arraignment, etc.), the P.D. sees defendants only at those places in their paths when they appear in the court he is manning. A given defendant may be "represented" by one P.D. at arraignment, another at preliminary hearing, a third at trial and a fourth when sentenced.

At the first interview with a client (initial interviews occur in the jail where attorneys go, *en masse*, to "pick up new defendants" in the afternoons) a file is prepared on the defendant. In each file is recorded the charge brought against the defendant and, among other things, his next court date. Each evening attorneys return new files to the central office where secretaries prepare court books for each courtroom that list the defendants due to appear in a given court on a given day. In the mornings, attorneys take the court books from the office and remove from the central file the files of those defendants due to appear in "their court" that day.

There is little communication between P.D. and client. After the first interview, the defendant's encounters with the P.D. are primarily in court. Only under special circumstances (to be discussed below) are there contacts between lawyers and defendants in the jail before and after appearances in court. The bulk of "preparation for court" (either trials or non-trial matters) occurs at the first interview. The attorney on station, the "attending attorney," is thus a stranger to "his client," and vice versa. Over the course of his proceedings, a defendant will have several attorneys (in one instance a man was "represented" by eight P.D.'s on a charge of simple assault). Defendants who come to court find a lawyer they don't know conducting their trials, entering their motions, making their pleas, and the rest. Often there is no introduction of P.D. to defendant; defendants are prepared to expect a strange face:

> Don't be surprised when you see another P.D. in court with you on Tuesday. You just do what he tells you to. He'll know all about your case.

P.D.s seldom talk about particular defendants among themselves. When they converse about trials, the facts of cases, etc., they do so not so much for briefing, e.g., "This is what I think you should do when you 'get him'," but rather as small talk, as "What have you got going today." The P.D. does not rely on the information about a case he receives from a previous attending attorney in order to know how to manage his "representation." Rather, the file is relied upon to furnish all the information essential for making an "appearance." These appearances range from morning calendar work (e.g., arraignments, motions, continuances, etc.) to trials on offenses from drunkenness to assault with a deadly weapon. In the course of a routine day, the P.D. will receive his batch of files in the morning and, seeing them for the first time that day, conduct numerous trials, preliminary hearings, calendar appearances, sentencing proceedings, etc. They do not study files overnight. Attorneys will often only look over a file a half hour or so before the jury trial begins.

THE FIRST INTERVIEW

As the first interview is often the only interview and as the file prepared there is central for the continuing "representation" of the defendant by other attorneys, it is important to examine these interviews and the file's contents. From the outset, the P.D. attends to establishing the typical character of the case before him and thereby instituting routinely employed reduction arrangements. The defendant's appearance, e.g., his race, demeanor, age, style of talk, way of attending to the occasion of his incarceration, etc., provides the P.D. with an initial sense of his place in the social structure. Knowing only that the defendant is charged with section 459 (Burglary) of the penal code, the P.D. employs his conception of typical burglars against which the character of the present defendant is assessed.

> ...he had me fooled for a while. With that accent of his and those Parliaments he was smoking I thought something was strange. It turned out to be just another burglary. You heard him about New York and the way he had a hold on him there that he was running away from. I just guess N.Y. is a funny place, you can never tell what kinds of people get involved in crimes there.

The initial fact of the defendant's "putting in a request to see the P.D." establishes his lower position in the class structure of the community:

> We just never get wealthier people here. They usually don't stay in jail overnight and then they call a private attorney. The P.D. gets everything at the bottom of the pile.

Searching over the criminal history (past convictions and arrests) the defendant provides when preliminary fact sheet data is recorded in the file, the P.D. gets a sense of the man's typical pattern of criminal activity. It is not the particular offenses for which he is charged that are crucial, but the constellation of prior offenses and the sequential pattern they take:

> I could tell as soon as he told me he had four prior drunk charges that he was just another of these skid row bums. You could look at him and tell.

> When you see a whole string of forgery counts in the past you pretty much know what kind of case you're dealing with. You either get those who commit an occasional forgery, or those that do nothing but.... With a whole bunch of prior checks (prior forgery convictions) you can bet that he cashes little ones. I didn't even have to ask for the amount you know. I seldom come across one over a hundred bucks.

> From the looks of him and the way he said "I wasn't doing anything, just playing with her," you know, its the usual kind of thing, just a little diddling or something. We can try to get it out on a simple assault.

When a P.D. puts questions to the defendant he is less concerned with recording nuances of the instant event (e.g., how many feet from the bar were you when the cops came in, did you break into the back gate or the front door), than with establishing its similarity with "events of this sort."

That similarity is established, not by discovering statutorily relevant events of the present case, but by locating the event in a sociologically constructed class of "such cases." The first questions directed to the defendant are of the character that answers to them either confirm or throw into question the assumed typicality. First questions with ADWs are of the order: "How long had you been drinking before this all started?"; with "child molestation cases": "How long were you hanging around before this began?"; with "forgery" cases: "Was this the second or third check you cashed in the same place?"

We shall present three short excerpts from three first interviews. They all begin with the first question asked after preliminary background data is gathered. The first is with a 288 (child molestation), the second with a 459 (burglary) and the last with a 11530 (possession of marijuana). Each interview was conducted by a different Public Defender. In each case the P.D. had no information about the defendant or this particular crime other than that provided by the penal code number:

288

P.D.: O.K., why don't you start out by telling me how this thing got started?

Def.: Well, I was at the park and all I did was to ask this little girl if she wanted to sit on my lap for awhile and you know, just sit on my lap. Well, about twenty minutes later I'm walkin' down the street about a block away from the park and this cop pulls up and there the same little girl is, you know, sitting in the back seat with some dame. The cop asks me to stick my head in the back seat and he asks the kid if I was the one and she says yes. So he puts me in the car and takes a statement from me and here I am in the joint. All I was doin was playin with her a little....

P.D.: (interrupting)...O.K. I get the story, let's see what we can do. If I can get this charge reduced to a misdemeanor then I would advise you to plead guilty, particularly since you have a record and that wouldn't look too well in court with a jury.

(the interview proceeded for another two or three minutes and the decision to plead guilty was made)

459

P.D.. Why don't you start by telling me where this place was that you broke into?

Def.: I don't know for sure...I think it was on 13th Street or something like that.

P.D.: Had you ever been there before?

Def.: I hang around that neighborhood you know, so I guess I've been in the place before, yeah.

P.D.: What were you going after?

Def.: I don't know, whatever there was so's I could get a little cash. Man, I was pretty broke that night.

P.D.: Was anyone with you?

Def.:   No, I was by myself.
P.D.:   How much did you break up the place?
Def.:   I didn't do nothing. The back window was open a little bit see and I just put my hand in there and opened the door. I was just walking in when I heard police comin so I turn around and start to run. And, they saw me down the block and that was that.
P.D.:   Were you drunk at the time?
Def.:   I wasn't drunk, no, I maybe had a drink or two that evening but I wasn't drunk or anything like that.

11530

P.D.:   Well Smith, why don't you tell me where they found it (the marijuana)?
Def.:   I was driving home from the drugstore with my friend and this cop car pulls me up to the side. Two guys get out, one of them was wearing a uniform and the other was a plain clothes man. They told us to get out of the car and then they searched me and then my friend. Then this guy without the uniform he looked over into the car and picked up this thing from the back floor and said something to the other one. Then he asked me if I had any more of the stuff and I said I didn't know what he was talking about. So he wrote something down on a piece of paper and made me sign it. Then he told my friend to go home and they took me down here to the station and booked me on possession of marijuana. I swear I didn't have no marijuana.
P.D.:   You told me you were convicted of possession in 1959.
Def.:   Yeah, but I haven't touched any of the stuff since then. I don't know what it was doing in my car, but I haven't touched the stuff since that last time.
P.D.:   You ought to know it doesn't make any difference whether or not they catch you using, just so long as they find it on your possession or in a car, or your house, or something.
Def.:   Man, I swear I don't know how it got there. Somebody must have planted it there.
P.D.   Look, you know as well as I do that with your prior conviction and this charge now that you could go away from here for five years or so. So just calm down a minute and let's look at this thing reasonably. If you go to trial and lose the trial, you're stuck. You'll be in the joint until you're 28 years old. If you plead to this one charge without the priors then we can get you into jail maybe, or a year or two at the most in the joint. If you wait until the preliminary hearing and then they charge the priors, boy you've had it, its too late.
Def.:   Well how about a trial?
        (After ten minutes, the defendant decided to plead guilty to one charge of possession, before the date of the preliminary hearing)

Let us consider, in light of the previous discussion, some of the features of these interviews.

1. In each case the information sought is not "data" for organizing the particular facts of the case for deciding proper penal code designations (or

with a view toward undermining the assignment of a designation in an anticipated trial). In the 288 instance, the P.D. interrupted when he had enough information to confirm his sense of the case's typicality and construct a typifying portrayal of the present defendant. The character of the information supplied by the defendant was such that it was specifically lacking detail about the particular occurrences, e.g., the time, place, what was said to the girl, what precisely did the defendant do or not do, his "state of mind," etc. The defendant's appearance and prior record (in this case the defendant was a fifty-five year old white, unemployed, unskilled laborer, with about ten prior drunk arrests, seven convictions, and two prior sex offense violations) was relied upon to provide the sense of the present occasion. The P.D. straightforwardly approached the D.A. and arranged for a "contributing to the delinquency of a minor" reduction. In the burglary case, the question, "Had you ever been there before?", was intended to elicit what was received, e.g., that the place was a familiar one to the defendant. Knowing that the place was in the defendant's neighborhood establishes its character as a skid row area business; that the First Federal Bank was not entered has been confirmed. "What were you going after?", also irrelevant to the 459 section of the penal code, provides him with information that there was no special motive for entering this establishment. The question, "Was anyone with you?", when answered negatively, placed the event in the typical class of "burglaries" as solitary, non-coordinated activities. The remaining questions were directed as well to confirming the typical character of the event, and the adequacy of the defendant's account is not decided by whether or not the P.D. can now decide whether the statutory definition of the contemplated reduction or the original charge is satisfied. Its adequacy is determined by the ability with which the P.D. can detect its normal character. The accounts provided thus may have the character of anecdotes, sketches, phrases, etc. In the first instance, with the 288, the prior record and the defendant's appearance, demeanor and style of talking about the event was enough to warrant his typical treatment.

2. The most important feature of the P.D.'s questioning is the presupposition of guilt that makes his proposed questions legitimate and answerable at the outset. To pose the question, "Why don't you start by telling me where this place was that you broke into?" as a lead question, the P.D. takes it that the defendant is guilty of a crime and the the crime for which he is charged probably describes what essentially occurred.

The P.D.'s activity is seldom geared to securing acquittals for clients. He and the D.A., as co-workers in the same courts, take it for granted that the persons who come before the courts are guilty of crimes and are to be treated accordingly.

> Most of them have records as you can see. Almost all of them have been through our courts before. And the police just don't make mistakes in this town. That's one thing about—, we've got the best police force in the state.

As we shall argue below, the way defendants are "represented" (the station manning rather than assignment of counselors to clients), the way trials are conducted, the way interviews are held and the penal code employed—all of the P.D.'s work is premised on the supposition that people charged with crimes have committed crimes.

This presupposition makes such first questions as "Why don't you start by telling me where this place was..." reasonable questions. When the answer comes: "What place? I don't know what you are talking about," the defendant is taken to be a phony, making an "innocent pitch." The conceivable first question: "Did you do it?", is not asked because it is felt that this gives the defendant the notion that he can try an "innocent pitch":

> I never ask them, "did you do it?", because on one hand I know they did and mainly because then they think that they can play games with us. We can always check their records and usually they have a string of offenses. You don't have to, though, because in a day or two they change their story and plead guilty. Except for the stubborn ones.

Of the possible answers to an opening question, bewilderment, the inability to answer or silence are taken to indicate that the defendant is putting the P.D. on. For defendants who refuse to admit anything, the P.D. threatens:

> Look, if you don't want to talk, that's your business. I can't help you. All I can say is that if you go to trial on this beef you're going to spend a long time in the joint. When you get ready to tell me the story straight, then we can see what can be done.

If the puzzlement comes because the wrong question is asked, e.g., "There wasn't any fight—that's not the way it happened," the defendant will start to fill in the story. The P.D. awaits to see if, how far, and in what ways the instant case is deviant. If the defendant is charged with burglary and a middle class establishment was burglarized, windows shattered, a large payroll sought after and a gun used, then the reduction to petty theft, generally employed for "normal burglaries," would be more difficult to arrange.

Generally, the P.D. doesn't have to discover the atypical kinds of cases through questioning. Rather, the D.A., in writing the original complaint, provides the P.D. with clues that the typical recipe, given the way the event occurred, will not be allowable. Where the way it occurs is such that it does not resemble normal burglaries and the routinely used penalty would reduce it *too far* commensurate with the way the crime occurred, the D.A. frequently charges various situationally included offenses, indicating to the P.D. that the procedure to employ here is to suggest "dropping" some of the charges, leaving the originally charged greatest offense as it stands.

In the general case he doesn't charge all those offenses that he legally might. He might charge "child molesting" and "loitering around a schoolyard" but typically only the greater charge is made. The D.A. does so so as to provide for a later reduction that will appear particularly lenient in that it seemingly involves a *change* in the charge. Were he to charge both molesting and loitering, he would be obliged, moreover, should the case come to trial, to introduce evidence for both offenses. The D.A. is thus always constrained not to set overly high charges or not situationally included multiple offenses by the possibility that the defendant will not plead guilty to a lesser offense and the case will go to trial. Of primary importance is that he doesn't charge multiple offenses so that the P.D. will be in the best position vis-à-vis the defendant. He thus charges the first complaint so as to provide for a "setup."

The alteration of charges must be made in open court. The P.D. requests to have a new plea entered:

> P.D.: Your honor, in the interests of justice, my client would like to change his plea of not guilty to the charge of burglary and enter a plea of guilty to the charge of petty theft.
> Judge: Is this new plea acceptable to the prosecution?
> D.A.: Yes, your honor.

The prosecutor knows beforehand that the request will be made, and has agreed in advance to allow it.

I asked a P.D. how they felt about making such requests in open court, i.e., asking for a reduction from one offense to another when the latter is obviously not necessarily included and often (as is the case in burglary-to-petty theft) not situationally included. He summarized the office's feeling:

> ...in the old days, ten or so years ago, we didn't like to do it in front of the judge. What we used to do when we made a deal was that the D.A. would dismiss the original charge and write up a new complaint altogether. That took a lot of time. We had to re-arraign him all over again back in the muni court and everything. Besides, in the same courtroom, everyone used to know what was going on anyway. Now, we just ask for a change of plea to the lesser charge regardless of whether it's included or not. Nobody thinks twice about asking for petty theft on burglary, or drunkenness on car theft, or something like that. It's just the way it's done.

Some restrictions are felt. Assaultive crimes (e.g., ADW, simple assault, attempted murder, etc.) will not be reduced to or from "money offenses" (burglary, robbery, theft) unless the latter involve weapons or some violence. Also, victimless crimes (narcotics, drunkenness) are not reduced to or from assaultive or "money offenses," unless there is some factual relation, e.g., drunkenness with a fight might turn out to be simple assault reduced to drunkenness.

For most cases that come before their courts, the P.D. and D.A. are able to employ reductions that are formulated for handling typical cases. While some burglaries, rapes, narcotics violations and petty thefts, are instigated in strange ways and involve atypical facts, some manipulation in the way the initial charge is made can be used to set up a procedure to replace the simple charge-alteration form of reducing.

RECALCITRANT DEFENDANTS

Most of the P.D.'s cases that "have to go to trial" are those where the P.D. is not able to sell the defendant on the "bargain." These are cases for which reductions are available, reductions that are constructed on the basis of the typicality of the offense and allowable by the D.A. These are normal crimes committed by "stubborn" defendants.

So-called "stubborn" defendants will be distinguished from a second class of offenders, those who commit *crimes which are atypical in their character (for this community, at this time, etc.) or who commit crimes which while typical (recurrent for this community, this time, etc.) are committed atypically.* The manner in which the P.D. and D.A. must conduct the representation and prosecution of these defendants is radically different. To characterize the special problems the P.D. has with each class of defendants, it is first necessary to point out a general feature of the P.D.'s orientation to the work of the courts that has hitherto not been made explicit. This orientation will be merely sketched here.

As we noticed, the defendant's guilt is not attended to. That is to say, the presupposition of guilt, as a *presupposition*, does not say "You are guilty" with a pointing accusatory finger, but "You are guilty, you know it, I know it, so let's get down to the business of deciding what to do with you." When a defendant agrees to plead guilty, he is not *admitting* his guilt; when asked to plead guilty, he is not being asked, "Come on, admit it, you know you were *wrong*," but rather, "Why don't you be sensible about this thing?" What is sought is not a *confession*, but reasonableness.

The presupposition of guilt as a way of attending to the treatment of defendants has its counterpart in the way the P.D. attends to the entire court process, prosecuting machinery, law enforcement techniques, and the community.

For P.D. and D.A. it is a routinely encountered phenomenon that persons in the community regularly commit criminal offenses, are regularly brought before the courts, and are regularly transported to the state and county penal institutions. To confront a "criminal" is, for D.A. and P.D., no special experience, nothing to tell their wives about, nothing to record as outstanding in the happenings of the day. Before "their court" scores of "criminals" pass each day.

The morality of the courts is taken for granted. The P.D. assumes that the D.A., the police, judge, the narcotics agents and others all conduct their business as it must be conducted and in a proper fashion. That the police may hide out to deceive petty violators; that narcotics agents may regularly employ illicit entrapment procedures to find suspects; that investigators may routinely arrest suspects before they have sufficient grounds and only later uncover warrantable evidence for a formal booking; that the police may beat suspects; that judges may be "tough" because they are looking to support for higher office elections; that some laws may be specifically prejudicial against certain classes of persons—whatever may be the actual course of charging and convicting defendants—all of this is taken, as one P.D. put it, "as part of the system and the way it has to be." And the P.D. is part of the team.

While it is common to overhear private attorneys call judges "bastards," policemen "hoodlums" and prosecutors "sadists," the P.D., in the presence of such talk, remains silent. When the P.D. "loses" a case—and we shall see that *losing* is an adequate description only for some circumstances—he is likely to say "I knew *he* couldn't win." Private attorneys, on the other hand, will not hesitate to remark, as one did in a recent case. "You haven't got a fucking chance in front of that son-of-a-bitch dictator." In the P.D. office, there is a total absence of such condemnation.

The P.D. takes it for granted and attends to the courts in accord with the view that "what goes on in this business is what goes on and what goes on is the way it should be." It is rare to hear a public defender voice protest against a particular law, procedure, or official. One of the attorneys mentioned that he felt the new narcotics law (which makes it mandatory that a high minimum sentence be served for "possession or sale of narcotics") wasn't too severe "considering that they wanted to give them the chair." Another indicated that the more rigid statute "will probably cure a lot of them because they'll be in for so long." One P.D. feels that wire-tapping would be a useful adjunct to police procedure. It is generally said, by everyone in the office, that ". . . is one of the best cities in the state when it comes to police."

In the P.D.'s interviews, the defendant's guilt only becomes a topic when the defendant himself attempts to direct attention to his innocence. Such attempts are never taken seriously by the P.D. but are seen as "innocent pitches," as "being wise," as "not knowing what is good for him." Defendants who make "innocent pitches" often find themselves able to convince the P.D. to have trials. The P.D. is in a professional and organizational bind in that he requires that his "clients" agree with whatever action he takes "on their behalf":

> Can you imagine what might happen if we went straight to the D.A. with a deal to which the client later refused to agree? Can you see him in court screaming how the P.D. sold him out? As it is, we get plenty of letters purporting to show why we don't do our job. Judges are swamped with letters condemning the P.D. Plenty of appeals get started this way.

Some defendants don't buy the offer of less time as constituting sufficient grounds for avoiding a trial. To others, it appears that "copping out" is worse than having a trial regardless of the consequences for the length of sentence. The following remarks, taken from P.D. files, illustrate the terms in which such "stubborn" defendants are conceived:

> Def wants a trial, but he is dead. In lieu of a possible 995, DA agreed to put note in his file recommending a deal. This should be explored and encouraged as big break for Def.

> Chance of successful defense negligible. Def realizes this but says he ain't going to cop to no strong-arm. See if we can set him straight.

> Dead case. Too many witnesses and...used in two of the transactions. However, Def is a very squirmy jailhouse lawyer and refuses to face facts.

> Possibly the DA in Sup/Ct could be persuaded into cutting her loose if she took the 211 and one of the narco counts. If not, the Def, who is somewhat recalcitrant and stubborn, will probably demand a JT (jury trial).

The routine trial, generated as it is by the defendant's refusal to make a lesser plea, is the "defendant's fault":

> What the hell are we supposed to do with them. If they can't listen to good reason and take a bargain, then it's their tough luck. If they go to prison, well, they're the ones who are losing the trials, not us.

When the P.D. enters the courtroom, he takes it that he is going to lose, e.g., the defendant is going to prison. When he "prepares" for trial, he doesn't prepare to "win." There is no attention given to "how am I going to construct a defense in order that I can get this defendant free of the charges against him." In fact, he doesn't "prepare for trial" in any "ordinary" sense (I use the term *ordinary* with hesitation; what *preparation for trial* might in fact involve with other than P.D. lawyers has not, to my knowledge, been investigated.)

For the P.D., "preparation for trial" involves, essentially, learning what "burglary cases" are like, what "rape cases" are like, what "assaults" are like. The P.D.'s main concern is to conduct his part of the proceedings in accord with complete respect for proper legal procedure. He raises objections to improper testimony; introduces motions whenever they seem called for; demands his "client's rights" to access to the prosecution's evidence before trial (through so-called "discovery proceedings"); cross examines all witnesses; does not introduce evidence that he expects will not be allowable; asks all those questions of all those people that he must in order to have addressed himself to the task of insuring that the *corpus delicti* has been established; carefully summarizes the evidence that has been presented in making a closing argument. Throughout, at every point, he conducts his "defense" in such a manner that no one can say of him "He has been negligent, there are grounds for appeal here." He systematically provides, in accord with the prescriptions of due process and the fourteenth amendment, a completely proper, "adequate legal representation."

At the same time, the district attorney, and the county which employs them both, can rely on the P.D. not to attempt to morally degrade police officers in cross examination; not to impeach the state's witnesses by trickery; not to attempt an exposition of the entrapment methods of narcotics agents; not to condemn the community for the "racial prejudice that produces our criminals" (the phrase of a private attorney during closing argument); not to challenge the prosecution of "these women who are trying to raise a family without a husband" (the statement of another private attorney during closing argument on a welfare fraud case); in sum, not to make an issue of the moral character of the administrative machinery of the local courts, the community or the police. He will not cause any serious trouble for the routine motion of the court conviction process. Laws will not be challenged, cases will not be tried to test the constitutionality of procedures and statutes, judges will not be personally degraded, police will be free from scrutiny to decide the legitimacy of their operations, and the community will not be condemned for its segregative practices against Negroes. The P.D.'s defense is completely proper, in accord with correct legal procedure, and specifically amoral in its import, manner of delivery, and perceived implications for the propriety of the prosecution enterprise.

In "return" for all this, the district attorney treats the defendant's guilt in a matter-of-fact fashion, doesn't get hostile in the course of the proceedings, doesn't insist that the jury or judge "throw the book," but rather "puts on a trial" (in their way of referring to their daily tasks) in order to, with a minimum of strain, properly place the defendant behind bars. Both prosecutor and public defender thus protect the moral character of the other's charges from exposure. Should the P.D. attend to demonstrating the innocence of his client by attempting to undermine the legitimate character of police operations, the prosecutor might feel obliged in return to employ devices to degrade the moral character of the P.D.'s client. Should the D.A. attack defendants in court, by pointing to the specifically immoral character of their activities, the P.D. might feel obligated, in response, to raise into relief the moral texture of the D.A.'s and police's and community's operations. Wherever possible, each holds the other in check. But the "check" need not be continuously held in place, or even attended to self consciously, for both P.D. and D.A. trust one another implicitly. The D.A. knows, with certainty, that the P.D. will not make a closing argument that resembles the following by a private attorney, from which I have paraphrased key excerpts:

> If it hadn't been for all the publicity that this case had in our wonderful local newspapers, you wouldn't want to throw the book at these men.

If you'd clear up your problems with the Negro in...maybe you wouldn't have cases like this in your courts.

(after sentence was pronounced) Your honor, I just would like to say one thing—that I've never heard or seen such a display of injustice as I've seen here in this court today. It's a sad commentary on the state of our community if people like yourself pay more attention to the local political machines than to the lives of our defendants. I think you are guilty of that, your Honor.

(At this last statement, one of the P.D.s who was in the courtroom turned to me and said, "He sure is looking for a contempt charge.")

The P.D. knows how to conduct his trials because he knows how to conduct "assault with deadly weapons" trials, "burglary" trials, "rape" trials, and the rest. The *corpus delicti here* provides him with a basis for asking "proper questions," making the "proper" cross examinations, and pointing out the "proper" things to jurors about "reasonable doubt." He need not extensively gather information about the specific facts of the instant case. Whatever is needed in the way of "facts of the case" arise in the course of the D.A.'s presentation. He employs the "strategy" of directing the same questions to the witness as were put by the D.A. with added emphasis on the question mark, or an inserted "Did you really see...?" His "defense" consists of attempting to "bring out" slightly variant aspects of the D.A.'s story by questioning his own witnesses (whom he seldom interviews before beginning trial but who are interviewed by the Office's two "investigators") and the defendant.

With little variation the same questions are put to all defendants charged with the same crimes. The P.D. learns with experience what to expect as the "facts of the case." These facts, in their general structure, portray social circumstances that he can anticipate by virtue of his knowledge of the normal features of offense categories and types of offenders. The "details" of the instant case are "discovered" over the course of hearing them in court. In this regard, the "information" that "comes out" is often as new to him as to the jury.

Employing a common sense conception of what criminal lawyers behave like in cross examination and argument, and the popular portrayal of their demeanor and style of addressing adversary witnesses, the onlooker comes away with the sense of having witnessed not a trial at all, but a set of motions, a perfunctorily carried off event. A sociological analysis of this sense would require a systematic attempt to describe the features of adversary trial conduct.

NOTES

1. For general histories of indigent defender systems in the United States, see The Association of the Bar of the City of New York, *Equal Justice for the Accused,* Garden City,

New York: 1959; and E.A. Brownell, *Legal Aid in the United States,* Rochester, New York: The Lawyer's Cooperative Publishing Company, 1951.

2. The experience of the Public Defender system is distinctly different in this regard from that of the Legal Aid Societies, which, I am told, have continually met very strong opposition to their establishment by local bar associations.

3. "Calendar part" consists of that portion of the court day, typically in the mornings, when all matters other than trials are heard, e.g., arraignments, motions, continuances, sentencing, probation reports, etc.

THEODORE M. NEWCOMB

Attitude Development as
a Function of Reference Groups:
The Bennington Study

In a membership group in which certain attitudes are approved (i.e., held by majorities, and conspicuously so by leaders), individuals acquire the approved attitudes to the extent that the membership group (particularly as symbolized by leaders and dominant subgroups) serves as a positive point of reference. The findings of the Bennington study seem to be better understood in terms of this thesis than any other. The distinction between membership group and reference group is a crucial one, in fact, although the original report did not make explicit use of it.

The above statement does not imply that no reference groups other than the membership group are involved in attitude formation; as we shall see, this is distinctly not the case. Neither does it imply that the use of the membership group as reference group necessarily results in adoption of the approved attitudes. It may also result in their rejection; hence the word *positive* in the initial statement. It is precisely these variations in degree and manner of relationship between reference group and membership group which must be known in order to explain individual variations in attitude formation, as reported in this study.

The essential facts about the Bennington membership group are as follows: (1) It was small enough (about 250 women students) so that data could be obtained from every member. (2) It was in most respects self-sufficient: college facilities provided not only the necessities of living and studying, but also a cooperative store, post office and Western Union office, beauty parlor, gasoline station, and a wide range of recreational opportunities. The average student visited the four-mile-distant village once a week and spent one week end a month away from the college. (3) It was self-conscious and enthusiastic, in large part because it was new (the

Prepared by the author from data originally reported in *Personality and Social Change* (New York: Dryden Press, 1943), and reprinted from M. Sherif, *An Outline of Social Psychology* (New York: Harper & Brothers, 1948), pp. 139-55, by permission of the author and the publisher. Copyright 1948 by Harper & Row, Publishers, Inc.

study was begun during the first year in which there was a senior class) and because of the novelty and attractiveness of the college's educational plan. (4) It was unusually active and concerned about public issues, largely because the faculty felt that its educational duties included the familiarizing of an oversheltered student body with the implications of a depression-torn America and a war-threatened world. (5) It was relatively homogeneous in respect to home background; tuition was very high, and the large majority of students came from urban, economically privileged families whose social attitudes were conservative.

Most individuals in this total membership group went through rather marked changes in attitudes toward public issues, as noted below. In most cases the total membership group served as the reference group for the changing attitudes. But some individuals changed little or not at all in attitudes during the four years of the study; attitude persistence was in some of these cases a function of the membership group as reference group and in some cases it was not. Among those who did change, moreover, the total membership group sometimes served as reference group but sometimes it did not. An oversimple theory of "assimilation into the community" thus leaves out of account some of those whose attitudes did and some of those whose attitudes did not change; they remain unexplained exceptions. A theory which traces the impact of other reference groups as well as the effect of the membership group seems to account for all cases without exception.

The general trend of attitude change for the total group is from freshman conservatism to senior nonconservatism (as the term was commonly applied to the issues toward which attitudes were measured). During the 1936 presidential election, for example, 62 percent of the freshmen and only 14 percent of the juniors and seniors "voted" for the Republican candidate, 29 percent of freshmen and 54 percent of juniors and seniors for Roosevelt, and 9 percent of freshmen as compared with 30 percent of juniors and seniors for the Socialist or Communist candidates. Attitudes toward nine specific issues were measured during the four years of the study, and seniors were less conservative in all of them than freshmen; six of the nine differences are statistically reliable. These differences are best shown by a Likert-type scale labeled Political and Economic Progressivism (PEP) which dealt with such issues as unemployment, public relief, and the rights of organized labor, which were made prominent by the New Deal. Its odd-even reliability was about .9, and it was given once or more during each of the four years of the study to virtually all students. The critical ratios of the differences between freshmen and juniors-seniors in four successive years ranged between 3.9 and 6.5; the difference between the average freshman and senior scores of 44 individuals (the entire class that graduated in 1939) gives a critical ratio of 4.3.

As might be anticipated in such a community, *individual prestige was associated with nonconservatism.* Frequency of choice as one of five students "most worthy to represent the College" at an intercollegiate gathering was used as a measure of prestige. Nominations were submitted in sealed envelopes of 99 percent of all students in two successive years, with almost identical results. The nonconservatism of those with high prestige is not merely the result of the fact that juniors and seniors are characterized by both high prestige and nonconservatism; in each class those who have most prestige are least conservative. For example, ten freshmen receiving 2 to 4 choices had an average PEP score of 64.6 as compared with 72.8 for freshmen not chosen at all (high scores are conservative); eight sophomores chosen 12 or more times had an average score of 63.6 as compared with 71.3 for those not chosen; the mean PEP score of five juniors and seniors chosen 40 or more times was 50.4 and of the fifteen chosen 12 to 39 times, 57.6, as compared with 69.0 for those not chosen. In each class, those intermediate in prestige are also intermediate in average PEP score.

Such were the attitudinal characteristics of the total membership group, expressed in terms of average scores. Some individuals, however, showed these characteristics in heightened form and others failed to show them at all. An examination of the various reference groups in relation to which attitude change did or did not occur, and of the ways in which they were brought to bear, will account for a large part of such attitude variance.

Information concerning reference groups was obtained both directly, from the subjects themselves, and indirectly, from other students and from teachers. Chief among the indirect procedures was the obtaining of indexes of "community citizenship" by a guess-who technique. Each of twenty-four students, carefully selected to represent every cross section and grouping of importance within the community, named three individuals from each of three classes who were reputedly most extreme in each of twenty-eight characteristics related to community citizenship. The relationship between reputation for community identification and nonconservatism is a close one, in spite of the fact that no reference was made to the latter characteristic when the judges made their ratings. A reputation index was computed, based upon the frequency with which individuals were named in five items dealing with identification with the community, minus the number of times they were named in five other items dealing with negative community attitude. Examples of the former items are: "absorbed in college community affairs," and "influenced by community expectations regarding codes, standards, etc."; examples of the latter are: "indifferent to activities of student committees," and "resistant to community expectations regarding codes, standards, etc." The mean senior PEP score of fifteen individuals whose index was +15 or more was 54.4; of sixty-three whose index was +4 to —4, 65.3; and of ten whose index was —15 or less, 68.2.

To have the reputation of identifying oneself with the community is not the same thing, however, as to identify the community as a reference group for a specific purpose—e.g., in this case, as a point of reference for attitudes toward public issues. In short, the reputation index is informative as to degree and direction of tendency to use the total membership group as a *general* reference group, but not necessarily as a group to which social attitudes are referred. For this purpose information was obtained directly from students.

Informal investigation had shown that whereas most students were aware of the marked freshman-to-senior trend away from conservatism, a few (particularly among the conservatives) had little or no awareness of it. Obviously, those not aware of the dominant community trend could not be using the community as a reference group for an attitude. (It does not follow, of course, that all those who are aware of it are necessarily using the community as reference group.) A simple measure of awareness was therefore devised. Subjects were asked to respond in two ways to a number of attitude statements taken from the PEP scale: first, to indicate agreement or disagreement (for example, with the statement: "The budget should be balanced before the government spends any money on social security"); and second, to estimate what percentage of freshmen, juniors and seniors, and faculty would agree with the statement. From these responses was computed an index of divergence (of own attitude) from the estimated majority of juniors and seniors. Thus a positive index on the part of a senior indicates the degree to which her own responses are more conservative than those of her classmates, and a negative index the degree to which they are less conservative. Those seniors whose divergence index more or less faithfully reflects the true difference between own and class attitude may (or may not) be using the class as an attitude reference group; those whose divergence indexes represent an exaggerated or minimized version of the true relationship between own and class attitude are clearly not using the class as an attitude reference group, or if so, only in a fictitious sense. (For present purposes the junior-senior group may be taken as representative of the entire student body, since it is the group which "sets the tone" of the total membership group.)

These data were supplemented by direct information obtained in interviews with seniors in three consecutive classes, just prior to graduation. Questions were asked about resemblance between own attitudes and those of class majorities and leaders, about parents' attitudes and own resemblance to them, about any alleged "social pressure to become liberal," about probable reaction if the dominant college influence had been conservative instead of liberal, etc. Abundant information was also available from the college personnel office and from the college psychiatrist. It was not possible to combine all of these sources of information into intensive studies of each individual, but complete data were assembled for (roughly) the most conservative and least conservative sixths of three consecutive graduating classes. The twenty-four nonconservative and nineteen conservative seniors thus selected for intensive study were classified according to their indexes of conservative divergence and of community reputation. Thus eight sets of seniors were identified, all individuals within each set having in common similar attitude scores, similar reputations for community identification, and similar degrees of awareness (based upon divergence index) of own attitude position relative to classmates. The following descriptions of these eight sets of seniors will show that there was a characteristic pattern of relationship between membership group and reference group within each of the sets.

1. *Conservatives, reputedly negativistic, aware of their own relative conservatism.* Four of the five are considered stubborn or resistant by teachers (all five, by student judges). Three have prestige scores of 0, scores of the other two being about average for their class. Four of the five are considered by teachers or psychiatrist, or by both to be overdependent upon one or both parents. All of the four who were interviewed described *their major hopes*, on entering college, *in terms of social rather than academic prestige:* all four felt that they had been defeated in this aim. The following verbatim quotations are illustrative:

E2: "Probably the feeling that (my instructors) didn't accept me led me to reject their opinions." (She estimates classmates as being only moderately less conservative than herself, but faculty as much less so.)

G32: "I wouldn't care to be intimate with those so-called 'liberal' student leaders." (*She claims to be satisfied with a small group of friends.* She is chosen as friend, in a sociometric questionnaire responded to by all students, only twice, and reciprocates both choices; both are conservative students.)

F22: "I wanted to disagree with all the noisy liberals, but I was afraid and I couldn't. *So I built up a wall inside me against what they said. I found I couldn't compete, so I decided to stick to my father's ideas. For at least two years I've been insulated against all college influences.*" (She is chosen but once as a friend, and does not reciprocate that choice.)

Q10: (who rather early concluded that she had no chance of social success in college) "It hurt me at first, but now I don't give a damn. *The things I really care about are mostly outside the college.* I think radicalism symbolizes the college for me more than anything else." (Needless to say, she has no use for radicals.)

For these four individuals (and probably for the fifth also) the community serves as reference group in a *negative* sense, and the home-and-family group in a positive sense. Thus their conservatism is dually reinforced.

2. *Conservatives, reputedly negativistic, unaware of their own relative conservatism.* All five are described by teachers, as well as by guess-who judges, to be stubborn or resistant. Four have prestige scores of 0, and the

fifth a less than average score. Each reciprocated just one friendship choice. Four are considered insecure in social relationships, and all five are regarded as extremely dependent upon parents. In interviews four describe with considerable intensity, and the fifth with more moderation, precollege experiences of rebuff, ostracism, or isolation, and all describe their hopes, on entering college, in terms of making friends or avoiding rebuff rather than in terms of seeking prestige. All five felt that their (rather modest) aims had met with good success. Each of the five denies building up any resistance to the acceptance of liberal opinions (but two add that they would have resented any such pressure, if felt). Three believe that only small, special groups in the college have such opinions, while the other two describe themselves as just going their own way, *paying no attention to anything but their own little circles and their college work.* Typical quotations follow:

> Q47: "I'm a perfect middle-of-the-roader, neither enthusiast nor critic. I'd accept anything if they just let me alone. . . . I've made all the friends I want." (Only one of her friendship choices is reciprocated.)

> Q19: *"In high school I was always thought of as my parents' daughter.* I never felt really accepted for myself. . . . I wanted to make my own way here, socially, but independence from my family has never asserted itself in other ways." (According to guess-who ratings, she is highly resistant to faculty authority.)

> L12: "What I most wanted was to get over being a scared bunny. . . . I always resent doing the respectable thing just because it's the thing to do, but I didn't realize I was so different, politically, from my classmates. At least I agree with the few people I ever talk to about such matters." (Sociometric responses place her in a small, conservative group.)

> Q81: "I hated practically all my school life before coming here. I had the perfect inferiority complex, and I pulled out of school social life—out of fear. I didn't intend to repeat that mistake here. . . . I've just begun to be successful in winning friendships, and I've been blissfully happy here." (She is described by teachers as "pathologically belligerent"; she receives more than the average number of friendship choices, but reciprocates only one of them.)

For these five individuals, who are negativistic in the sense of being near-isolates rather than rebels, the community does not serve as reference group for public attitudes. To some extent, their small friendship groups serve in this capacity, but in the main they still refer such areas of their lives to the home-and-family group. They are too absorbed in their own pursuits to use the total membership group as a reference group for most other purposes, too.

3. *Conservatives, not reputedly negativistic, aware of their own relative conservatism.* Three of the five are described by teachers as "cooperative"

and "eager," and none as stubborn or resistant. Four are above average in
prestige. Four are considered by teachers or by guess-who raters, or both,
to retain very close parental ties. All four who were interviewed had more
of less definite ambitions for leadership on coming to college, and all felt
that they had been relatively successful—though, in the words of one of
them, none ever attained the "really top-notch positions." All four are
aware of conflict between parents and college community in respect to
public attitudes, and all quite consciously decided to "string along" with
parents, feeling self-confident of holding their own in college in spite of
being atypical in this respect. Sample quotations follow:

> Q73: *"I'm all my mother has in the world. It's considered intellectually
> superior here to be liberal or radical. This puts me on the defensive,* as
> I refuse to consider my mother beneath me intellectually, as so many
> other students do. Apart from this, I have loved every aspect of college
> life." (A popular girl, many of whose friends are among the non-
> conservative college leaders.)
>
> Q78: *"I've come to realize how much my mother's happiness depends on
> me, and the best way I can help her is to do things with her at home as
> often as I can.* This has resulted in my not getting the feel of the college
> in certain ways, and I know my general conservatism is one of those
> ways. But it has not been important enough to me to make me feel
> particularly left out. If you're genuine and inoffensive about your
> opinions, no one really minds here if you remain conservative."
> (Another popular girl, whose friends were found among many groups.)
>
> F32: *"Family against faculty has been my struggle here.* As soon as I felt
> really secure here I decided not to let the college atmosphere affect me
> too much. Every time I've tried to rebel against my family I've found
> out how terribly wrong I am, and so I've naturally kept to my parents'
> attitudes. (While not particularly popular, she shows no bitterness and
> considerable satisfaction over her college experience.)
>
> Q35: "I've been aware of a protective shell against radical ideas. When I
> found several of my best friends getting that way, I either had to go
> along or just shut out that area entirely. I couldn't respect myself if I
> had changed my opinions just for that reason, and so I almost
> deliberately lost interest—really, *it was out of fear of losing my
> friends."* (A very popular girl, with no trace of bitterness, who is not
> considered too dependent upon parents.)

For these five the total membership group does not serve as reference
group in respect to public attitudes, but does so serve for most other
purposes. At some stage in their college careers the conflict between
college community and home and family as reference group for public
attitudes was resolved in favor of the latter.

4. *Conservatives, not reputedly negativistic, not aware of their own
relative conservatism.* All four are consistently described by teachers as
conscientious and cooperative; three are considered overdocile and un-

critical of authority. All are characterized by feelings of inferiority. All are low in prestige, two receiving scores of 0; all are low in friendship choices, but reciprocate most of these few choices. Two are described as in conflict about parental authority, and two as dependent and contented. All four recall considerable anxiety as to whether they would fit into the college community; all feel that they have succeeded better than they had expected. Sample statements from interviews follow:

D22: "I'd like to think like the college leaders, but I'm not bold enough and I don't know enough. So the college trend means little to me; I didn't even realize how much more conservative I am than the others. *I guess my family influence has been strong enough to counterbalance the college influence.*" (This girl was given to severe emotional upsets, and according to personnel records, felt "alone and helpless except when with her parents.")

M12: "It isn't that I've been resisting any pressure to become liberal. The influences here didn't matter enough to resist, I guess. *All that's really important that has happened to me occurred outside of the college,* and so I never became very susceptible to college influences." (*Following her engagement to be married, in her second year, she had "practically retired" from community life.*)

Q68: "If I'd had more time here I'd probably have caught on to the liberal drift here. But I've been horribly busy making money and trying to keep my college work up. *Politics and that sort of thing I've always associated with home instead of with the college.*" (A "town girl" of working-class parentage.)

Q70: "Most juniors and seniors, if they really *get excited about their work, forget about such community enthusiasms as sending telegrams to Congressmen.* It was so important to me to be accepted, I mean intellectually, *that I naturally came to identify myself in every way with the group which gave me this sort of intellectual satisfaction.*" (One of a small group of science majors nearly all conservative, who professed no interests other than science and who were highly self-sufficient socially.)

For none of the four was the total membership group a reference group for public attitudes. Unlike the nonnegativistic conservatives who are aware of their relative conservatism, they refer to the total membership group for few if any other purposes. Like the negativistic conservatives who are unaware of their relative conservatism, their reference groups for public attitudes are almost exclusively those related to home and family.

5. *Nonconservatives, reputedly community-identified, aware of their relative non-conservatism.* Each of the seven is considered highly independent by teachers, particularly in intellectual activities; all but one are referred to as meticulous, perfectionist, or overconscientious. Four are very high in prestige, two high, and one average; all are "good group members," and all but one a "leader." None is considered overdependent

upon parents. All have come to an understanding with parents concerning their "liberal" views; five have "agreed to differ," and the other two describe one or both parents as "very liberal." All take their public attitudes seriously, in most cases expressing the feeling that they have bled and died to achieve them. Interview excerpts follow:

> B72: "*I bend in the direction of community expectation*—almost more than I want to. I constantly have to check myself to be sure it's real self-conviction and not just social respect." (An outstanding and deeply respected leader.)

> M42: "My family has always been liberal, but the influences here made me go further, and for a while I was pretty far left. Now I'm pretty much in agreement with my family again, but it's my own and it means a lot. It wouldn't be easy for me to have friends who are very conservative." (Her friendship choices are exclusively given to nonconservatives.)

> E72: "I had been allowed so much independence by my parents that I needed desperately to identify myself with an institution with which I could conform conscientiously. Bennington was perfect. I drank up everything the college had to offer, including social attitudes, though not uncritically. I've become active in radical groups and constructively critical of them." (Both during and after college she worked with C.I.O. unions.)

> H32: "I accepted liberal attitudes here because *I had always secretly felt that my family was narrow and intolerant, and because such attitudes had prestige value.* It was all part of my generally expanding personality—*I had never really been part of anything before.* I don't accept things without examining things, however, and I was sure I meant it before I changed." (One of those who has "agreed to differ" with parents.)

> Q43: "It didn't take me long to see that liberal attitudes had prestige value. But all the time I felt inwardly superior to persons who want public acclaim. Once I had arrived at a feeling of personal security, I could see that it wasn't important—it wasn't enough. *So many people have no security at all. I became liberal at first because of its prestige value.* I remain so because the problems around which my liberalism centers are important. What I want now is to be effective in solving the problems." (Another conspicuous leader, active in and out of college in liberal movements.)

The total membership clearly serves as reference group for these individuals' changing attitudes, but by no means as the only one. For those whose parents are conservative, parents represent a negative reference group, from whom emancipation was gained via liberal attitudes. And for several of them the college community served as a bridge to outside liberal groups as points of reference.

6. *Nonconservatives, reputedly community-identified, not aware of their own relative nonconservatism.* The word *enthusiastic* appears constantly in the records of each of these six. All are considered eager,

ambitious, hard-working, and anxious to please. Four are very high in prestige, the other two about average. None is considered overdependent upon parents, and only two are known to have suffered any particular conflict in achieving emancipation. Each one came to college with ambitions for leadership, and each professes extreme satisfaction with her college experience. Sample quotations follow:

Qx: "Every influence I felt tended to push me in the liberal direction: my underdog complex, *my need to be independent of my parents, and my anxiousness to be a leader here.*"

Q61: "I met a whole body of new information here; I took a deep breath and plunged. When I talked about it at home my family began to treat me as if I had an adult mind. *Then too, my new opinions gave me the reputation here of being open-minded and capable of change.* I think I could have got really radical but I found it wasn't the way to get prestige here." (She judges most of her classmates to be as nonconservative as herself.)

Q72: "I take everything hard, and so of course I reacted hard to all the attitudes I found here. I'm 100-percent enthusiastic about Bennington, and that includes liberalism (but not radicalism, though I used to think so). Now I know that you can't be an *extremist if you're really devoted to an institution,* whether it's a labor union or a college." (A conspicuous leader who, like most of the others in this set of six, *judges classmates to be only slightly more conservative than herself.*)

Q63: "*I came to college to get away from my family,* who never had any respect for my mind. Becoming a radical meant thinking for myself and, figuratively, thumbing my nose at my family. *It also meant intellectual identification with the faculty and students that I most wanted to be like.*" (She has always felt oppressed by parental respectability and sibling achievements.)

Q57: "It's very simple. *I was so anxious to be accepted that I accepted the political complexion of the community here.* I just couldn't stand out against the crowd unless I had many friends and strong support." (Not a leader, but many close friends among leaders and nonconservatives.)

For these six, like the preceding seven, the membership group serves as reference group for public affairs. They differ from the preceding seven chiefly in that they are less sure of themselves and are careful "not to go too far." Hence they tend to repudiate "radicalism," and to judge classmates as only slightly less conservative than themselves.

7. *Nonconservatives, not reputedly community-identified, aware of own relative nonconservatism.* Each of the six is described as highly independent and critical-minded. Four are consistently reported as intellectually outstanding, and the other two occasionally so. All describe their ambitions on coming to college in intellectual rather than in social terms. Four of the five who were interviewed stated that in a conservative college they would be "even more radical than here." Two are slightly

above average in prestige, two below average, and two have 0 scores. Three have gone through rather severe battles in the process of casting off what they regard as parental shackles; none is considered overdependent upon parents. Sample interview excerpts follow:

Q7:   *"All my life I've resented the protection of governesses and parents.* What I most wanted here was the intellectual approval of teachers and the more advanced students. Then I found you can't be reactionary and be intellectually respectable." (Her traits of independence became more marked as she achieved academic distinction.)

Q21:   "I simply got filled with new ideas here, and the only possible formulation of all of them was to adopt a radical approach. *I can't see my own position in the world in any other terms. The easy superficiality with which so many prestige-hounds here get 'liberal' only forced me to think it out more intensely."* (A highly gifted girl, considered rather aloof.)

C32:   *"I started rebelling against my pretty stuffy family before I came to college.* I felt apart from freshmen here, because I was older. Then I caught on to faculty attempts to undermine prejudice. I took sides with the faculty immediately, against the immature freshmen. I crusaded about it. *It provided just what I needed by way of family rebellion,* and bolstered up my self-confidence, too." (A very bright girl, regarded as sharp-tongued and a bit haughty.)

J24:   *"I'm easily influenced by people whom I respect,* and the people who rescued me when I was down and out, intellectually, gave me a radical intellectual approach; they included both teachers and advanced students. *I'm not rebelling against anything.* I'm just doing what I had to do to stand on my own feet intellectually." (Her academic work was poor as a freshman, but gradually became outstanding.)

For these six students it is not the total membership group, but dominant sub-groups (faculty, advanced students) which at first served as positive reference groups, and for many of them the home group served as a negative point of reference. Later, they developed extracollege reference groups (left-wing writers, etc.). In a secondary sense, however, the total membership group served as a negative point of reference—i.e., they regarded their nonconservatism as a mark of personal superiority.

8. *Nonconservatives, not reputedly community-identified, not aware of own relative nonconservatism.* Each of the five is considered hardworking, eager, and enthusiastic but (especially during the first year or two) unsure of herself and too dependent upon instructors. They are "good citizens," but in a distinctly retiring way. Two are above average in prestige, and the other three much below average. None of the five is considered overdependent upon parents; two are known to have experienced a good deal of conflict in emancipating themselves. All regard themselves as "pretty average persons," with strong desire to conform; they describe their ambitions in terms of social acceptance instead of social or intellectual prestige. Sample excerpts follow:

E22: "*Social security is the focus of it all with me.* I became steadily less conservative as long as I was *needing to gain in personal security, both with students and with faculty.* I developed some resentment against a few extreme radicals who don't really represent the college viewpoint, and that's why I changed my attitudes so far and no further." (A girl with a small personal following, otherwise not especially popular.)

D52: "*Of course there's social pressure here to give up your conservatism.* I'm glad of it, because for me this became the *vehicle for achieving independence from my family.* So changing my attitudes has gone hand in hand with two *very important things: establishing my own independence and at the same time becoming a part of the college organism.*" (She attributes the fact that her social attitudes changed, while those of her younger sister, also at the college, did not, to the fact that she had greater need both of family independence and of group support.)

Q6: "I was ripe for developing liberal or even radical opinions because so many of my friends at home were doing the same thing. So it was really wonderful that I could agree with all the people I respected here and the same time move in the direction that my home friends were going." (A girl characterized by considerable personal instability at first, but showing marked improvement.)

Qy: "I think my change of opinions has given me *intellectual and social self-respect at the same time.* I used to be too timid for words, and I never had an idea of my own. As I gradually became more successful in my work and made more friends, I came to feel that it didn't matter so much whether I agreed with my parents. It's all part of the feeling that I really belong here." (Much other evidence confirms this; she was lonely and pathetic at first, but really belonged later.)

These five provide the example *par excellence* of individuals who came to identify themselves with "the community" and whose attitudes change *pari passu* with the growing sense of identity. Home-and-family groups served as supplementary points of reference, either positive or negative. To varying degrees, subgroups within the community served as focal points of reference. But, because of *their need to be accepted, it was primarily the membership group as such which served as reference group for these five.*

SUMMARY

In this community, as presumably in most others, all individuals belong to the total membership group, but such membership is not necessarily a point of reference for every form of social adaptation, e.g., for acquiring attitudes toward public issues. *Such attitudes, however, are not acquired in a social vacuum. Their acquisition is a function of relating oneself to some group or groups, positively or negatively.* In many cases (perhaps in all) the referring of social attitudes to one group negatively leads to referring them to another group positively, or vice versa, so that the attitudes are dually reinforced.

An individual is, of course, "typical" in respect to attitudes if the total membership group serves as a positive point of reference for that purpose, but "typicality" may also result from the use of other reference groups. It does not follow from the fact that an individual is "atypical" that the membership group does not serve for reference purposes; it may serve as negative reference group. Even if the membership group does not serve as reference group at all (as in the case of conservatives in this community who are unaware of the general freshman-to-senior trend), it cannot be concluded that attitude development is not a function of belonging to the total membership group. The unawareness of such individuals is itself a resultant adaptation of particular individuals to a particular membership group. The fact that such individuals continue to refer attitudes toward public issues primarily to home-and-family groups is, in part at least, a result of the kind of community in which they have membership.

In short, the Bennington findings seem to support the thesis that, in a community characterized by certain approved attitudes, the individual's attitude development is a function of the way in which he relates himself both to the total membership group and to one or more reference groups.

BRUNO BETTELHEIM

Individual and
Mass Behavior in
Extreme Situations

PURPOSE OF THE INVESTIGATION

The author spent approximately one year in the two biggest German concentration camps for political prisoners, at Dachau and at Buchenwald. During this time he made observations and collected material, part of which will be presented in this paper. It is not the intention of this presentation to recount once more the horror story of the German concentration camp for political prisoners.

It is assumed that the reader is roughly familiar with it, but it should be reiterated that the prisoners were deliberately tortured.[1] They were inadequately clothed, but nevertheless exposed to heat, rain, and freezing temperatures as long as seventeen hours a day, seven days a week. They suffered from extreme malnutrition, but had to perform hard labor.[2] Every single moment of their lives was strictly regulated and supervised. They were never permitted to see any visitors, nor a minister. They were not entitled to any medical care, and when they received it, it was rarely administered by medically trained persons.[3] The prisoners did not know exactly why they were imprisoned, and never knew for how long. This may explain why we shall speak of the prisoners as persons finding themselves in an "extreme" situation.

The acts of terror committed in these camps arouse in the minds of civilized persons justified and strong emotions, and those emotions lead them sometimes to overlook that terror is, as far as the Gestapo is concerned, only a means for attaining certain ends.[4] By using extravagant means which fully absorb the investigator's interest, the Gestapo only too often succeeds in hiding its real purposes. One of the reasons that this happens so frequently in respect to the concentration camps is that the persons most able to discuss them are former prisoners, who obviously are more interested in what happened to them than in why it happened. If one

Excerpted and reprinted by permission of the author and the American Psychological Association from *Journal of Abnormal and Social Psychology*, 1943, pp. 417-52.

desires to understand the purposes of the Gestapo, and the ways in which they are attained, emphasis on what happened to particular persons would be erroneous. According to the well-known ideology of the Nazi state the individual as such is either nonexistent or of no importance. An investigation of the purposes of the concentration camps must, therefore, emphasize not individual acts of terror, but their trans-individual purposes and results. . . .

In this paper, which, considering the complexity of the problem with which it is dealing, is comparatively short, an effort will be made to deal adequately with at least one aspect of it, namely, with *the concentration camp as a means of producing changes in the prisoners which will make them more useful subjects* of the Nazi state.

These changes are produced by exposing the prisoners to situations particularly suitable for this purpose. Their nature is such as to warrant calling them extreme. By means of their extreme character they force the prisoners to adapt themselves entirely and with the greatest speed. This adaptation produces interesting types of private, individual, and mass behavior. We call "private" behavior that which originates to a large degree in a subject's particular background and personality, rather than in the experiences to which the Gestapo exposed him, although these experiences were instrumental in bringing about the private behavior. We call "individual" behavior that which, although developed by individuals more or less independently of one another, is clearly the result of experiences common to all prisoners. The pattern of these behaviors was similar in nearly all prisoners with only slight deviations from the average, these deviations originating in the prisoners' particular background and personality. We call "mass" behavior those phenomena which could be observed *only* in a group of prisoners when functioning as a more or less unified mass. Although these three types of behavior were somewhat overlapping and a sharp discrimination between them seems difficult, the subdivision seems advisable for this paper. We shall restrict our discussion mainly to individual and mass behavior, as the title indicates. One example of private behavior will be discussed on the following pages.

If we thus assume that what happens in the camp has, among others, the purpose of changing the prisoners into useful subjects of the Nazi state, and if this purpose is attained by means of exposing them to extreme situations, then a legitimate way to carry on our investigation is by an historical account of what occurred in the prisoners from the moment they had their first experience with the Gestapo up to the time when the process of adaptation to the camp situation was practically concluded. In analyzing this development different stages can be recognized, which will furnish us with appropriate subdivisions. The first of these stages centers around *the initial shock of finding oneself unlawfully imprisoned.* The main event of the second stage is *the transportation into the camp and the first experiences in it.* The next stage is characterized by a slow process of changing the prisoner's life and personality. It occurs step by step, continuously. It is *the adaptation to the camp situation.* During this process it is difficult to recognize the impact of what is going on. One way to make it more obvious is to compare two groups of prisoners, one in whom the process has only started, namely, the "new" prisoners, with another one in whom the process is already far advanced. This other group will consist of the "old" prisoners. The final stage is reached when *the prisoner has adapted himself to the life in the camp.* This last stage seems to be characterized, among other features, by a definitely changed attitude to, and evaluation of, the Gestapo....

THE TRANSPORTATION INTO THE CAMP AND THE FIRST EXPERIENCES IN IT

After having spent several days in prison, the prisoners were brought into the camp. During this transportation they were exposed to constant tortures of various kinds. Many of them depended on the fantasy of the particular Gestapo member in charge of a group of prisoners. Still, a certain pattern soon became apparent. Corporal punishment, consisting of whipping, kicking, slapping, intermingled with shooting and wounding with the bayonet, alternated with tortures the obvious goal of which was extreme exhaustion. For instance, the prisoners were forced to stare for hours into glaring lights, to kneel for hours, and so on. From time to time a prisoner got killed; no prisoner was permitted to take care of his or another's wounds. These tortures alternated with efforts on the part of the guards to force the prisoners to hit one another, and to defile what the guards considered the prisoners' most cherished values. For instance, the prisoners were forced to curse their God, to accuse themselves of vile actions, accuse their wives of adultery and of prostitution. This continued for hours and was repeated at various times. According to reliable reports, this kind of initiation never took less than 12 hours and frequently lasted 24 hours. If the number of prisoners brought into the camp was too large, or if they came from nearby places, the ceremony took place during the first day in camp.

The purpose of the tortures was to break the resistance of the prisoners, and to assure the guards that they were really superior to them. This can be seen from the fact that the longer the tortures lasted, the less violent they became. The guards became slowly less excited, and at the end even talked with the prisoners. As soon as a new guard took over, he started with new acts of terror, although not as violent as in the beginning, and he eased up sooner than his predecessor. Sometimes prisoners who had already spent time in camp were brought back with a group of new prisoners. These old prisoners were not tortured if they could furnish evidence that they had already been in the camp. That these tortures were planned can be seen from the fact that during the author's transportation into the camp after several prisoners had died and many had been wounded in tortures lasting for 12 hours, the command, "Stop mistreating the prisoners," came and from this moment on the prisoners were left in peace till they arrived in the camp when another group of guards took over and started anew to take advantage of them.

It is difficult to ascertain what happened in the minds of the prisoners during the time they were exposed to this treatment. Most of them became so exhausted that they were only partly conscious of what happened. In general, prisoners remembered the details and did not mind talking about them, but they did not like to talk about what they had felt and thought during the time of torture. The few who volunteered information made vague statements which sounded like devious rationalizations, invented for the purpose of justifying that they had endured treatment injurious to their self-respect without trying to fight back. The few who had tried to fight back could not be interviewed; they were dead.

The writer can vividly recall his extreme weariness, resulting from a bayonet wound he had received early in the course of transportation and from a heavy blow on the head. Both injuries led to the loss of a con-siderable amount of blood, and made him groggy. He recalls vividly, nevertheless, his thoughts and emotions during the transportation. He wondered all the time that man can endure so much without committing suicide or going insane. He wondered that the guards really tortured prisoners in the way it had been described in books on the concentration camps; that the Gestapo was so simple-minded as either to enjoy forcing prisoners to defile themselves or to expect to break their resistance in this way. He wondered that the guards were lacking in fantasy when selecting the means to torture the prisoners; that their sadism was without imagination. He was rather amused by the repeated statement that guards do not shoot the prisoners but kill them by beating them to death because a bullet costs six pfennigs, and the prisoners are not worth even so much. Obviously the idea that these men, most of them formerly influential persons, were not worth such a trifle impressed the guards considerably. On the basis of this introspection it seems that the writer gained emotional strength from the following facts: that things happened according to expectation; that, therefore, his future in the camp was at least partly predictable from what he already was experiencing and from what he had read; and that the Gestapo was more stupid than he had expected, which eventually provided small satisfaction. Moreover, he felt pleased with himself that the tortures did not change his ability to think or his general point of view. In retrospect these considerations seem futile, but they ought to be mentioned because, if the author should be asked to sum up in one sentence what, all during the time he spent in the camp, was his main problem, he would say: *to safeguard his ego in such a way, that, if by any*

good luck he should regain liberty, he would be approximately the same
person he was when deprived of liberty.

He has no doubt that he was able to endure the transportation, and all
that followed, because right from the beginning he became convinced that
these horrible and degrading experiences somehow did not happen to
"him" as a subject, but only to "him" as an object. The importance of this
attitude was corroborated by many statements of other prisoners,
although none would go so far as to state definitely that an attitude of this
type was clearly developed already during the time of the transportation.
They couched their feelings usually in more general terms such as, "The
main problem is to remain alive and unchanged," without specifying what
they meant as unchanged. From additional remarks it became apparent
that what should remain unchanged was individually different and
roughly covered the person's general attitudes and values.

All the thoughts and emotions which the author had during the transportation were extremely detached. It was as if he watched things happening in which he only vaguely participated. Later he learned that many
prisoners had developed this same feeling of detachment, as if what
happened really did not matter to oneself. It was strangely mixed with a
conviction that "this cannot be true, such things just do not happen." Not
only during the transportation but all through the time spent in camp, the
prisoners had to convince themselves that this was real, was really happening, and not just a nightmare. They were never wholly successful.[5]

This feeling of detachment which rejected the reality of the situation in
which the prisoners found themselves might be considered a mechanism
safeguarding the integrity of their personalities. Many prisoners behaved
in the camp as if their life there would have no connection with their
"real" life; they went so far as to insist that this was the right attitude.
Their statements about themselves, and their evaluation of their own and
other persons' behavior, differed considerably from what they would have
said and thought outside of camp. This separation of behavior patterns
and schemes of values inside and outside of camp was so strong that it
could hardly be touched in conversation; it was one of the many "taboos"
not to be discussed.[6] The prisoners' feelings could be summed up by the
following sentence: "What I am doing here, or what is happening to me,
does not count at all; here everything is permissible as long and insofar as
it contributes to helping me to survive in the camp."

One more observation made during the transportation ought to be
mentioned. No prisoner fainted. To faint meant to get killed. In this
particular situation fainting was no device protecting a person against
intolerable pain and in this way facilitating his life; it endangered a
prisoner's existence because anyone unable to follow orders was killed.
Once the prisoners were in the camp the situation changed and a prisoner

who fainted sometimes received some attention or was usually no longer tortured. The result of this changed attitude of the guards was that prisoners who did not faint under the more severe strains during the transportation, in the camp usually fainted when exposed to great hardships, although they were not as great as those endured during the transportation. . . .

THE ADAPTATION TO THE CAMP SITUATION

DIFFERENCES IN THE RESPONSE TO EXTREME AND TO SUFFERING EXPERIENCES

It seems that camp experiences which remained within the normal frame of reference of a prisoner's life experience were dealt with by means of the normal psychological mechanisms. Once the experience transcended this frame of reference, the normal mechanisms seemed no longer able to deal adequately with it and new psychological mechanisms were needed. The experience during the transportation was one of those transcending the normal frame of reference and the reaction to it may be described as "unforgettable, but unreal."

The prisoners' dreams were an indication that the extreme experiences were not dealt with by the usual mechanisms. Many dreams expressed aggression against Gestapo members, usually combined with wish fulfillment in such a way that the prisoner was taking his revenge on them. Interestingly enough, the reason he took revenge on them—if a particular reason could be ascertained—was always for some comparatively small mistreatment, never an extreme experience. The author had had some previous experience concerning his reaction to shocks in dreams. He expected that his dreams after the transportation would follow the pattern of repetition of the shock in dreams, the shock becoming less vivid and the dream finally disappearing. He was astonished to find that in his dreams the most shocking events did not appear. He asked many prisoners whether they dreamed about the transportation and he was unable to find a single one who could remember having dreamed about it.

Attitudes similar to those developed toward the transportation could be observed in other extreme situations. On a terribly cold winter night when a snow storm was blowing, all prisoners were punished by being forced to stand at attention without overcoats—they never wore any—for hours.[7] This, after having worked for more than 12 hours in the open, and having received hardly any food. They were threatened with having to stand all through the night. After about 20 prisoners had died from exposure the discipline broke down. The threats of the guards became ineffective. To be exposed to the weather was a terrible torture; to see one's friends die without being able to help, and to stand a good chance of dying, created a situation similar to the transportation, except that the prisoners had by now more experience with the Gestapo. Open resistance was impossible, as impossible as it was to do anything definite to safeguard oneself. A feeling of utter indifference swept the prisoners. They did not care whether the guards shot them; they were indifferent to acts of torture committed by the guards. The guards had no longer any authority, the spell of fear and death was broken. It was again as if what happened did not "really" happen to oneself. There was again the split between the "me" to whom it happened and the "me" who really did not care and was just an interested but detached observer. Unfortunate as the situation was, they felt free from fear and therefore were actually happier than at most other times during their camp experiences.

Whereas the extremeness of the situation probably produced the split mentioned above, a number of circumstances concurred to create the feeling of happiness in the prisoners. Obviously it was easier to withstand unpleasant experiences when all found themselves in "the same boat." Moreover, since everybody was convinced that his chances to survive were slim, each felt more heroic and willing to help others than he would feel at other moments when helping others might endanger him. This helping and being helped raised the spirits. Another factor was that they were not only free of the fear of the Gestapo, but the Gestapo had actually lost its power, since the guards seemed reluctant to shoot all prisoners.[8] After more than 80 prisoners had died, and several hundred had their extremities so badly frozen that they had later to be amputated, the prisoners were permitted to return to the barracks. They were completely exhausted, but did not experience that feeling of happiness which some of them had expected. They felt relieved that the torture was over, but felt at the same time that they no longer were free from fear and no longer could strongly rely on mutual help. Each prisoner as an individual was now comparatively safer, but he had lost the safety originating in being a member of a unified group. This event was again freely discussed, in a detached way, and again the discussion was restricted to facts; the prisoners' emotions and thoughts during this night were hardly ever mentioned. The event itself and its details were not forgotten, but no particular emotions were attached to them; nor did they appear in dreams.

The psychological reactions to events which were somewhat more within the sphere of the normally comprehensible were decidedly different from those to extreme events. It seems that prisoners dealt with less extreme events in the same way as if they had happened outside of the camp. For example, if a prisoner's punishment was not of an unusual kind, he seemed ashamed of it, he tried not to speak about it. A slap in one's face was embarrassing, and not to be discussed. One hated individual guards who had kicked one, or slapped one, or verbally abused one much more than the guard who really had wounded one seriously. In the latter case one eventually hated the Gestapo as such, but not so much the individual inflicting the punishment. Obviously this differentiation was unreasonable, but it seemed to be inescapable. One felt deeper and more violent aggressions against particular Gestapo members who had committed minor vile acts than one felt against those who had acted in a much more terrible fashion....

DIFFERENCES IN THE PSYCHOLOGICAL ATTITUDES OF OLD AND NEW PRISONERS

In the following discussion we refer by the term "new prisoners" to those who had not spent more than one year in the camp; "old" prisoners are those who have spent at least three years in the camp. As far as the old prisoners are concerned the author can offer only observations but no findings based on introspection.

It has been mentioned that the main concern of the new prisoners seemed to be to remain intact as a personality and to return to the outer world the same persons who had left it; all their emotional efforts were directed towards this goal. Old prisoners seemed mainly concerned with the problem of how to live as well as possible within the camp. Once they had reached this attitude, everything that happened to them, even the worst atrocity, was "real" to them. No longer was there a split between one to whom things happened and the one who observed them. Once this stage was reached of taking everything that happened in the camp as "real," there was every indication that the prisoners who had reached it were afraid of returning to the outer world. They did not admit it directly, but from their talk it was clear that they hardly believed they would ever return to this outer world because they felt that only a cataclysmic event—a world war and world revolution—could free them; and even then they doubted that they would be able to adapt to this new life. They seemed aware of what had happened to them while growing older in the camp. They realized that they had adapted themselves to the life in the camp and that this process was coexistent with a basic change in their personality.

The most drastic demonstration of this realization was provided by the case of a formerly very prominent radical German politician. He declared that according to his experience nobody could live in the camp longer than five years without changing his attitudes so radically that he no longer could be considered the same person he used to be. He asserted that he did not see any point in continuing to live once his real life consisted in being a prisoner in a concentration camp, that he could not endure developing those attitudes and behaviors he saw developing in all old prisoners. He therefore had decided to commit suicide on the sixth anniversary of his being brought into the camp. His fellow prisoners tried to watch him carefully on this day, but nevertheless he succeeded.

There was, of course, considerable variation among individuals in the time it took them to make their peace with the idea of having to spend the rest of their lives in the camp. Some became part of the camp life rather soon, some probably never. When a new prisoner was brought into the camp, the older ones tried to teach him a few things which might prove helpful in his adjustment. The new prisoners were told that they should try by all means to survive the first days and not to give up the fight for their lives, that it would become easier the longer time they spent in camp. They said, "If you survive the first three months you will survive the next three years." This despite the fact that the yearly mortality was close to 20 per cent.[9] This high death rate was mostly due to the large number of new prisoners who did not survive the first few weeks in the camp, either because they did not care to survive by means of adapting themselves to the life in camp or because they were unable to do so. How long it took a prisoner to cease to consider life outside the camp as real depended to a great extent on the strength of his emotional ties to his family and friends. The change to accepting camp life as real never took place before spending two years in camp. Even then everyone was overtly longing to regain freedom. Some of the indications from which one could learn about the changed attitude were: scheming to find oneself a better place in the camp rather than trying to contact the outer world,[10] avoiding speculation about one's family, or world affairs,[11] concentrating all interest on events taking place inside of the camp. When the author expressed to some of the old prisoners his astonishment that they seemed not to be interested in discussing their future life outside the camp, they frequently admitted that they no longer could visualize themselves living outside the camp, making free decisions, taking care of themselves and their families. The changes in attitudes toward their families and to events taking place in the outside world were not the only ones which could be observed in old prisoners; other differences between old and new prisoners could be recognized in their hopes for their future lives, in the degree to which they regressed to infantile behavior, and in many other ways. When discussing these differences between old and new prisoners it should be borne in mind that there were great individual variations, that all statements are only approximations and generalizations, and that the categories are interrelated....

Old prisoners did not like to be reminded of their families and former friends. When they spoke about them, it was in a very detached way. They liked to receive letters, but it was not very important to them, partly because they had lost contact with the events related in them. It has been mentioned that they had some realization of how difficult it might be for them to find their way back, but there was another contributing factor, namely, the prisoners' hatred of all those living outside of the camp, who "enjoyed life as if we were not rotting away."

This outside world which continued to live as if nothing had happened was in the minds of the prisoners represented by those whom they used to know, namely, by their relatives and friends. But even this hatred was very subdued in the old prisoners. It seemed that, as much as they had forgotten to love their kin, they had lost the ability to hate them. *They had learned to direct a great amount of aggression against themselves so as not to get into too many conflicts with the Gestapo, while the new prisoners still directed their aggressions against the outer world, and—when not supervised—against the Gestapo.* Since the old prisoners did not show much emotion either way, they were unable to feel strongly about anybody.

Old prisoners did not like to mention their former social status or their former activities, whereas new prisoners were rather boastful about them. New prisoners seemed to try to back their self-esteem by letting others know how important they had been, with the very obvious implication that they still were important. Old prisoners seemed to have accepted their state of dejection, and to compare it with their former splendor—and anything was magnificent when compared with the situation in which they found themselves—was probably too depressing. . . .

REGRESSION INTO INFANTILE BEHAVIOR

The prisoners developed types of behavior which are characteristic of infancy or early youth. Some of these behaviors developed slowly, others were immediately imposed on the prisoners and developed only in intensity as time went on. Some of these more or less infantile behaviors have already been discussed, such as ambivalence to one's family, despondency, finding satisfaction in daydreaming rather than in action.

Whether some of these behavior patterns were deliberately produced by the Gestapo is hard to ascertain. Others were definitely produced by it, but again we do not know whether it was consciously done. It has been mentioned that even during the transportation the prisoners were tortured in a way in which a cruel and domineering father might torture a helpless child; here it should be added that the prisoners were also debased by techniques which went much further into childhood situations. They were forced to soil themselves. In the camp the defecation was strictly regulated; it was one of the most important daily events, discussed in great detail. During the day the prisoners who wanted to defecate had to obtain the permission of the guard. It seemed as if the education to cleanliness would be once more repeated. It seemed to give pleasure to the guards to hold the power of granting or withholding the permission to visit the latrines. (Toilets were mostly not available.) This pleasure of the guards found its counterpart in the pleasure the prisoners derived from visiting the latrines, because there they usually could rest for a moment, secure from the whips of the overseers and guards. They were not always so secure, because sometimes enterprising young guards enjoyed interfering with the prisoners even at these moments.

The prisoners were forced to say "thou" to one another, which in Germany is indiscriminately used only among small children. They were not permitted to address one another with the many titles to which middle-

and upper-class Germans are accustomed. On the other hand, they had to address the guards in the most deferential manner, giving them all their titles.

The prisoners lived, like children, only in the immediate present; they lost the feeling for the sequence of time, they became unable to plan for the future or to give up immediate pleasure satisfactions to gain greater ones in the near future. They were unable to establish durable object-relations. Friendships developed as quickly as they broke up. Prisoners would, like early adolescents, fight one another tooth and nail, declare that they would never even look at one another or speak to one another, only to become close friends within a few minutes. They were boastful, telling tales about what they had accomplished in their former lives, or how they succeeded in cheating foremen or guards, and how they sabotaged the work. Like children they felt not at all set back or ashamed when it became known that they had lied about their prowess.

Another factor contributing to the regression into childhood behavior was the work the prisoners were forced to perform. New prisoners particularly were forced to perform nonsensical tasks, such as carrying heavy rocks from one place to another, and after a while back to the place where they had picked them up. On other days they were forced to dig holes in the ground with their bare hands, although tools were available. They resented such nonsensical work, although it ought to have been immaterial to them whether their work was useful. They felt debased when forced to perform "childish" and stupid labor, and preferred even harder work when it produced something that might be considered useful. There seems to be no doubt that the tasks they performed, as well as the mistreatment by the Gestapo which they had to endure, contributed to their disintegration as adult persons.

The author had a chance to interview several prisoners who before being brought into the camp had spent a few years in prison, some of them in solitary confinement. Although their number was too small to permit valid generalizations, it seems that to spend time in prison does not produce the character changes described in this paper. As far as the regression into childhood behaviors is concerned, the only feature prison and camp seem to have in common is that in both the prisoners are prevented from satisfying their sexual desires in a normal way, which eventually leads them to the fear of losing their virility. In the camp this fear added strength to the other factors detrimental to adult types of behavior and promoted childlike types of behavior. . . .

THE FINAL ADJUSTMENT TO THE LIFE IN THE CAMP

A prisoner had reached the final stage of adjustment to the camp situation when he had changed his personality so as to accept as his own the values of the Gestapo. A few examples may illustrate how this acceptance expressed itself.

The Gestapo considered, or pretended to consider, the prisoners the scum of the earth. They insisted that none of them was any better than the others. One of the reasons for this attitude was probably to impress the young guards who received their training in the camp that they were superior to even the most outstanding prisoner and to demonstrate to them that the former foes of the Nazis were now subdued and not worthy of any special attention. If a formerly prominent prisoner had been treated better, the simple guard would have thought that he is still influential; if he had been treated worse, they might have thought that he is still dangerous. This was in line with the desire to impress the guards that even a slight degree of opposition against the Nazi system led to the entire destruction of the person who dared to oppose, and that the degree of opposition made no difference in this respect. Occasional talks with these guards revealed that they really believed in a Jewish-capitalistic world conspiracy against the German people, and whoever opposed the Nazis participated in it and was therefore to be destroyed, independent of his role in the conspiracy. So it can be understood why their behavior to the prisoners was that normally reserved for dealing with one's vilest enemy.

The prisoners found themselves in an impossible situation due to the steady interference with their privacy on the part of the guards and other prisoners. So a great amount of aggression accumulated. In the new prisoners it vented itself in the way it might have done in the world outside the camp. But slowly prisoners accepted, as expression of their verbal aggressions, terms which definitely did not originate in their previous vocabularies, but were taken over from the very different vocabulary of the Gestapo. From copying the verbal aggressions of the Gestapo to copying their form of bodily aggressions was one more step, but it took several years to make this step. It was not unusual to find old prisoners, when in charge of others, behaving worse than the Gestapo, in some cases because they were trying to win favor with the Gestapo in this way but more often because they considered this the best way to behave toward prisoners in the camp.

Practically all prisoners who had spent a long time in the camp took over the Gestapo's attitude toward the so-called unfit prisoners. Newcomers presented the old prisoners with difficult problems. Their complaints about the unbearable life in camp added new strain to the life in the barracks, so did their inability to adjust to it. Bad behavior in the labor gang endangered the whole group. So a newcomer who did not stand up well under the strain tended to become a liability for the other prisoners. Moreover, weaklings were those most apt eventually to turn traitors. Weaklings usually died during the first weeks in the camp anyway, so it seemed as well to get rid of them sooner. So old prisoners were sometimes instrumental in getting rid of the unfit, in this way making a feature of Gestapo ideology a feature of their own behavior. This was one of the many situations in which old prisoners demonstrated toughness and molded their way of treating other prisoners according to the example set by the Gestapo. That this was really a taking-over of Gestapo attitudes can be seen from the treatment of traitors. Self-protection asked for their elimination, but the way in which they were tortured for days and slowly killed was taken over from the Gestapo.

Old prisoners who seemed to have a tendency to identify themselves with the Gestapo did so not only in respect to aggressive behavior. They would try to arrogate to themselves old pieces of Gestapo uniforms. If that was not possible, they tried to sew and mend their uniforms so that they would resemble those of the guards. The length to which prisoners would go in these efforts seemed unbelievable, particularly since the Gestapo punished them for their efforts to copy Gestapo uniforms. When asked why they did it they admitted that they loved to look like one of the guards.

The identification with the Gestapo did not stop with the copying of their outer appearance and behavior. Old prisoners accepted their goals and values, too, even when they seemed opposed to their own interests. It was appalling to see how far formerly even politically well-educated prisoners would go in this identification. . . .

When old prisoners accepted Nazi values as their own they usually did not admit it, but explained their behavior by means of rationalizations. For instance, prisoners collected scrap in the camp because Germany was low on raw materials. When it was pointed out that they were thus helping the Nazis, they rationalized that through the saving of scrap Germany's working classes, too, became richer. When erecting buildings for the Gestapo, controversies started whether one should build well. New prisoners were for sabotaging, a majority of the old prisoners for building well. They rationalized that the new Germany will have use for these buildings. When it was pointed out that a revolution will have to destroy the fortresses of the Gestapo, they retired to the general statement that one ought to do well any job one has to do. It seems that the majority of the old prisoners had realized that they could not continue to work for the Gestapo unless they could convince themselves that their work made some sense, so they had to convince themselves of this sense.

The satisfaction with which some old prisoners enjoyed the fact that, during the twice daily counting of the prisoners, they really had stood well at attention can be explained only by the fact that they had entirely accepted the values of the Gestapo as their own. Prisoners prided themselves of being as tough as the Gestapo members. This identification with their torturers went so far as copying their leisure-time activities. One of the games played by the guards was to find out who could stand to be hit longest without uttering a complaint. This game was copied by the old prisoners, as though they had not been hit often and long enough without needing to repeat this experience as a game.

Often the Gestapo would enforce nonsensical rules, originating in the whims of one of the guards. They were usually forgotten as soon as formulated, but there were always some old prisoners who would continue to follow these rules and try to enforce them on others long after the Gestapo had forgotten about them. Once, for instance, a guard on inspecting the prisoners' apparel found that the shoes of some of them were dirty on the inside. He ordered all prisoners to wash their shoes inside and out with water and soap. The heavy shoes treated this way became hard as stone. The order was never repeated, and many prisoners did not even execute it when given. Nevertheless there were some old prisoners who not only continued to wash the inside of their shoes every day but cursed all others who did not do so as negligent and dirty. These prisoners firmly believed that the rules set down by the Gestapo were desirable standards of human behavior, at least in the camp situation.

NOTES

1. For an official report on life in these camps see: *Papers concerning the treatment of German nationals in Germany.* London: His Majesty's Stationery Office, 1939.

2. The daily food the prisoners received yielded approximately 1800 calories, whereas for the labor they were forced to perform the average caloric requirement is from 3000 to 3300 calories.

3. Surgical operations, for instance, were performed by a former printer. There were many M.D.'s in the camp, but no prisoner was permitted to work in the camp in his civilian capacity because that would not have implied a punishment.

4. The concentration camps for political prisoners are administered by the "Elite" formations of the "SS" groups, called "Deathhead" regiments. Every member of these regiments has to spend at least three months of his training as a guard in these camps. If he does not perform satisfactorily in this capacity, he is transferred back to the non-elite formations of the "SS."

There are many types of concentration camps in Germany. If the author speaks of concentration camps, the meaning is always camps for political prisoners. Up to the time of the war there were three big camps of this type and a few smaller ones, all for men, and one small camp for women. Up to that time the total of prisoners in these camps never exceeded 60,000. Contrary to widespread opinion, only a small minority of them were Jews.

The many other German concentration camps, such as those for forced labor, were not administered by the Gestapo, and the conditions in them were very different.

5. There were good indications that most guards embraced a similar attitude, although for different reasons. They tortured the prisoners partly because they enjoyed demonstrating their superiority, partly because their superiors expected it of them. But, having been educated in a world which rejected brutality, they felt uneasy about what they were doing. It seems that they, too, had an emotional attitude toward their acts of brutality which might be described as a feeling of unreality. After having been guards in the camp for some time, they got accustomed to inhuman behavior, they became "conditioned" to it; it then became part of their "real" life.

6. Some aspects of this behavior seem similar to those described in literature as "depersonalization," still there seem to be so many differences between the phenomena discussed in this paper and the phenomenon of depersonalization that it seemed not advisable to use this term.

7. The reason for this punishment was that two prisoners had tried to escape. On such occasions all prisoners were always punished very severely, so that in the future they would give away secrets they had learned, because otherwise they would have to suffer. The idea was

that every prisoner ought to feel responsible for any act committed by any other prisoner. This was in line with the principle of the Gestapo to force the prisoners to feel and act as a group, and not as individuals.

8. This was one of the occasions in which the antisocial attitudes of certain middle-class prisoners... became apparent. Some of them did not participate in the spirit of mutual help, some even tried to take advantage of others for their own benefit.

9. The prisoners in charge of a barrack kept track of what happened to the inhabitants of their barrack. In this way it was comparatively easy to ascertain how many died and how many were released. The former were always in the majority.

10. New prisoners would spend all their money on efforts to smuggle letters out of the camp or to receive communications without having them censored. Old prisoners did not use their money for such purposes. They used it for securing for themselves "soft" jobs, such as clerical work in the offices of the camp or work in the shops where they were at least protected against the weather while at work.

11. It so happened that on the same day news was received of a speech by President Roosevelt, denouncing Hitler and Germany, and rumors spread that one officer of the Gestapo would be replaced by another. The *new* prisoners discussed the speech excitedly, and paid no attention to the rumors, the *old* prisoners paid no attention to the speech, but devoted all their conversations to the changes in camp officers.

JOHN HORTON

Order and Conflict Theories of Social Problems as Competing Ideologies

A recent best seller, *The One Hundred Dollar Misunderstanding*,[1] should be required reading for every student of social problems and deviant behavior. The novel makes clear what is often dimly understood and rarely applied in sociology—the fundamentally social and symbolic character of existing theories of behavior. In the novel a square, white college boy and a Lolitaesque Negro prostitute recount their shared weekend experience. But what they have shared in action, they do not share in words. Each tells a different story. Their clashing tales express different vocabularies and different experiences. Gover stereotypically dramatizes a now hackneyed theme in the modern theater and novel—the misunderstandings generated by a conflict of viewpoints, a conflict between subjective representations of "objective" reality.

Paradoxically, this familiar literary insight has escaped many social scientists. The escape is most baffling and least legitimate for the sociologists of deviant behavior and social problems. Social values define their phenomena; their social values color their interpretations. Whatever the possibilities of developing empirical theory in the social sciences, only normative theory is appropriate in the sociology of social problems. I would accept Don Martindale's definitions of empirical and normative theory:

> The ultimate materials of empirical theory are facts; the ultimate materials of normative theory are value-imperatives...empirical theory is formed out of a system of laws. Normative theory converts facts and laws into requisite means and conditions and is unique in being addressed to a system of objectives desired by the formulator or by those in whose service he stands.[2]

The problem for the sociologist is not that normative theories contain values, but that these values may go unnoticed so that normative theories

Reprinted with the permission of the University of Chicago Press and the author from "Order and Conflict Theories of Social Problems as Competing Ideologies," *American Journal of Sociology* 71 (May 1966): 701-13.

pass for empirical theories. When his own values are unnoticed, the sociologist who studies the situation of the American Negro, for example, is a little like the middle-class white boy in Gover's novel, except that only one story is told, and it is represented as *the* story. The result could be a rather costly misunderstanding: the Negro may not recognize himself in the sociological story; worse, he may not even learn to accept it.

One of the tasks of the sociologist is to recognize his own perspective and to locate this and competing perspectives in time and social structure. In this he can use Weber, Mills, and the sociology of knowledge as guides. Following Weber's work, he might argue that in so far as we are able to theorize about the social world, we must use the vocabularies of explanation actually current in social life.[3] This insight has been expanded by C. W. Mills and applied to theorizing in general and to the character of American theorizing in particular. The key words in Mills's approach to theorizing are "situated actions" and "vocabularies of motive." His position is that theories of social behavior can be understood sociologically as typical symbolic explanations associated with historically situated actions.[4] Thus, Mills argues that the Freudian terminology of motives is that of an upper-bourgeois patriarchal group with a strong sexual and individualistic orientation. Likewise explanations current in American sociology reflect the social experience and social motives of the American sociologist. Mills contends that for a period before 1940, a single vocabulary of explanation was current in the American sociologist's analysis of social problems and that these motives expressed a small town (and essentially rural) bias.[5] He interpreted the contemporary sociological vocabulary as a symbolic expression of a bureaucratic and administrative experience in life and work.[6]

Continuing in the tradition of Weber and Mills, I attempt to do the following: (1) propose a method of classifying current normative theories of deviant behavior and social problems; (2) discuss liberal and sociological approaches to the race question as an example of one of these theories; and (3) point out the implications of the normative character of theory for sociology. My general discussion of competing theories will be an elaboration of several assumptions:

1. All definitions and theories of deviation and social problems are normative. They define and explain behavior from socially situated value positions.

2. Existing normative theories can be classified into a limited number of typical vocabularies of explanation. Contemporary sociological theories of deviation are adaptations of two fundamental models of analysis rooted in nineteenth-century history and social thought. These are *order* and *conflict* models of society. Order models imply an *anomy* theory of societal discontent and an *adjustment* definition of social deviation. Conflict models imply an *alienation* theory of discontent and a *growth* definition of deviation.

3. In general, a liberalized version of order theory pervades the American sociological approach to racial conflict, juvenile delinquency, and other social problems. I use the term "liberal" because the sociological and the politically liberal vocabularies are essentially the same. Both employ an order model of society; both are conservative in their commitment to the existing social order.

4. Alternatives to the liberal order approach exist both within the context of sociological theory and in the contemporary social and political fabric of American society. More radical versions of order models have been used by European sociologists such as Émile Durkheim; radical versions of order models are presently being used in American society by political rightists. The conflict vocabulary has been most clearly identified with Karl Marx and continues today in the social analysis of socialists and communists, while an anarchistic version of conflict theory pervades the politics of the so-called new left.

5. Current vocabularies for the explanation of social problems can be located within the social organization of sociology and the broader society. As a generalization, groups or individuals committed to the maintenance of the social status quo employ order models of society and equate deviation with non-conformity to institutionalized norms. Dissident groups, striving to institutionalize new claims, favor a conflict analysis of society and an alienation theory of their own discontents. For example, this social basis of preference for one model is clear in even the most superficial analysis of stands taken on civil rights demonstrations by civil rights activists and members of the Southern establishment. For Governor Wallace of Alabama, the 1965 Selma-Montgomery march was a negative expression of anomy; for Martin Luther King it was a positive and legitimate response to alienation. King argues that the Southern system is maladaptive to certain human demands; Wallace that the demands of the demonstrators are dysfunctional to the South. However, if one considers their perspectives in relationship to the more powerful Northern establishment, King and not Wallace is the order theorist.

In sociology, order analysis of society is most often expressed by the professional establishment and its organs of publication. Alienation analysis is associated with the "humanitarian" and "political" mavericks outside of, opposed to, or in some way marginal to the established profession of sociology.

ORDER AND CONFLICT THEORIES: ANOMY AND ALIENATION ANALYSIS OF SOCIAL PROBLEMS AS IDEAL TYPES

The terms "alienation" and "anomy" current in the analysis of social problems derive historically from two opposing models of society—order and conflict models.[7] A comparison of the works of Marx and Mills (classical and contemporary conflict models) and Durkheim and Merton or Parsons (classical and contemporary order models) highlights the differences between the two social vocabularies. These competing vocabularies can be abstracted into ideal types of explanation, that is, exaggerated and ideologically consistent models which are only approximated in social reality.

THE ORDER VOCABULARY

Order theories have in common an image of society as a system of action unified at the most general level by shared culture, by agreement on values (or at least on modes) of communication and political organization. System analysis is synonymous with structural-functional analysis. System analysis consists of *statics*—the classification of structural regularities in social relations (dominant role and status clusters, institutions, etc.)—and *dynamics*—the study of the intrasystem processes: strategies of goal definition, socialization, and other functions which maintain system balance. A key concept in the analysis of system problems (social problems, deviation, conflict) is anomy. Social problems both result from and promote anomy. Anomy means system imbalance or social disorganization—a lack of or breakdown in social organization reflected in weakened social control, inadequate institutionalization of goals, inadequate means to achieve system goals, inadequate socialization, etc. At a social psychological level of analysis, anomy results in the failure of individuals to meet the maintenance needs of the social system.

Order theories imply consensual and adjustment definitions of social health and pathology, of conformity and deviation. The standards for defining health are the legitimate values of the social system and its requisites for goal attainment and maintenance. Deviation is the opposite of social conformity and means the failure of individuals to perform their legitimate social roles; deviants are out of adjustment.

A contemporary example of an order approach to society and an adjustment interpretation of health and pathology has been clearly stated in Talcott Parsons' definition of mental health and pathology:

> Health may be defined as the state of optimum *capacity* of an individual for the effective performance of the roles and tasks for which he has been socialized. It is thus defined with reference to the individual's participation in the social system. It is also defined as *relative* to his "status" in the society, i.e., to differentiated type of role and corresponding task structure, e.g., by sex or age, and by level of education which he has attained and the like.[8]

THE CONFLICT VOCABULARY

Conflict theorists are alike in their rejection of the order model of contemporary society. They interpret order analysis as the strategy of a ruling group, a reification of their values and motivations, a rationalization for more effective social control. Society is a natural system for the order analyst; for the conflict theorist it is a continually contested political struggle between groups with opposing goals and world views. As an anarchist, the conflict theorist may oppose any notion of stable order and authority. As a committed Marxist, he may project the notion of order into the future. Order is won, not through the extension of social control, but through the radical reorganization of social life: order follows from the condition of social organization and not from the state of cultural integration.

Conflict analysis is synonymous with historical analysis: the interpretation of intersystem processes bringing about the transformation of social relations. A key concept in the analysis of historical and social change (as new behavior rather than deviant behavior) is alienation—separation, not from the social system as defined by dominant groups, but separation from man's universal nature or a desired state of affairs. Change is the progressive response to alienation; concepts of disorganization and deviation have no real meaning within the conflict vocabulary; they are properly part of the vocabulary of order theory where they have negative connotations as the opposites of the supreme values of order and stability. Within the conflict framework, the question of normality and health is ultimately a practical one resolved in the struggle to overcome alienation.

Conflict theory, nevertheless, implies a particular definition of health, but the values underlying this definition refer to what is required to grow and change, rather than to adjust to existing practices and hypothesized requirements for the maintenance of the social system. Health and pathology are defined in terms of postulated requirements for individual or social growth and adaptation. Social problems and social change arise from the exploitive and alienating practices of dominant groups; they are responses to the discrepancy between what is and what is in the process of becoming. Social problems, therefore, reflect, not the administrative problems of the social system, nor the failure of individuals to perform their system roles as in the order of explanation, but the adaptive failure of society to meet changing individual needs.

A growth definition of health based on a conflict interpretation of society is implicit in Paul Goodman's appraisal of the causes of delinquency in American society. Unlike Parsons, he does not define pathology as that which does not conform to system values; he argues that delinquency is not the reaction to exclusion from these values, nor is it a problem of faulty socialization. Existing values and practices are absurd standards because they do not provide youth with what they need to grow and mature:

> As was predictable, most of the authorities and all of the public spokesmen explain it (delinquency) by saying there has been a failure of socialization.

They say that background conditions have interrupted socialization and must be improved. And, not enough effort has been made to guarantee belonging, there must be better bait or punishment.

But perhaps there has *not* been a failure of communication. Perhaps the social message has been communicated clearly to the young men and is unacceptable.

In this book I shall, therefore, take the opposite tack and ask, "Socialization to what? to what dominant society and available culture?" And if this question is asked, we must at once ask the other question, "Is the harmonious organization to which the young are inadequately socialized, perhaps against human nature, or not worthy of human nature, and *therefore* there is difficulty in growing up?"[9]

The conflict theorist invariably questions the legitimacy of existing practices and values; the order theorist accepts them as the standard of health.

PARADIGM FOR THE ANALYSIS OF CONFLICT AND ORDER APPROACHES TO SOCIAL PROBLEMS

In order more sharply to compare order and conflict models in terms of their implications for explanations of deviation and social problems, essential differences can be summarized along a number of parallel dimensions. These dimensions are dichotomized into order and conflict categories. The resulting paradigm can be used as a preliminary guide for the content analysis of contemporary as well as classical studies of social problems.

ORDER PERSPECTIVE	CONFLICT PERSPECTIVE

1. UNDERLYING SOCIAL PERSPECTIVE AND VALUE POSITIONS (IDEAL)

a. Image of man and society

Society as a natural boundary-maintaining system of action	Society as a contested struggle between groups with opposed aims and perspectives
Transcendent nature of society, an entity *sui generis,* greater than and different from the sum of its parts; lack of transcendence as lack of social control means anomy	Immanent conception of society and the social relationship; men are society; society is the extension of man, the indwelling of man; the transcendence of society is tantamount to the alienation of man from his own social nature
Positive attitude toward the maintenance of social institutions	Positive attitude toward change

b. Human nature

Homo duplex, man half egoistic (self-nature), half altruistic (socialized nature), ever in need of restraints for the collective good or *Tabula rasa,* man equated with the socialization process or	*Homo laborans* existential man, the active creator of himself and society through practical and autonomous social action

ORDER PERSPECTIVE	CONFLICT PERSPECTIVE
Homo damnatus, the division into morally superior and morally inferior men	

c. *Values*

| The social good: balance, stability, authority, order, quantitative growth ("moving equilibrium") | Freedom as autonomy, change, action, qualitative growth |

2. MODES OF "SCIENTIFIC" ANALYSIS

Natural science model: quest for general and universal laws and repeated patterns gleaned through empirical research Structural-functional analysis	Historical model: quest for understanding (Verstehen) through historical analysis of unique and changing events; possible use of ideal type of generalization based on historically specific patterns
Multiple causality; theory characterized by high level of abstraction, but empirical studies marked by low level of generalization (separation of theory from application)	Unicausality; high or low level of theoretical generalization; union of theory and practice in social research and social action
Conditions of objectivity: accurate correspondence of concepts to facts; rigid separation of observer and facts observed—passive, receptive theory of knowledge	Utility in terms of observer's interests; objectivity discussed in the context of subjectivity—activistic theory of knowledge
Analysis begins with culture as major determinant of order and structure and proceeds to personality and social organization	Analysis begins with organization of social activities or with growth and maintenance needs of man and proceeds to culture
Dominant concepts: ahistorical; high level of generality; holistic; supra-individual concepts; ultimate referent for concepts—system needs considered universally (i.e., the functional prerequisites of any social system) or relativistically (i.e., present maintenance requirements of a particular social system)	Historical, dynamic; low level of generality and high level of historical specificity; ultimate referent for concepts—human needs considered universally (i.e., man's species nature) or relativistically (demands of particular contenders for power); referent often the future or an unrealized state of affairs

3. ORDER AND CONFLICT THEORIES OF SOCIAL PROBLEMS AND DEVIATION

a. *Standards for the definition of health and pathology*

| Health equated with existing values of a postulated society (or a dominant group in the society), ideological definition | Health equated with unrealized standards (the aspirations of subordinate but rising groups), utopian definition |

b. *Evaluation of deviant behavior*

| Pathological to the functioning of the social system | Possibly progressive to the necessary transformation of existing relationships |

c. *Explanation of deviation or a social problem*

| A problem of anomy in adequate control over competing groups in the social system; dis-equilibrium in the existing society | A problem of self-alienation, being thwarted in the realization of individual and group goals; a problem of illegitimate social control and exploitation |

ORDER PERSPECTIVE	CONFLICT PERSPECTIVE
d. Implied ameliorative action	
Extension of social control (further and more efficient institutionalization of social system values); adjustment of individuals to system needs; working within the system; the administrative solution	Rupture of social control; radical transformation of existing patterns of interaction; revolutionary change of the social system

4. ORDER AND CONFLICT THEORIES AS SOCIALLY SITUATED VOCABULARIES

Dominant groups: the establishment and administrators of the establishment	Subordinate groups aspiring for greater power
Contemporary representatives: Parsonian and Mertonian approach to social problems as a liberal variant of order models; politically conservative approaches	C. W. Mills, new left (SNCC, SDS, etc.) approaches and old left (socialistic and communistic)

The order and conflict models as outlined represent polar ideal types which are not consistently found in the inconsistent ideologies of actual social research and political practice. If the models have any utility to social scientists, it will be in making more explicit and systematic the usually implicit value assumptions which underlie their categories of thinking. In this paper as an exercise in the use of conflict-order models, I examine some of the normative assumptions which can be found in the approach of the sociologist and the political liberal to the Negro question. My thinking is intentionally speculative. I am not trying to summarize the vast literature on race relations, but merely showing the existence of an order pattern.

LIBERALS AND SOCIOLOGISTS ON THE AMERICAN NEGRO: A CONTEMPORARY ADAPTATION OF ORDER THEORY

Contemporary liberalism has been popularly associated with a conflict model of society; actually it is a variant of conservative order theory. Within the model, conflict is translated to mean institutionalized (reconciled) conflict or competition for similar goals within the same system. Conflict as confrontation of opposed groups and values, conflict as a movement toward basic change of goals and social structures is anathema.

The liberal tendency of American sociology and the essentially conservative character of contemporary liberalism are particularly marked in the sociological analysis of the Negro question. In the field of race relations, an order model can be detected in (1) consensual assumptions about man and society: the "oversocialized" man and the plural society; (2) a selective pattern of interpretation which follows from these assumptions: (*a*) the explanation of the problem as a moral dilemma and its solution as one requiring adjustment through socialization and social control; (*b*) the explanation of the minority group as a reaction-formation to exclusion from middle-class life; (*c*) an emphasis on concepts useful in the explanation of order (shared values as opposed to economic and political differences); an emphasis on concepts useful in the explanation of disorder or anomy within an accepted order (status competition rather than class conflict, problems of inadequate means rather than conflicting goals).

THE LIBERAL VIEW OF MAN: EGALITARIAN WITHIN AN ELITIST, CONSENSUAL FRAMEWORK: ALL MEN ARE SOCIALIZABLE TO THE AMERICAN CREED

No one can see an ideological assumption as clearly as a political opponent. Rightist and leftist alike have attacked the liberal concept of man implicit in the analysis of the Negro question: conservatives because it is egalitarian, radicals because it is elitist and equated with a dominant ideology. The rightist believes in natural inequality; the leftist in positive, historical differences between men; the liberal believes in the power of socialization and conversion.

A certain egalitarianism is indeed implied in at least two liberal assertions: (1) Negroes along with other men share a common human nature socializable to the conditions of society; (2) their low position and general inability to compete reflect unequal opportunity and inadequate socialization to whatever is required to succeed within the American system. These assertions are, in a sense, basically opposed to the elitist-conservative argument that the Negro has failed to compete because he is naturally different or has voluntarily failed to take full advantage of existing opportunities.[10]

The conservative, however, exaggerates liberal egalitarianism; it is tempered with elitism. Equality is won by conformity to a dominant set of values and behavior. Equality means equal opportunity to achieve the same American values; in other words, equality is gained by losing one identity and conforming at some level to another demanded by a dominant group. As a leftist, J. P. Sartre has summarized this liberal view of man, both egalitarian and elitist. What he has termed the "democratic" attitude toward the Jew applies well to the American "liberal" view of the Negro:

> The Democrat, like the scientist, fails to see the particular case; to him the individual is only an ensemble of universal traits. It follows that his defense of the Jew saves the latter as a man and annihilates him as a Jew . . . he fears that the Jew will acquire a consciousness of Jewish collectivity. . . ."There are no Jews," he says, "there is no Jewish question." This means that he wants to separate the Jew from his religion, from his family, from his ethnic com-

munity, in order to plunge him into the democratic crucible whence he will emerge naked and alone, an individual and solitary particle like all other particles.[11]

The conservative would preserve a Negro identity by pronouncing the Negro different (inferior), the radical by proclaiming him part of the superior vanguard of the future society; but the liberal would transform him altogether by turning him into another American, another individual competing in an orderly fashion for cars, television sets, and identification with the American Creed. In their attack on the liberal definition of man, the conservative and leftist agree on one thing: the liberal seems to deny basic differences between groups. At least differences are reconcilable within a consensual society.

THE LIBERAL SOCIETY: STRUCTURAL PLURALISM WITHIN A CONSENSUAL FRAMEWORK

Thus, the liberal fate of minorities, including Negroes, is basically containment through socialization to dominant values. Supposedly this occurs in a plural society where some differences are maintained. But liberal pluralism like liberal egalitarianism allows differences only within a consensual framework. This applies both to the liberal ideal and the sociological description: the plural-democratic society *is* the present society.

This consensual pluralism should be carefully distinguished from the conflict variety. J. S. Furnivall has called the once colonially dominated societies of tropical Asia plural in the latter sense:

> In Burma, as in Java, probably the first thing that strikes the visitor is the medley of peoples—European, Chinese, Indian, native. It is in the strictest sense a medley, for they mix but do not combine. Each group holds to its own religion, its own culture and language, its own ideas and ways. As individuals they meet, but only in the marketplace, in buying and selling. There is a plural society, with different sections of the community living side by side, but separately, within the same political unit. Even in the economic sphere there is a division along racial lines.[12]

For Furnivall, a plural society has no common will, no common culture. Order rests on political force and economic expediency. For liberals and sociologists, American society has a common social will (the American Creed). Order rests on legitimate authority and consensus. The whole analysis of the Negro question has generally been predicated on this belief that American society, however plural, is united by consensus on certain values. Gunnar Myrdal's influential interpretation of the Negro question has epitomized the social will thesis:

> Americans of all national origins, classes, regions, creeds, and colors, have something in common: a social ethos, a political creed. . . . When the

American Creed is once detected the cacophony becomes a melody . . . as principles which ought to rule, the Creed has been made conscious to everyone in American society. . . . America is continuously struggling for its soul. The cultural unity of the nation is sharing of both the consciousness of sin and the devotion to high ideals.[13]

In what sense can a consensual society be plural? It cannot tolerate the existence of separate cultural segments. Robin M. Williams in a recent book on race relations writes: "The United States is a plural society which cannot settle for a mosaic of separate cultural segments, nor for a caste system."[14] Norman Podhoretz, a political liberal who has written often on the Negro question has stated the issue more bluntly. In his review of Ralph Ellison's *Shadow and the Act,* a series of essays which poses a threat of conflict pluralism by asserting the positive and different "cultural" characteristics of Negroes, Podhoretz states his consensual realism:

> The vision of a world in which many different groups live together on a footing of legal and social equality, each partaking of a broad general culture and yet maintaining its own distinctive identity: this is one of the noble dreams of the liberal tradition. Yet the hard truth is that very little evidence exists to suggest that such a pluralistic order is possible. Most societies throughout history have simply been unable to suffer the presence of distinctive minority groups among them; and the fate of minorities has generally been to disappear, either through being assimilated into the majority, or through being expelled, or through being murdered.[15]

The liberal and the sociologist operating with an order ideology positively fear the conflict type of pluralism. As Sartre rightly observed, the liberal who is himself identified with the establishment, although avowedly the friend of the minority, suspects any sign of militant minority consciousness. He wants the minority to share in American human nature and compete like an individual along with other individuals for the same values.

As Podhoretz has observed, pluralism never really meant the co-existence of quite different groups:

> For the traditional liberal mentality conceives of society as being made up not of competing economic classes and ethnic groups, but rather of competing *individuals* who confront a neutral body of law and a neutral institutional complex.[16]

How then can ethnic groups be discussed within the plural but consensual framework? They must be seen as separate but assimilated (contained) social structures. Among sociologists, Milton Gordon has been most precise about this pluralism as a description of ethnic groups in American society.

Behavioral assimilation or acculturation has taken place in America to a considerable degree. . . . Structural assimilation, then, has turned out to be the rock on which the ships of Anglo-conformity and the melting pot have foundered. To understand the behavioral assimilation (or acculturation) without massive structural intermingling in primary relationships has been the dominant motif in the American experience of creating and developing a nation out of diverse peoples is to comprehend the most essential sociological fact of that experience. It is against the background of "structural pluralism" that strategies of strengthening inter-group harmony, reducing ethnic discrimination and prejudice, and maintaining the rights of both those who stay within and those who venture beyond their ethnic boundaries must be thoughtfully devised.[17]

Clearly then the liberal vocabulary of race relations is predicated on consensual assumptions about the nature of man and society. The order explanation of the Negro problem and its solution may be summarized as follows:

1. *An order or consensual model of society.*—American society is interpreted as a social system unified at its most general level by acceptance of certain central political, social, and economic values. Thus, the Negro population is said to have been acculturated to a somewhat vaguely defined American tradition; at the most, Negro society is a variant or a reaction to that primary tradition.

2. *Social problems as moral problems of anomy or social disorganization within the American system.*—Social problems and deviant behavior arise from an imbalance between goals and means. The problems of the Negro are created by unethical exclusion from equal competition for American goals.

3. *The response to anomy: social amelioration as adjustment and extension of social control.*—Liberal solutions imply further institutionalization of the American Creed in the opportunity structure of society and, therefore, the adjustment of the deviant to legitimate social roles.

THE RACE QUESTION AS A MORAL DILEMMA

A familiar expression of liberal-consensualism is Gunnar Myrdal's interpretation of the American race question as a moral dilemma. According to this thesis, racial discrimination and its varied effects on the Negro—the development of plural social structures, high rates of social deviation, etc.—reflect a kind of anomy in the relationship between the American Creed and social structure. Anomy means a moral crisis arising from an incongruity between legitimate and ethical social goals (for example, success and equality of opportunity) and socially available opportunities to achieve these goals. American society is good and ethical, but anomic because the American Creed of equality has not been fully institutionalized; the ethic is widely accepted in theory but not in practice. Sidney Hook as a political liberal has likewise insisted that American society is essentially ethical and that the Negro problem should be discussed in these ethical terms:

> Of course, no society has historically been organized on the basis of ethical principles, but I don't think we can understand how any society functions without observing the operation of the ethical principles within it. And if we examine the development of American society, we certainly can say that we have made *some* progress, to be sure, but progress nevertheless—by virtue of the extension of our ethical principles to institutional life. If we want to explain the progress that has been made in the last twenty years by minority groups in this country—not only the Negroes, but other groups as well—I believe we have to take into account the effect of our commitment to democracy, imperfect though it may be.[18]

THE SOLUTION: WORKING WITHIN THE SYSTEM

The liberal solution to the racial question follows from the American-dilemma thesis: the belief in the ethical nature and basic legitimacy of American institutions. Amelioration, therefore, becomes exclusively a question of adjustment within the system; it calls for administrative action: how to attack anomy as the imbalance of goals and means. The administrator accepts the goals of his organization and treats all problems as errors in administration, errors which can be rectified without changing the basic framework of the organization. Karl Mannheim has aptly characterized the bureaucratic and administrative approach to social problems. What he says about the perspective of the Prussian bureaucrat applies only too well to his counterpart in American society:

> The attempt to hide all problems of politics under the cover of administration may be explained by the fact that the sphere of activity of the official exists only within the limits of laws already formulated. Hence the genesis or the development of law falls outside the scope of his activity. As a result of his socially limited horizon, the functionary fails to see that behind every law that has been made there lie the socially fashioned interests and the *Weltanschauungen* of a specific social group. He takes it for granted that the specific order prescribed by the concrete law is equivalent to order in general. He does not understand that every rationalized order is only one of many forms in which socially conflicting irrational forces are reconciled.[19]

The liberal administrator's solution to the Negro question entails the expansion of opportunities for mobility within the society and socialization of the deviant (the Negro and the anti-Negro) to expanding opportunities. Hence, the importance of education and job training; they are prime means to success and higher status. Given the assumption that the American Creed is formally embodied in the political structure, the liberal also looks to legislation as an important and perhaps sole means of reenforcing the Creed by legitimizing changes in the American opportunity structure.

NEGRO LIFE AS A REACTION FORMATION

Another important deduction has followed from the assumption of the political and cultural assimilation of the American Negro: whatever is different or distinct in his life style represents a kind of negative reaction to exclusion from the white society. The Negro is the creation of the white. Like the criminal he is a pathology, a reaction-formation to the problem of inadequate opportunities to achieve and to compete in the American system.

Myrdal states:

> The Negro's entire life and, consequently, also his opinions on the Negro problem are, in the main, to be considered as secondary reactions to more primary pressures from the side of the dominant white majority.[20]

More recently Leonard Broom has echoed the same opinion:

> Negro life was dominated by the need to adjust to white men and to take them into account at every turn. . . . Taken as a whole, the two cultures have more common than distinctive elements. Over the long run, their convergence would seem inevitable. . . . Because Negro life is so much affected by poverty and subservience, it is hard to find distinctive characteristics that can be positively evaluated. In the stereotype, whatever is admirable in Negro life is assumed to have been adopted from the white man, while whatever is reprehensible is assumed to be inherently Negro.[21]

CONFLICT THEORIST LOOKS AT
ORDER THEORIST LOOKING AT THE NEGRO

A liberal order model—consensual pluralism, with its corollary approach to the race question as moral dilemma and reaction-formation—colors the sociological analysis of the race question. It is interesting that the fundamental assumption about consensus on the American Creed has rarely been subjected to adequate empirical test.[22] Lacking any convincing evidence for the order thesis, I can only wonder who the sociologist is speaking for. He may be speaking for himself in that his paradigm answers the question of how to solve the Negro problem without changing basic economic and political institutions. He probably speaks least of all for the Negro. The liberal sociologists will have some difficulty describing the world from the viewpoint of Negro "rioters" in Los Angeles and other cities. In any case, he will not agree with anyone who believes (in fact or in ideology) that the Negro may have a separate and self-determining identity. Such a view suggests conflict and would throw doubt on the fixations of consensus, anomy, and reaction-formation.

Conflict interpretations are minority interpretations by definition. They are rarely expressed either by sociologists or by ethnic minorities. However, a few such interpretations can be mentioned to imply that the end of ideology and, therefore, the agreement on total ideology has not yet arrived.

Ralph Ellison, speaking from a conflict and nationalistic perspective, has made several salient criticisms of the liberal American dilemma thesis. He has argued that Myrdal's long discussion of American values and conclusion of multiple causality have conveniently avoided the inconvenient question of power and control in American society.

> All this, of course, avoids the question of power *and* the question of who manipulates that power. Which to us seems more of a stylistic maneuver than a scientific judgment....Myrdal's stylistic method is admirable. In presenting his findings he uses the American ethos brilliantly to disarm all American social groupings, by appealing to their stake in the American Creed, and to locate the psychological barriers between them. But he also uses it to deny the existence of an American class struggle, and with facile economy it allows him to avoid admitting that actually there exist two American moralities, kept in balance by social science.[23]

Doubting the thesis of consensus, Ellison is also in a position to attack Myrdal's interpretation of the American Negro as a reaction-formation and assimilation to the superior white society as his only solution.

> But can a people (its faith in an idealized American Creed notwithstanding) live and develop for over three hundred years simply by reacting? Are American Negroes simply the creation of white men, or have they at least helped to create themselves out of what they found around them? Men have made a way of life in caves and upon cliffs, why cannot Negroes have made a life upon the horns of the white men's dilemma?
> Myrdal sees Negro culture and personality simply as the product of a "social pathology." Thus he assumes that "it is to the advantage of American Negroes as individuals and as a group to become assimilated into American culture, to acquire the traits held in esteem by the dominant white American." This, he admits, contains the value premise that "*here in America,* American culture is 'highest' in the pragmatic sense. ..." Which aside from implying that Negro culture is not also American, assumes that Negroes should desire nothing better than what whites consider highest. But in the "pragmatic" sense lynching and Hollywood, fadism and radio advertising are products of "higher" culture, and the Negro might ask, "Why, if my culture is pathological, must I exchange it for these?"
> ...What is needed in our country is not an exchange of pathologies, but a change of the basis of society.[24]

CONCLUSION

The hostile action of Negro masses destroying white property is perhaps a more convincing demonstration of conflict theory than the hopes of Negro intellectuals. But as a sociologist I am not really interested in raising the question of whether a conflict definition of the race question is more correct than the more familiar order model. Each view is correct in a normative and practical sense in so far as it conforms to a viable political and social experience. What indeed is a correct interpretation of the Negro problem or any social problem? The answer has as much to do with consensus as with correspondence to the facts. Normative theories are not necessarily affected by empirical evidence because they seek to change or to maintain the world, not describe it.

Whenever there is genuine conflict between groups and interpretations, correctness clearly becomes a practical matter of power and political persuasion. This seems to be the situation today, and one can expect more heated debate. If conflict continues to increase between whites and Negroes in the United States, the liberal sociologist studying the "Negro problem" had better arm himself with more than his questionnaire. A militant Negro respondent may take him for the social problem, the sociologist as an agent of white society and the scientific purveyor of order theory and containment policy.

This clash of perspectives would be an illustration of my general argument: explanations of the Negro question or any other social problem invariably involve normative theory, values, ideologies, or whatever one may care to call the subjective categories of our thinking about society. Concepts of deviation and social problems can be discussed only in the context of some social (and therefore contestable) standard of health, conformity, and the good society. Terms like "moral dilemma," "pluralism," "assimilation," "integration" describe motives for desirable action: they are definitions placed on human action, not the action itself independent of social values.

The error of the sociologist is not that he thinks politically and liberally about his society, but that he is not aware of it. Awareness may help him avoid some of the gross errors of myopia: (1) mistaking his own normative categories for "objective" fact; thus, the liberal sociologist may mistake his belief in the consensual society for actual consensus; (2) projecting a normative theory appropriate to the experience of one group on to another group; this is what Ellison means when he says that the liberal sociologist is not necessarily speaking for the Negro. Indeed, the errors of myopia are perhaps greatest whenever the middle-class sociologist presumes to describe the world and motivation of persons in lower status. Seeing the lower-class Negro within a white liberal vocabulary may be very realistic politics, but it is not very accurate sociology.

Once the sociologist is involved in the study of anything that matters, he has the unavoidable obligation of at least distinguishing his vocabulary from that of the groups he is supposedly observing rather than converting. As a scientist, he must find out what perspectives are being employed, where they are operating in the society, and with what effect. Perhaps this awareness of competing perspectives occurs only in the actual process of conflict and debate. Unfortunately, this is not always the situation within an increasingly professionalized sociology. The more professionalized the field, the more standardized the thinking of sociologists and the greater the danger of internal myopia passing for objectivity. But outside sociology debate is far from closed; conflict and order perspectives are simultaneously active on every controversial social issue. The liberal order model may not long enjoy uncontested supremacy.

NOTES

1. Robert Gover, *The One Hundred Dollar Misunderstanding* (New York: Ballantine Books, 1961).

2. Don Martindale, "Social Disorganization: The Conflict of Normative and Empirical Approaches," in Howard Becker and Alvin Boskoff (eds.), *Modern Sociological Theory* (New York: Dryden Press, 1959), p. 341.

3. For Weber's discussion of explanation in the social sciences see *Max Weber: The Theory of Social and Economic Organization*, trans. A.M. Henderson and Talcott Parsons (Glencoe, Ill.: Free Press, 1947), pp. 87-114.

4. C. Wright Mills, "Situated Actions and Vocabularies of Motive," *American Sociological Review*, V (December, 1940), 904-13.

5. C. Wright Mills, "The Professional Ideology of the Social Pathologists," *American Journal of Sociology*, XLIX (September, 1942), 165-80.

6. C. Wright Mills, *The Sociological Imagination* (New York: Oxford University Press, 1959.)

7. In contemporary sociology, the concepts of alienation and anomy are often used synonymously. In practice, this usually means that alienation, a key term in conflict analysis, has been translated into a more conservative-order vocabulary; for a discussion of differences between past and present uses of these concepts see John Horton, "The Dehumanization of Anomie and Alienation," *British Journal of Sociology*, XV (December, 1964), 283-300.

8. Talcott Parsons, "Definitions of Health and Illness in the Light of American Values and Social Structure," in E. Gartley Jaco (ed.), *Patients, Physicians and Illness* (Glencoe Ill.: Free Press, 1963), p. 176.

9. Paul Goodman, *Growing Up Absurd* (New York: Random House, 1960), p. 11.

10. For a conservative argument, see, among many others, Carleton Putnam, *Race and Reason* (Washington, D.C.: Public Affairs Press, 1961).

11. Jean-Paul Sartre, *Anti-Semite and Jew*, trans. George J. Becker (New York: Grove Press, 1962), pp. 56-57.

12. J. S. Furnivall, *Colonial Policy and Practice* (London: Cambridge University Press, 1948), p. 304.

13. Gunnar Myrdal, *An American Dilemma* (New York: Harper & Bros., 1944), pp. 3-4.

14. Robin M. Williams, Jr., *Strangers Next Door* (Englewood Cliffs, N.J.: Prentice-Hall, Inc., 1964), p. 386.

15. Norman Podhoretz, "The Melting Pot Blues," *Washington Post*, October 25, 1964.

16. Norman Podhoretz, as quoted in "Liberalism and the American Negro—a Round Table Discussion," with James Baldwin, Nathan Glazer, Sidney Hook, Gunnar Myrdal, and Norman Podhoretz (moderator), *Commentary*, XXXVII (March 1964), 25-26.

17. Milton Gordon, "Assimilation in America: Theory and Reality," *Daedalus*, XC (Spring, 1961), 280, 283.

18. Sidney Hook, "Liberalism and the American Negro—a Round-Table Discussion," *Commentary*, XXXVII (March, 1964), p. 31.

19. Karl Mannheim, *Ideology and Utopia* (New York: Harcourt, Brace & World, 1936), p. 118.

20. Gunnar Myrdal as quoted by Ralph Ellison, "An American Dilemma: A Review," in *Shadow and the Act* (New York: Random House, 1964), p. 315.

21. Leonard Broom, *The Transformation of the American Negro* (New York: Harper & Row, 1965), pp. 22-23.

22. For a recent attempt to test the American dilemma thesis see Frank R. Westie, "The American Dilemma: An Empirical Test," *American Sociological Review,* XXX (August, 1965), 527-38.

23. Ralph Ellison, *Shadow and the Act, op. cit.,* p. 315.

24. *Ibid.,* pp. 316-17.

PART III

Symbols, Culture, and Socialization

IN THIS SECTION AND THE NEXT ONE WE WANT TO illustrate some of the diversity among social scientists by looking more closely at two major areas of study. The first of these includes the organization of ideas, the patterns of values, beliefs, and rules that are found in human organizations, and the processes that lead to the development and reinforcement of these patterns. The second includes the organization of people, the patterns of relationships among them, and the relationships between different patterns and human behavior. This section takes up the first of these two areas.

The overarching concept in this area is *culture*, which is variously defined. In one selection that follows Hoebel defines culture as "the sum total of learned behavior traits which are manifested and shared by the members of a society." It might also be defined as the patterns of values, beliefs, and rules found in a society. The two definitions are really not that different from each other because it is the values, beliefs, and rules in the latter definition that shape the learned behavior traits that Hoebel speaks about. Common to most definitions

of culture are that it is learned, that it constrains or shapes
human behavior, and that it tends to be patterned. But how is
it created? How is it learned or transmitted? What happens
when it is not learned? These and other questions are taken
up in this section.

The selection from Leslie White's book *The Science of
Culture* discusses the role of the symbol in human life. People
develop jointly shared meanings for objects, qualities, and
ideas which are manifested in the form of symbols. Symbols,
White proposes, are the basic element of culture. As the small
child (or the adult, for that matter) learns symbols he is also
learning culture: he is internalizing the constraints that will
shape his behavior. He learns that behaving one way is
"good" while another way is "bad." But more subtly, many of
the seemingly neutral symbols are conveyed to him in a way
that dresses them in ethical or emotional terms. The symbols
"black" and "white" denote colors but they also have other
meanings. White is good, but black is bad, sad or funereal. In
the Vietnamese culture these symbols have exactly the opposite connotations. In sum the conversion of the newborn
infant into a socially skilled adult is based on the process of
developing shared meanings for symbols. This is the process
of socialization.

What happens if this process does not occur? The second
selection deals with this question. Kingsley Davis did a careful
study of two children who had reached the age of six without
experiencing much human contact involving symbols. In
Isabelle's case she and her mother were isolated in an attic for
years by the embarrassed grandparents of the illegitimate
child. Since her mother was a deaf-mute of very limited intelligence, the usual symbol-building processes between
parent and child did not occur. When the authorities
discovered the child at age six, she was still crawling on all
fours and making the random sounds usually heard only from
babies. In other words, without symbolic interaction the child

had made no progress toward mental and social maturity.

The line of reasoning pursued by Leslie White and others has led to the development of the concept of *self*. To the extent that individuals share common meanings for symbols, they have a basis for understanding each other's values, beliefs, and motives. Further, the individual can make some estimate of himself as others see him because he can interpret the signs and symbols they use with him: e.g., looking bored, avoiding him, smiling when they see him, or talking with or about him. The selection by Francis Merrill reviews the development of the concept of self and some of the research that has been done using that concept.

Adamson Hoebel provides a useful statement on the concept of culture. He explains what is meant by pattern or consistency in culture and many of the other concepts that are used to analyze cultures. In the third volume in this series, *American Society*, this theme of self will be taken up again to show how some of the characteristics of our society affect our images of our self and our self-esteem.

The final two articles illustrate aspects of culture. The first by John Brewer describes the argot used in ghetto subcultures and how it relates to problems of ghetto life. In the second, Horace Miner discusses some of the exotic and even bizarre practices which can be associated with a culture.

LESLIE WHITE

The
Symbol

I

In July, 1939, a celebration was held at Leland Stanford University to commemorate the hundredth anniversary of the discovery that the cell is the basic unit of all living tissue. Today we are beginning to realize and to appreciate the fact that the symbol is the basic unit of all human behavior and civilization.

All human behavior originates in the use of symbols. It was the symbol which transformed our anthropoid ancestors into men and made them human. All civilizations have been generated, and are perpetuated, only by the use of symbols. It is the symbol which transforms an infant of Homo sapiens into a human being; deaf mutes who grow up without the use of symbols are not human beings. All human behavior consists of, or is dependent upon, the use of symbols. Human behavior is symbolic behavior; symbolic behavior is human behavior. The symbol is the universe of humanity.

II

The great Darwin declared in *The Descent of Man* that "there is no fundamental difference between man and the higher mammals in their mental faculties," that the difference between them consists *solely* in his [man's] almost infinitely larger power of associating together the most diversified sounds and ideas...the mental powers of higher animals do not differ *in kind,* though greatly *in degree,* from the corresponding powers of man" (Chs. 3, 18; emphasis ours).

This view of comparative mentality is held by many scholars today. Thus, F.H. Hankins, a prominent sociologist, states that "in spite of his large brain, it cannot be said that man has any mental traits that are

Reprinted with the permission of Leslie White and Farrar, Straus & Giroux, Inc., from *Science of Culture* (New York: Farrar, Straus and Cudahy [Grove Press Inc. Edition], 1949), pp. 22-36. Copyright ©1949 (1969) by Leslie White.

peculiar to him. . . All of these human superiorities are merely relative or differences of degree." Professor Ralph Linton, an anthropologist, writes in *The Study of Man:* "The differences between men and animals in all these [behavior] respects are enormous, but they seem to be differences in quantity rather than in quality." "Human and animal behavior can be shown to have so much in common," Linton observes, "that the gap [between them] ceases to be of great importance." Dr. Alexander Goldenweiser, likewise an anthropologist, believes that "In point of sheer psychology, mind as such, man is after all no more than a talented animal" and that "the difference between the mentality here displayed [by a horse and a chimpanzee] and that of man is merely one of degree."

That there are numerous and impressive similarities between the behavior of man and that of ape is fairly obvious; it is quite possible that chimpanzees and gorillas in zoos have noted and appreciated them. Fairly apparent, too, are man's behavioral similarities to many other kinds of animals. Almost as obvious, but not easy to define, is a difference in behavior which distinguishes man from all other living creatures. I say 'obvious' because it is quite apparent to the common man that the non-human animals with which he is familiar do not and cannot enter, and participate in, the world in which he, as a human being, lives. It is impossible for a dog, horse, bird, or even an ape, to have any understanding of the meaning of the sign of the cross to a Christian, or of the fact that black (white among the Chinese) is the color of mourning. No chimpanzee or laboratory rat can appreciate the difference between Holy water and distilled water, or grasp the meaning of *Tuesday, 3,* or *sin.* No animal save man can distinguish a cousin from an uncle, or a cross cousin from a parallel cousin. Only man can commit the crime of incest or adultery; only he can remember the Sabbath and keep it Holy. It is not, as we well know, that the lower animals can do these things but to a lesser degree than ourselves; they cannot perform these acts of appreciation and distinction *at all.* It is, as Descartes said long ago, "not only that the brutes have less Reason than man, but that they have none at all."

But when the scholar attempts to *define* the mental difference between man and other animals he sometimes encounters difficulties which he cannot surmount and, therefore, ends up by saying that the difference is merely one of degree: man has a bigger mind, "larger power of association," wider range of activities, etc. We have a good example of this in the distinguished physiologist, Anton J. Carlson. After taking note of "man's present achievements in science, in the arts (including oratory), in political and social institutions," and noting "at the same time the apparent paucity of such behavior in other animals," he, as a common man "is tempted to conclude that in these capacities, at least, man has a qualitative superiority over other mammals." But, since, as a scientist, Professor Carlson cannot *define* this qualitative difference between man and other animals, since as a physiologist he cannot explain it, he refuses to admit it—". . . the physiologist does not accept the great development of articulate speech in man as something qualitatively new; . . ."—and suggests helplessly that some day we may find some new "building stone," an "additional lipoid, phosphatid, or potassium ion," in the human brain which will explain it, and concludes by saying that the difference between the mind of man and that of non-man is "probably only one of degree."

The thesis that we shall advance and defend here is that there is a *fundamental* difference between the mind of man and the mind of non-man. This difference is one of kind, not one of degree. And the gap between the two types is of the greatest importance—at least to the science of comparative behavior. Man uses symbols; no other creature does. An organism has the ability to symbol or it does not; there are no intermediate stages.

III

A symbol may be defined as a thing the value or meaning of which is bestowed upon it by those who use it. I say 'thing' because a symbol may have any kind of physical form; it may have the form of a material object, a color, a sound, an odor, a motion of an object, a taste.

The meaning, or value, of a symbol is in no instance derived from or determined by properties intrinsic in its physical form: the color appropriate to mourning may be yellow, green, or any other color; purple need not be the color of royalty; among the Manchu rulers of China it was yellow. The meaning of the word "see" is not intrinsic in its phonetic (or pictorial) properties. "Biting one's thumb at"* someone might mean anything. The meanings of symbols are derived from and determined by the organisms who use them; meaning is bestowed by human organisms upon physical things or events which thereupon become symbols. Symbols "have their signification," to use John Locke's phrase, "from the arbitrary imposition of men."

All symbols must have a physical form otherwise they could not enter our experience. This statement is valid regardless of our theory of experiencing. Even the exponents of "Extra-Sensory Perception" who have challenged Locke's dictum that "the knowledge of the existence of any other thing [besides ourselves and God] we can have only by sensation," have been obliged to work with physical rather than ethereal forms. But the meaning of a symbol cannot be discovered by mere sensory examination of its physical form. One cannot tell by looking at an x in an algebraic equation what it stands for; one cannot ascertain with the ears alone the symbolic value of the phonetic compound *si;* one cannot tell

---

*"Do you bite your thumb at us, sir?"—*Romeo and Juliet,* Act I, Sc. 1.

merely by weighing a pig how much gold he will exchange for; one cannot tell from the wave length of a color whether it stands for courage or cowardice, "stop" or "go"; nor can one discover the spirit in a fetish by any amount of physical or chemical examination. The meaning of a symbol can be grasped only by non-sensory, symbolic means.

The nature of symbolic experience may be easily illustrated. When the Spaniards first encountered the Aztecs, neither could speak the language of the other. How could the Indians discover the meaning of santo, or the significance of the crucifix? How could the Spaniards learn the meaning of *calli*, or appreciate Tlaloc? These meanings and values could not be communicated by sensory experience of physical properties alone. The finest ears will not tell you whether *santo* means "holy" or "hungry." The keenest senses cannot capture the value of holy water. Yet, as we all know, the Spaniards and the Aztecs did discover each other's meanings and appreciate each other's values. But not with sensory means. Each was able to enter the world of the other only by virtue of a faculty for which we have no better name than *symbol*.

But a thing which in one context is a symbol is, in another context, not a symbol but a sign. Thus, a word is a symbol only when one is concerned with the distinction between its meaning and its physical form. This distinction *must* be made when one bestows value upon a sound-combination or when a previously bestowed value is discovered for the first time; it may be made at other times for certain purposes. But after value has been bestowed upon, or discovered in, a word, its meaning becomes identified, in use, with its physical form. The word then functions as a sign, rather than as a symbol. Its meaning is then grasped with the senses.

We define a *sign* as a physical thing or event whose function is to indicate some other thing or event. The meaning of a sign may be inherent in its physical form and its context, as in the case of the height of a column of mercury in a thermometer as an indication of temperature, or the return of robins in the spring. Or, the meaning of a sign may be merely identified with its physical form as in the case of a hurricane signal or a quarantine flag. But in either case, the meaning of the sign may be ascertained by sensory means. The fact that a thing may be both a symbol (in one context) and a sign (in another context) has led to confusion and misunderstanding.

Thus Darwin says: "That which distinguishes man from the lower animals is not the understanding of articulate sounds, for as everyone knows, dogs understand many words and sentences," (Ch. III, *The Descent of Man*).

It is perfectly true, of course, that dogs, apes, horses, birds, and perhaps creatures even lower in the evolutionary scale, can be taught to respond in a specific way to a vocal command. Little Gua, the infant chimpanzee in the Kelloggs' experiment, was, for a time, "considerably superior to the child in responding to human words." But it does not follow that no difference exists between the meaning of "words and sentences" to a man and to an ape or dog. Words are both signs and symbols to man; they are merely signs to a dog. Let us analyze the situation of vocal stimulus and response.

A dog may be taught to roll over at the command "Roll over!" A man may be taught to stop at the command "Halt!" The fact that a dog can be taught to roll over in Chinese, or that he can be taught to "go fetch" at the command "roll over" (and, of course, the same is true for a man) shows that there is no necessary and invariable relationship between a particular sound combination and a specific reaction to it. The dog or the man can be taught to respond in a certain manner to *any* arbitrarily selected combination of sounds, for example, a group of nonsense syllables, coined for the occasion. On the other hand, any one of a great number and variety of responses may become evocable by a given stimulus. Thus, so far as the *origin* of the relationship between vocal stimulus and response is concerned, the nature of the relationship, i.e., the meaning of the stimulus, is not determined by properties intrinsic in the stimulus.

But, once the relationship has been established between vocal stimulus and response, the meaning of the stimulus becomes *identified with the sounds;* it is then *as if* the meaning were intrinsic in the sounds themselves. Thus, "halt" does not have the same meaning as "hilt" or "malt," and these stimuli are distinguished from one another with the auditory mechanism. A dog may be conditioned to respond in a certain way to a sound of a given wave length. Sufficiently alter the pitch of the sound and the response will cease to be forthcoming. The meaning of the stimulus has become identified with its physical form; its value is appreciated with the senses.

Thus in *sign* behavior we see that in *establishing* a relationship between a stimulus and a response the properties intrinsic in the stimulus do not determine the nature of the response. But, *after the relationship has been established* the meaning of the stimulus is *as if* it were *inherent* in its physical form. It does not make any difference what phonetic combination we select to evoke the response of terminating self-locomotion. We may teach a dog, horse, or man to stop at any vocal command we care to choose or devise. But once the relationship has been established between sound and response, the meaning of the stimulus becomes identified with its physical form and is, therefore, perceivable with the senses.

So far we have discovered no difference between the dog and the man; they appear to be exactly alike. And so they are as far as we have gone. But we have not told the whole story yet. No difference between dog and man is discoverable so far as learning to respond appropriately to a vocal stimulus is concerned. But we must not let an impressive similarity conceal an important difference. A porpoise is not yet a fish.

The man differs from the dog—and all other creatures—in that *he can and does play an active role in determining what value the vocal stimulus is to have, and the dog cannot.* The dog does not and cannot play an active part in determining the value of the vocal stimulus. Whether he is to roll over or go fetch at a given stimulus, or whether the stimulus for roll over be one combination of sounds or another is a matter in which the dog has nothing whatever to "say." He plays a purely passive role and can do nothing else. He learns the meaning of a vocal command just as his salivary glands may learn to respond to the sound of a bell. But man plays an active role and thus becomes a creator: let *x* equal three pounds of coal and it does equal three pounds of coal; let removal of the hat in a house of worship indicate respect and it becomes so. This creative faculty, that of freely, actively, and arbitrarily bestowing the value upon things, is one of the most commonplace as well as *the* most important characteristic of man. Children employ it freely in their play: "Let's pretend that this rock is a wolf."

The difference between the behavior of man and other animals then, is that the lower animals may receive new values, may acquire new meanings, but they cannot create and bestow them. Only man can do this. To use a crude analogy, lower animals are like a person who has only the receiving apparatus for wireless messages: he can receive messages but cannot send them. Man can do both. And this difference is one of kind, not of degree: a creature can either "arbitrarily impose signification," can either create and bestow values, or he cannot. There are no intermediate stages. This difference may appear slight, but, as a carpenter once told William James in discussing differences between men, "It's very important." All *human* existence depends upon it and it alone.

The confusion regarding the nature of words and their significance to men and the lower animals is not hard to understand. It arises, first of all, from a failure to distinguish between the two quite different contexts in which words function. The statements, "The meaning of a word cannot be grasped with the senses," and "The meaning of a word can be grasped with the senses," though contradictory, are nevertheless equally true. In the *symbol* context the meaning cannot be perceived with the senses; in the *sign* context it can. This is confusing enough. But the situation has been made worse by using the words "symbol" and "sign" to label, not the *different contexts,* but *one and the same thing:* the word. Thus a word is a symbol *and* a sign, two different things. It is like saying that a vase is a *doli* and a *kana*—two different things—because it may function in two contexts, esthetic and commercial. . . .

VI

All culture (civilization) depends upon the symbol. It was the exercise of the symbolic faculty that brought culture into existence and it is the use of symbols that makes the perpetuation of culture possible. Without the symbol there would be no culture, and man would be merely an animal, not a human being.

Articulate speech is the most important form of symbolic expression. Remove speech from culture and what would remain? Let us see.

Without articulate speech we would have no *human* social organization. Families we might have, but this form of organization is not peculiar to man; it is not *per se, human.* But we would have no prohibitions of incest, no rules prescribing exogamy and endogamy, polygamy or monogamy. How could marriage with a cross cousin be prescribed, marriage with a parallel cousin proscribed, without articulate speech? How could rules which prohibit plural mates possessed simultaneously but permit them if possessed one at a time, exist without speech?

Without speech we would have no political, economic, ecclesiastic, or military organization; no codes of etiquette or ethics; no laws; no science, theology, or literature; no games or music, except on an ape level. Rituals and ceremonial paraphernalia would be meaningless without articulate speech. Indeed, without articulate speech we would be all but toolless: we would have only the occasional and insignificant use of the tool such as we find today among the higher apes, for it was articulate speech that transformed the non-progressive tool-using of the ape into the progressive, cumulative tool-using of man, the human being.

In short, without symbolic communication in some form, we could have no culture. "In the Word was the beginning" of culture—and its perpetuation also.

To be sure, with all his culture man is still an animal and strives for the same ends that all other living creatures strive for: the preservation of the individual and the perpetuation of the race. In concrete terms these ends are food, shelter from the elements, defense from enemies, health, and offspring. The fact that man strives for these ends just as all other animals do has, no doubt, led many to declare that there is "no fundamental difference between the behavior of man and of other creatures." But man does differ, not in *ends* but in *means.* Man's means are cultural means: culture is simply the human animal's way of living. And, since these means, culture, are dependent upon a faculty possessed by man alone, the ability to use symbols, the difference between the behavior of man and of all other creatures is not merely great, but basic and fundamental.

VII

The behavior of man is of two distinct kinds: symbolic and non-symbolic. Man yawns, stretches, coughs, scratches himself, cries out in pain, shrinks with fear, "bristles" with anger, and so on. Non-symbolic behavior of this sort is not peculiar to man; he shares it not only with the other primates but with many other animal species as well. But man communicates with his fellows with articulate speech, uses amulets, confesses sins, makes laws, observes codes of etiquette, explains his dreams, classifies his relatives in designated categories, and so on. This kind of behavior is unique; only man is capable of it; it is peculiar to man because it consists of, or is dependent upon, the use of symbols. The non-symbolic behavior of Homo sapiens is the behavior of man the animal; the symbolic behavior is that of man the human being. It is the symbol which has transformed man from a mere animal to a human animal.

Because *human* behavior is symbol behavior and since the behavior of infra-human species is non-symbolic, it follows that we can learn nothing about human behavior from observations upon or experiments with the lower animals. Experiments with rats and apes have indeed been illuminating. They have thrown much light upon mechanisms and processes of behavior among mammals or the higher vertebrates. But they have contributed nothing to an understanding of *human* behavior because the symbol mechanism and all of its consequences are totally lacking among the lower species. And as for neuroses in rats, it is of course interesting to know that rats can be made neurotic. But science probably had a better understanding of psychopathic behavior among human beings before neuroses were produced experimentally in rats than they now have of the neuroses of the rats. Our understanding of human neuroses has helped us to understand those of rats; we have, as a matter of fact, interpreted the latter in terms of *human* pathology. But I cannot see where the neurotic laboratory rats have served to deepen or enlarge our understanding of *human* behavior.

As it was the symbol that made *mankind* human so it is with each member of the species. A baby is not a *human* being until he begins to symbol. Until the infant begins to talk there is nothing to distinguish his behavior qualitatively from that of a very young ape, as *The Ape and the Child* showed. As a matter of fact, one of the impressive results of this fascinating experiment by Professor and Mrs. Kellogg was the demonstration of how ape-like an infant of Homo sapiens is before he begins to talk. The baby boy acquired exceptional proficiency in climbing in association with the little chimpanzee, and even acquired her "food bark"! The Kelloggs speak of how the little ape "humanized" during her sojourn in their home. But what the experiment demonstrated so conclusively was the ape's utter inability to learn to talk or even to make *any* progress in this direction—in short, her inability to become "humanized" at all.

The infant of the species *Homo sapiens* becomes human only when and as he exercises his symbol faculty. Only through articulate speech—not necessarily vocal—can he enter the world of human beings and take part in their affairs. The questions asked earlier may be repeated now. How could a growing child know and appreciate such things as social organization, ethics, etiquette, ritual, science, religion, art and games without symbolic communication? The answer is of course that he could know nothing of these things and have no appreciation of them at all.

KINGSLEY DAVIS

Final Note on
a Case of
Extreme Isolation

Early in 1940 there appeared in this *Journal* an account of a girl called Anna.[1] She had been deprived of normal contact and had received a minimum of human care for almost the whole of her first six years of life. At that time observations were not complete and the report had a tentative character. Now, however, the girl is dead, and, with more information available,[2] it is possible to give a fuller and more definitive description of the case from a sociological point of view.

Anna's death, caused by hemorrhagic jaundice, occurred on August 6, 1942. Having been born on March 1 or 6,[3] 1932, she was approximately ten and a half years of age when she died. The previous report covered her development up to the age of almost eight years; the present one recapitulates the earlier period on the basis of new evidence and then covers the last two and a half years of her life.

EARLY HISTORY

The first few days and weeks of Anna's life were complicated by frequent changes of domicile. It will be recalled that she was an illegitimate child, the second such child born to her mother, and that her grandfather, a widowed farmer in whose house her mother lived, strongly disapproved of this new evidence of the mother's indiscretion. This fact led to the baby's being shifted about.

Two weeks after being born in a nurse's private home, Anna was brought to the family farm, but the grandfather's antagonism was so great that she was shortly taken to the house of one of her mother's friends. At this time a local minister became interested in her and took her to his house with an idea of possible adoption. He decided against adoption,

Reprinted with the permission of the University of Chicago Press and author from "Final Note on a Case of Extreme Isolation," *American Journal of Sociology* 52 (March 1947): 432-37.

however, when he discovered that she had vaginitis. The infant was then taken to a children's home in the nearest large city. This agency found that at the age of only three weeks she was already in a miserable condition, being "terribly galled and otherwise in very bad shape." It did not regard her as a likely subject for adoption but took her in for a while anyway, hoping to benefit her. After Anna had spent nearly eight weeks in this place, the agency notified her mother to come to get her. The mother responded by sending a man and his wife to the children's home with a view to their adopting Anna, but they made such a poor impression on the agency that permission was refused. Later the mother came herself and took the child out of the home and then gave her to this couple. It was in the home of this pair that a social worker found the girl a short time thereafter. The social worker went to the mother's home and pleaded with Anna's grandfather to allow the mother to bring the child home. In spite of threats, he refused. The child, by then more than four months old, was next taken to another children's home in a near-by town. A medical examination at this time revealed that she had impetigo, vaginitis, umbilical hernia, and a skin rash.

Anna remained in this second children's home for nearly three weeks, at the end of which time she was transferred to a private foster-home. Since, however, the grandfather would not, and the mother could not, pay for the child's care, she was finally taken back as a last resort to the grandfather's house (at the age of five and a half months). There she remained, kept on the second floor in an attic-like room because her mother hesitated to incur the grandfather's wrath by bringing her downstairs.

The mother, a sturdy woman weighing about 180 pounds, did a man's work on the farm. She engaged in heavy work such as milking cows and tending hogs and had little time for her children. Sometimes she went out at night, in which case Anna was left entirely without attention. Ordinarily, it seems, Anna received only enough care to keep her barely alive. She appears to have been seldom moved from one position to another. Her clothing and bedding were filthy. She apparently had no instruction, no friendly attention.

It is little wonder that, when finally found and removed from the room in the grandfather's house at the age of nearly six years, the child could not talk, walk, or do anything that showed intelligence. She was in an extremely emaciated and undernourished condition, with skeleton-like legs and a bloated abdomen. She had been fed on virtually nothing except cow's milk during the years under her mother's care.

Anna's condition when found, and her subsequent improvement, have been described in the previous report. It now remains to say what happened to her after that.

LATER HISTORY

In 1939, nearly two years after being discovered, Anna had progressed, as previously reported, to the point where she could walk, understand simple commands, feed herself, achieve some neatness, remember people, etc. But she still did not speak, and, though she was much more like a normal infant of something over one year of age in mentality, she was far from normal for her age.

On August 30, 1939, she was taken to a private home for retarded children, leaving the county home where she had been for more than a year and a half. In her new setting she made some further progress, but not a great deal. In a report of an examination made November 6 of the same year, the head of the institution pictured the child as follows:

Anna walks about aimlessly, makes periodic rhythmic motions of her hands, and, at intervals, makes guttural and sucking noises. She regards her hands as if she had seen them for the first time. It was impossible to hold her attention for more than a few seconds at a time—not because of distraction due to external stimuli but because of her inability to concentrate. She ignored the task in hand to gaze vacantly about the room. Speech is entirely lacking. Numerous unsuccessful attempts have been made with her in the hope of developing initial sounds. I do not believe that this failure is due to negativism or deafness but that she is not sufficiently developed to accept speech at this time.....The prognosis is not favorable....

More than five months later, on April 25, 1940, a clinical psychologist, the late Professor Francis N. Maxfield, examined Anna and reported the following: large for her age; hearing "entirely normal"; vision apparently normal; able to climb stairs; speech in the "babbling stage" and "promise for developing intelligible speech later seems to be good." He said further that "on the Merrill-Palmer scale she made a mental score of 19 months. On the Vineland social maturity scale she made a score of 23 months."[4]

Professor Maxfield very sensibly pointed out that prognosis is difficult in such cases of isolation. "It is very difficult to take scores on tests standardized under average conditions of environment and experience," he wrote, "and interpret them in a case where environment and experience have been so unusual." With this warning he gave it as his opinion at that time that Anna would eventually "attain an adult mental level of six or seven years."[5]

The school for retarded children, on July 1, 1941, reported that Anna had reached 46 inches in height and weighed 60 pounds. She could bounce and catch a ball and was said to conform to group socialization, though as a follower rather than a leader. Toilet habits were firmly established. Food habits were normal, except that she still used a spoon as her sole implement. She could dress herself except for fastening her clothes. Most remarkable of all, she had finally begun to develop speech. She was characterized as being at about the two-year level in this regard. She could call attendants by name and bring in one when she was asked to. She had a few complete sentences to express her wants. The report concluded that there was nothing peculiar about her, except that she was feebleminded— "probably congenital in type."[6]

A final report from the school, made on June 22, 1942, and evidently the last report before the girl's death, pictured only a slight advance over that given above. It said that Anna could follow directions, string beads, identify a few colors, build with blocks, and differentiate between attractive and unattractive pictures. She had a good sense of rhythm and loved a doll. She talked mainly in phrases but would repeat words and try to carry on a conversation. She was clean about clothing. She habitually washed her hands and brushed her teeth. She would try to help other children. She walked well and could run fairly well, though clumsily. Although easily excited, she had a pleasant disposition.

INTERPRETATION

Such was Anna's condition just before her death. It may seem as if she had not made much progress, but one must remember the condition in which she had been found. One must recall that she had no glimmering of speech, absolutely no ability to walk, no sense of gesture, not the least capacity to feed herself even when the food was put in front of her, and no comprehension of cleanliness. She was so apathetic that it was hard to tell whether or not she could hear. And all this at the age of nearly six years. Compared with this condition, her capacities at the time of her death seem striking indeed, though they do not amount to much more than a two-and-a-half-year mental level. One conclusion therefore seems safe, namely, that her isolation prevented a considerable amount of mental development that was undoubtedly part of her capacity. Just what her original capacity was, of course, is hard to say; but her development after her period of confinement (including the ability to walk and run, to play, dress, fit into a social situation, and, above all, to speak) shows that she had at least this much capacity—capacity that never could have been realized in her original condition of isolation.

A further question is this: What would she have been like if she had received a normal upbringing from the moment of birth? A definitive answer would have been impossible in any case, but even an approximate answer is made difficult by her early death. If one assumes, as was tentatively surmised in the previous report, that it is "almost impossible for any child to learn to speak, think, and act like a normal person after a long period of early isolation," it seems likely that Anna might have had a normal or near-normal capacity, genetically speaking. On the other hand, it was pointed out that Anna represented "a marginal case, [because] she was discovered before she had reached six years of age," an age "young enough to allow for some plasticity."[7] While admitting, then, that Anna's isolation *may* have been the major cause (and was certainly a minor cause) of her lack of rapid mental progress during the four and a half years following her rescue from neglect, it is necessary to entertain the hypothesis that she was congenitally deficient.

In connection with this hypothesis, one suggestive though by no means conclusive circumstance needs consideration, namely, the mentality of Anna's forebears. Information on this subject is easier to obtain, as one might guess, on the mother's than on the father's side. Anna's maternal grandmother, for example, is said to have been college educated and wished to have her children receive a good education, but her husband, Anna's stern grandfather, apparently a shrewd, hard-driving, calculating farmowner, was so penurious that her ambitions in this direction were thwarted. Under the circumstances her daughter (Anna's mother) managed, despite having to do hard work on the farm, to complete the eighth grade in a country school. Even so, however, the daughter was evidently not very smart. "A schoolmate of [Anna's mother] stated that she was retarded in school work; was very gullible at this age; and that her morals even at this time were discussed by other students." Two tests administered to her on March 4, 1938, when she was thirty-two years of age, showed that she was mentally deficient. On the Stanford Revision of the Binet-Simon Scale her performance was equivalent to that of a child of eight years, giving her an I.Q. of 50 and indicating mental deficiency of "middle-grade moron type."[8]

As to the identity of Anna's father, the most persistent theory holds that he was an old man about seventy-four years of age at the time of the girl's birth. If he was the one, there is no indication of mental or other biological deficiency, whatever one may think of his morals. However, someone else may actually have been the father.

To sum up: Anna's heredity is the kind that *might* have given rise to innate mental deficiency, though not necessarily.

COMPARISON WITH ANOTHER CASE

Perhaps more to the point than speculations about Anna's ancestry would be a case for comparison. If a child could be discovered who had been isolated about the same length of time as Anna but had achieved a much quicker recovery and a greater mental development, it would be a stronger indication that Anna was deficient to start with.

Such a case does exist. It is the case of a girl found at about the same time as Anna and under strikingly similar circumstances. A full description of the details of this case has not been published, but, in addition to newspaper reports, an excellent preliminary account by a speech specialist, Dr. Marie K. Mason, who played an important role in the handling of the child, has appeared.[9] Also the late Dr. Francis N. Maxfield, clinical psychologist at Ohio State University, as was Dr. Mason, has written an as yet unpublished but penetrating analysis of the case.[10] Some of his observations have been included in Professor Zingg's book on feral man.[11] The following discussion is drawn mainly from these enlightening materials. The writer, through the kindness of Professors Mason and Maxfield, did have a chance to observe the girl in April, 1940, and to discuss the features of her case with them.

Born apparently one month later than Anna, the girl in question, who has been given the pseudonym Isabelle, was discovered in November, 1938, nine months after the discovery of Anna. At the time she was found she was approximately six and a half years of age. Like Anna, she was an illegitimate child and had been kept in seclusion for that reason. Her mother was a deaf-mute, having become so at the age of two, and it appears that she and Isabelle had spent most of their time together in a dark room shut off from the rest of the mother's family. As a result Isabelle had no chance to develop speech; when she communicated with her mother, it was by means of gestures. Lack of sunshine and inadequacy of diet had caused Isabelle to become rachitic. Her legs in particular were affected; they "were so bowed that as she stood erect the soles of her shoes came nearly flat together, and she got about with a skittering gait."[12] Her behavior toward strangers, especially men, was almost that of a wild animal, manifesting much fear and hostility. In lieu of speech she made only a strange croaking sound. In many ways she acted like an infant. "She was apparently utterly unaware of relationships of any kind. When presented with a ball for the first time, she held it in the palm of her hand, then reached out and stroked my face with it. Such behavior is comparable to that of a child of six months."[13] At first it was even hard to tell whether or not she could hear, so unused were her senses. Many of her actions resembled those of deaf children.

It is small wonder that, once it was established that she could hear, specialists working with her believed her to be feebleminded. Even on nonverbal tests her performance was so low as to promise little for the future. Her first score on the Stanford-Binet was 19 months, practically at the zero point of the scale. On the Vineland social maturity scale her first score was 39, representing an age level of two and a half years.[14] "The general impression was that she was wholly uneducable and that any attempt to teach her to speak, after so long a period of silence, would meet with failure."[15]

In spite of this interpretation, the individuals in charge of Isabelle launched a systematic and skilful program of training. It seemed hopeless at first. The approach had to be through pantomime and dramatization, suitable to an infant. It required one week of intensive effort before she even made her first attempt at vocalization. Gradually she began to respond, however, and, after the first hurdles had at last been overcome, a curious thing happened. She went through the usual stages of learning characteristic of the years from one to six not only in proper succession but far more rapidly than normal. In a little over two months after her first vocalization she was putting sentences together. Nine months after that she could identify words and sentences on the printed page, could write well, could add to ten, and could retell a story after hearing it. Seven months beyond this point she had a vocabulary of 1,500-2,000 words and was asking complicated questions. Starting from an educational level of between one and three years (depending on what aspect one considers), she had reached a normal level by the time she was eight and a half years old. In short, she covered in two years the stages of learning that ordinarily require six.[16] Or, to put it another way, her I.Q. trebled in a year and a half.[17] The speed with which she reached the normal level of mental development seems analogous to the recovery of body weight in a growing child after an illness, the recovery being achieved by an extra fast rate of growth for a period after the illness until normal weight for the given age is again attained.

When the writer saw Isabelle a year and a half after her discovery, she gave him the impression of being a very bright, cheerful, energetic little girl. She spoke well, walked and ran without trouble, and sang with gusto and accuracy. Today she is over fourteen years old and has passed the sixth grade in a public school. Her teachers say that she participates in all school activities as normally as other children. Though older than her classmates, she has fortunately not physically matured too far beyond their level.[18]

Clearly the history of Isabelle's development is different from that of Anna's. In both cases there was an exceedingly low, or rather blank, intellectual level to begin with. In both cases it seemed that the girl might be congenitally feeble minded. In both a considerably higher level was reached later on. But the Ohio girl achieved a normal mentality within two years, whereas Anna was still marked inadequate at the end of four and a half years. This difference in achievement may suggest that Anna had less initial capacity. But an alternative hypothesis is possible.

One should remember that Anna never received the prolonged and expert attention that Isabelle received. The result of such attention, in the case of the Ohio girl, was to give her speech at an early stage, and her subsequent rapid development seems to have been a consequence of that. "Until Isabelle's speech and language development, she had all the characteristics of a feeble-minded child." Had Anna, who, from the standpoint of psychometric tests and early history, closely resembled this girl at the start, been given a mastery of speech at an earlier point by intensive training, her subsequent development might have been much more rapid.[19]

The hypothesis that Anna began with a sharply inferior mental capacity is therefore not established. Even if she were deficient to start with, we have no way of knowing how much so. Under ordinary conditions she might have been a dull normal or, like her mother, a moron. Even after the blight of her isolation, if she had lived to maturity, she might have finally reached virtually the full level of her capacity, whatever it may have been. That her isolation did have a profound effect upon her mentality, there can be no doubt. This is proved by the substantial degree of change during the four and a half years following her rescue.

Consideration of Isabelle's case serves to show, as Anna's case does not clearly show, that isolation up to the age of six, with failure to acquire any form of speech and hence failure to grasp nearly the whole world of cultural meaning, does not preclude the subsequent acquisition of these. Indeed, there seems to be a process of accelerated recovery in which the child goes through the mental stages at a more rapid rate than would be the case in normal development. Just what would be the maximum age at which a person could remain isolated and still retain the capacity for full cultural acquisition is hard to say. Almost certainly it would not be as high as age fifteen; it might possibly be as low as age ten. Undoubtedly various individuals would differ considerably as to the exact age.

Anna's is not an ideal case for showing the effects of extreme isolation, partly because she was possibly deficient to begin with, partly because she did not receive the best training available, and partly because she did not live long enough. Nevertheless, her case is instructive when placed in the record with numerous other cases of extreme isolation. This and the previous article about her are meant to place her in the record. It is to be hoped that other cases will be described in the scientific literature as they are discovered (as unfortunately they will be), for only in these rare cases of extreme isolation is it possible "to observe *concretely separated* two factors in the development of human personality which are always otherwise only analytically separated, the biogenic and the sociogenic factors."[20]

NOTES

1. Kingsley Davis, "Extreme Social Isolation of a Child," *American Journal of Sociology,* XLV (January, 1940), 554-65.

2. Sincere appreciation is due to the officials in the Department of Welfare, Commonwealth of Pennsylvania, for their kind co-operation in making available the records

concerning Anna and discussing the case frankly with the writer. Helen C. Hubbell, Florentine Hackbusch, and Eleanor Meckelnburg were particularly helpful, as was Fanny L. Matchette. Without their aid neither of the reports on Anna could have been written.

3. The records are not clear as to which day.

4. Letter to one of the state officials in charge of the case.

5. *Ibid.*

6. Progress report of the school.

7. Davis, *op. cit.*, p. 564.

8. The facts set forth here as to Anna's ancestry are taken chiefly from a report of mental tests administered to Anna's mother by psychologists at a state hospital where she was taken for this purpose after the discovery of Anna's seclusion. This excellent report was not available to the writer when the previous paper on Anna was published.

9. Marie K. Mason, "Learning To Speak after Six and One-Half Years of Silence," *Journal of Speech Disorders,* VII (1942), 295-304.

10. Francis N. Maxfield, "What Happens When the Social Environment of a Child Approaches Zero." The writer is greatly indebted to Mrs. Maxfield and to Professor Horace B. English, a colleague of Professor Maxfield, for the privilege of seeing this manuscript and other materials collected on isolated and feral individuals.

11. J.A.L. Singh and Robert M. Zingg, *Wolf-Children and Feral Man* (New York: Harper & Bros., 1941), pp. 248-51.

12. Maxfield, unpublished manuscript cited above.

13. Mason, *op. cit.*, p. 299.

14. Maxfield, unpublished manuscript.

15. Mason, *op. cit.*, p. 299.

16. *Ibid.*, pp. 300-304.

17. Maxfield, unpublished manuscript.

18. Based on a personal letter from Dr. Mason to the writer, May 13, 1946.

19. This point is suggested in a personal letter from Dr. Mason to the writer, October 22, 1946.

20. Singh and Zingg, *op. cit.*, pp. xxi-xxii, in a foreword by the writer.

FRANCIS E. MERRILL

The Self and the Other:
An Emerging Field of
Social Problems

This paper will explore some of the further implications of a shift in social problems resulting from recent changes in the social climate. An earlier paper examined some of the general relationships between social character and social problems and suggested that many traditional problems are on the way to amelioration and eventual solution. Among these problems are illiteracy, poverty, child labor, unemployment, undernourishment, old-age insecurity, infant mortality, endemic disease, and similar difficulties which have recently come within the purview of democratic government. These situations are by no means completely eliminated in the United States, much less in the underdeveloped parts of the world. But the technical knowledge and productive capacity to deal constructively with them are part of the heritage of modern democratic societies.

In place of these former concerns, a new type of problem situation has emerged, which likewise reflects a particular sociocultural climate with its own values and norms. This is the growing preoccupation with what might be called "self-other" problems, in which individuals and groups are concerned with interpersonal relationships in general and those involving the self and the other(s) in particular. Central to this preoccupation is the social self, as the product of the perceived and imagined appraisals of others. The investigation of the social self was pioneered by Baldwin, Cooley, and Dewey and given a systematic theoretical structure by Mead. Harry Stack Sullivan further developed this approach and made it the center of his conceptual system and therapeutic technique. In the present context, however, the self-other approach is applied to social problems, rather than to psychotherapy.

Reprinted with the permission of the Society for the Study of Social Problems and the late author's wife from "The Self and the Other: An Emerging Field of Social Problems," *Social Problems* 4 (January 1957): 200-207.

A social problem involves a situation, a value, and social action. The action is intended to alleviate or eliminate the situation and thereby enhance the value. Problems of the self and the other(s) are as crucial as they are intangible. Status is as important as material comfort and the deprivation of status as devastating as hunger. Technological and industrial development may eventually solve such problems as unemployment, but, for example, self-other problems of prejudice remain. Basic anxiety is the heritage of the new social climate, and the attempt to minimize this anxiety motivates social action. The latter ranges from informal efforts to win friends and influence people to formal attempts to understand small-group interaction.

THE SOCIAL SELF

The social self has been called "a subject which is its own object." Each person loves himself, hates himself, praises himself, blames himself, and punishes himself. Both the subject and the object of these verbs are the self. Motivation for this action is in large part derived from others, as each projects himself into the minds of others and takes their role toward himself. The social self thus arises in interaction with others, as the individual looks at himself through others' eyes. He feels happy or sad as he evokes praise or blame from those whose roles he takes in his imagination. In so doing, he develops self-attitudes, which range from blissful self-love to extreme self-denigration. The sources of these attitudes are the "significant others" in his environment, whose opinions about him matter very much.

The social self has been viewed in terms of the pronouns "I" and "me." The former is the subject of the self-attitudes, the latter their object. The "I" is the active part of the self, whereas the "me" reflects the attitudes of others. These elements are in constant interaction and give rise to what Sullivan has termed the "good-me" and the "bad-me." The former is the part of the self which reflects affection, tenderness, and generally pleasant treatment from others. The latter reflects dissatisfaction and anxiety arising from lack of affection and approval by the "significant others." People try to avoid thinking and talking about the "bad-me," because it makes them anxious and unhappy to do so. They prefer to think about the "good-me," because this gives them pleasure and generally enhances their self-feeling.

Both the "good-me" and the "bad-me" reflect the actual or imputed judgments of others. The nature of the social self therefore predisposes the person to a concern with these "reflected appraisals." In Mead's words: "The individual...enters his own experience as a self or individual...only insofar as he first becomes an object to himself...and he becomes an object to himself only by taking the attitudes of other individuals toward himself within a social environment. . . in which both he and they are involved."[1]

Under these conditions, the individual tries to maximize the "good-me" and minimize the "bad-me." Comparative inability to reach this goal, together with anxiety concerning the judgments of others, generates social problems of the self-other type. The individual does not receive as much love, affection, understanding, acceptance, or status as he has learned to expect. He desires more of these intangible but vital values so that he may incorporate them into his social self. He is somewhat like Arnold W. Green's unhappy middle-class male child, who has been reared in an atmosphere of comforting security and (sometimes) suffocating affection and is thenceforth unable to recapture this infantile paradise. Self-other problems are thus literally *social* problems, rather than economic, political, or moral problems. As people "take each other into account" and view themselves through the eyes of others, they are acting in a specifically social fashion.

SOCIAL STRUCTURE AND SELF-OTHER PROBLEMS

Social problems reflect social structure. As the patterned behavior of society has changed, the problems have changed accordingly, albeit with a time lag. Some of the traditional social problems reflected an economy of scarcity, in which technological knowledge, productive capacity, and distributive organization were inadequate. As suggested elsewhere, many of those problems are giving way before expanding industrial facilities. Other traditional social problems involved conflicts in social values. The way of life of the Old South incorporates values which are not the same as those of the American creed. Similarly, value conflicts are at the heart of such problems as child labor, slum clearance, sexual laxity, and divorce.

Each society has its own structure and its own accompanying problems. The present article suggests that social problems of the self-other type are emerging as increasingly important in American society. Among the structural factors responsible for this trend are the following:

ACHIEVED STATUS.   The emphasis in our society upon achieved, as contrasted to ascribed, status needs no documentation. In an earlier day, achievement was gained by physical activity, whether clearing a wilderness, building a factory, or constructing a railroad. Although these activities actually required cooperation with others, the individual could entertain the illusion that he was acting as an independent and self-sufficient individual. Under present conditions, this illusion is no longer possible. In the bureaucratic structure of the large corporation, each man is at the mercy of his fellows, a fact of which he is acutely aware. From the moment he enters the bank, the railroad, or the plant, the aspiring young man is constantly taking the roles of others and viewing himself through their eyes.

SOCIAL MOBILITY. In his movements up (or down) the status ladder, the individual is continually conscious of the attitudes of others toward himself. The "empathic responses" are at a premium, and the person who is deficient in the ability to take the role of the other is at a disadvantage. Both those going up and those going down derive their self-attitudes from the reflected appraisals of others. These self-attitudes tend to determine their attitudes toward the world in general. In their study of intolerance among veterans of World War II, Bruno Bettelheim and Morris Janowitz discovered that men who were losing status were much more prejudiced than those who were either gaining status or staying in the same place.

COMPETITION. In societies which emphasize peaceful cooperation, the individual is presumably not so aware of other selves in opposition to himself. But the pervasive emphasis in our society upon competition for scarce goals means that self-appraisal is dependent upon competitive success, which in turn directly affects the attitudes of others. Money is the most important of these goals, and the status of the breadwinner is dependent upon his skill and acumen in this respect. Individuals also compete for status, love, and prestige, which can be gained only from others. Attitudes of others toward the self thus enter into many relationships which are arranged by custom in other societies. Manipulation of others is another element in competitive interaction, and here again each person is made aware of other selves and his own in relation to them. He must take others consciously into account, which increases his awareness of self-other relationships. The more bitter the competition, the more aware he is.

CLASS DIFFERENTIALS. In their study of communication differences between classes, Leonard Schatzman and Anselm Strauss found that the lower class showed a deficiency in the ability to take the role of the other. Persons on this social level communicated with others in terms interesting and significant only to themselves, rather than to their listeners, who were middle-class. In another study, class differences appeared in the tendency to blame, censure, and otherwise act aggressively toward the self. Middle-class persons indicated a strong degree of self-aggression, which appeared as self-discipline, self-blame, and even self-hatred. In contrast, lower-class persons directed their aggressions against others. A society with middle-class values would thus presumably be more concerned with self-other relationships than one where either lower-class or upper-class values predominated.

MASS MEDIA. In their depiction of "personalities" and celebrities, the mass media make private emotions and self-conceptions a matter of public interest. The movies, radio, television, and the mass-circulation magazines are concerned, in one way or another, with the glorification of the self as seen through the eyes of others. In this case, the "others" comprise the bulk of the reading, listening, and viewing population. The love-life of a prominent movie actress becomes a matter of national importance, and millions of persons rapturously identify themselves with her. Interpersonal relations become vitally important and adolescents of both sexes and all ages view their own self-other problems as crucial. The mass media depict interpersonal situations because of the informal taboo against "controversial" topics, such as politics, religion, prejudice, or power. The least common denominator is the problem theme which stresses the self and the other.

TYPES OF SELF-OTHER PROBLEMS

Problems of the self and the other are thus intensified by the nature of the culture and the social structure. In one sense, these relationships are basic in *any* social setting, in that the social self is necessarily the product of the reflected appraisals of others. Under present conditions, however, this situation has been intensified by the emphasis upon these relationships and the corresponding individual self-consciousness. Examples of these emerging social problems have been anticipated in the foregoing discussion; they may now be discussed in more detail.

ROLE-PLAYING. A generic problem of a self-conscious society is the inability of the individual to play the roles expected of him. Social roles are an integral part of the social self, and self-feeling reflects the ability to fulfill the expectations of one's roles. The more complex the society, the more difficult this feat becomes. The person who is chronically anxious about his role-*playing* ability (as distinguished from his role-*taking* ability) is often inadequate in the performance of a role, which further increases his anxiety. He thus becomes prey, in Sullivan's words, to an "anticipated unfavorable appraisal of one's current activity by someone whose opinion is significant." This is an interpersonal, rather than an individual, situation, inasmuch as both the conception of the role and the sense of adequacy (or inadequacy) in playing it come from other persons. Failure in role-playing may cause the individual to distrust his status, his motives, his fellows, and hence, himself. Many of the most pressing problems of the present society derive from role-failure. These roles include those of parent and child, peer-group member, adolescent, lover, mistress, husband, wife, group member, and "100 percent American."

PARENT-CHILD RELATIONSHIPS. In an earlier generation, parents were primarily concerned with the physical safety, material comfort, and intellectual development of their children. For all practical purposes, these matters are no longer of immediate concern, because they are substantially under control; infant mortality, childhood disease, and material deprivation have been alleviated or virtually eliminated. In this self-conscious generation, however, parents are increasingly aware of the impact of their own personalities upon those of their children. Permissive or nonpermissive training, methods of discipline, relations with other children, and demonstrations of affection are still vital questions.

PEER-GROUP ACCEPTANCE. In his relations with the peer-group, the child is first introduced to self-other problems in all their stark reality. In the peer-group, from an early age through high school and college, the interactionist conception of the self is perhaps more clearly demonstrated than in any other context. The child is soon made aware of the attitudes of his peers toward himself, and these attitudes are often brutally expressed with no effort to soften the blow. Parents and siblings are ordinarily restrained by affection, custom, and in-group loyalty from expressing their true feelings toward the child. Not so his peer-group. Acceptance by this body is vital to self-respect, and status is made very clear. The child is provided with a virtual running market report on his status. The peer-group reaches its greatest influence during adolescence, when the child is trying to break away from his parents and has not yet attained adult status. In his marginal world, the adolescent looks largely to his peers for guidance, moral support, and self-realization.

DATING. Dating is a competitive game, in which the winner is "loved" because he is successful and successful because he is "loved." Boys and girls who are in demand as dates have prima facie evidence of their acceptance. High self-appraisal follows such acceptance and low self-feelings accompany a failure in this respect. *Nothing succeeds like success*, and an initial convergence of favorable self-judgments is prolonged into subsequent relationships with the opposite sex. The practice of "going steady" at an early age is a cautious attempt (which has become increasingly structured) to insure the adolescent of at least a modicum of success in dating. Boys and girls who are going steady are always assured of a date and need not run the risk of rejection.

LOVE AND MARRIAGE. Closely related to self-other problems of dating are those of love and marriage. In both cases, the self is bolstered by the affectionate responses of another. When one is loved, he feels that he is a better person than before and is correspondingly grateful to the other for thus bolstering his self-attitudes. Lovers enhance each other's self-feelings, a process which may continue throughout their lives. Conversely, those who are unilaterally in love suffer an impairment in self-attitudes and self-respect. Romantic love as a prelude to marriage is one form of this desire for self-approval. Lost or frustrated love after marriage is a major self-other problem.

CONFORMITY AND NONCONFORMITY. In a stable society, adaptation to group demands is comparatively spontaneous and unreflecting. The members have the same general cultural patterns and are not *consciously* concerned with conformity. In a heterogeneous society, conceptions of the self require a more deliberate and self-conscious adjustment to the group.

The mobile population is so large that, in many urban neighborhoods, a large proportion of the residents are and will continue to be "strangers" to each other. This is as true in middle-class suburbs as in lower-class slums. Acceptance requires (or is believed to require) a strong conformity to the superficial patterns of the mass culture. Those who conform will presumably be accepted, and those who do not, will not. This emphasis upon conformity has a stifling effect upon the society and increases intolerance on the part of those who are uneducated and provincial. The most pressing future social problems will involve acceptance of the individual by the group.

MINORITY-GROUP STATUS. The problem of minority-group status has ramifications ranging from the marginal status of some third-generation Americans to overt ethnic and racial discrimination. In each case, a self-constituted in-group rejects a designated out-group, with resultant impairment of self-feelings. Members of minority groups view themselves through the eyes of the majority, inasmuch as the latter, by definition, dominate the society and impose their definitions upon it. The Negro in America has for generations viewed his social self in terms of the white man's appraisal. The practice of segregation—whether formal or informal, legal or illegal, overt or covert—reacts negatively upon the self-attitudes of the segregated individual. The member of the majority group who holds a violent prejudice is himself marked by insecurity and self-hatred. His own self-feelings form the basis for his hatred of the minority group. In the resulting deprivation of status, the self-feeling of the minority group suffers accordingly. This situation constitutes perhaps the most widespread and corrosive social problem of our society.

SOCIAL ACTION AND SELF-OTHER PROBLEMS

Social problems are believed capable of solution by human action, whether or not any solution has demonstrably been reached. Many of the problems of an earlier day are in a fair way to ultimate elimination in the United States, although not yet in the rest of the world. Problems of the self and the other, however, are infinitely more difficult, if indeed they can ever be "solved" in any meaningful sense. Love, happiness, acceptance, and the rest are "infinite" values, which cannot be gained once and for all, as many of the "old-fashioned" material values can. The quest for self-other values is a never-ending one, and the related problems can perhaps never be completely "solved."

But this does not keep people from trying. A basic goal of the individual, in this or any other society, is to gain status from his fellows and, through reflected self-appraisals, enhance his own self-feelings. In our society, as noted, this process is more self-conscious and contrived. From play-group to the board of directors, the individual spends much of his energy in the sedulous cultivation of his social self.

Each individual works in a number of ways to solve this problem to his own satisfaction. The methods may be classified into two general types: common-sense action and scientific action. This distinction is clearly not absolute and considerable overlapping is apparent. But approaches to problems of the self and the other take two basic forms—the one spontaneous and empirical, the other derived from the sciences of human behavior.

COMMON SENSE ACTION. In his efforts to solve problems of the self and the other, the individual engages in a variety of activities, some deliberate and conscious and others spontaneous and haphazard. The reflected nature of the self provides the rationale behind efforts to "win friends and influence people," to sell oneself, to make oneself the center of group attention, to call the attention of the boss (or the boss' daughter) to one's qualifications, to be "popular" with the boys (or the girls), to be a charming and knowledgeable hostess, and to excel in the leisure arts of an increasingly leisure-conscious society. The individual is no longer judged by his ability as a producer but his knowledge and skill as a consumer. Leisure is an important consumption commodity, and this consumption requires considerable *savoir faire* and *savoir vivre*.

Problems of the self and the other are at the heart of much of modern advertising copy. The unhappy person who is afflicted with halitosis, dandruff, body odor, or dishpan hands is continually exhorted (a) to beware of his self-image, and (b) to do something about it. Men are reminded that they must dress for other men as well as for women, if they are to retain their male self-image. Women need little urging to accept their obligation to look attractive, seductive, or smart, depending upon the time and circumstance. The buyer of a Cadillac is happily secure in the knowledge that he owns a prominent status-symbol, and prospective owners are lured in the same way. Other automobiles are made to look as much like a Cadillac as possible, so that their owners may bask in this reflected glory.

In the field of industrial relations, much "personnel" work is devoted to individual adjustment to the group and hence to bolstering the worker's self-feeling. In this endeavor, the personnel director makes use of some of the insights of applied psychology, but his efforts are still largely common-sense. The satisfied worker is presumably the efficient worker, and one way to bring about satisfaction is to make him happy about his role in the production process. Although recent research has questioned this all-out self-identification with the job, most programs still act as if a strong self-involvement were a vital prerequisite to industrial efficiency.

SCIENTIFIC ACTION. Much of the work in the behavioral sciences involves, directly or indirectly, social action toward the amelioration of self-other problems. To be sure, most scientific work is geared to the *understanding* of interpersonal relations rather than to the application of this knowledge to self-other problems. At some point, however, the ordered knowledge will presumably be applied to the basic values of society. Science has a reason for being that is more than idle curiosity, however remote this reason may be from the day-to-day processes of scientific investigation. In their efforts to appear "scientific," the behavioral sciences have protested too much their indifference to human values and goals. The older sciences have no such compulsion to declare themselves remote from all consideration, proximate or remote, of human welfare.

Whether they like it or not, therefore, the researches of the "pure" scientists in the behavioral area will be applied to the enhancement of social values. One of these values is the social self. Among the specific subject matters related to ordered knowledge of self-other relationships are the following: (a) the study of social interaction in the small group; (b) investigations subsumed under the general title of sociometry; (c) empirical work on dating among high school and college students; (d) the study of the personality needs, both conscious and unconscious, that determine marital choice; (e) the extensive research in child psychology; (f) the investigation of interpersonal relations in marriage and the family; (g) the study of the relationships between culture and personality; (h) the study of social stratification; (i) the analysis of minority-group relationships; and (j) the study of ethnic, religious, and racial prejudice.

These fields of scientific investigation are by no means concerned exclusively with problems of the self and the other. But they all bear upon this field in one way or another. The most direct use of this information is made by psychiatrists and case workers, who are concerned directly with strengthening and rehabilitating individual self-feelings in an increasingly self-conscious society. Marriage counselors, clinical psychologists, clergymen, teachers, doctors, and lawyers are likewise called upon to deal with self-other problems with or without the knowledge derived from the above scientific disciplines.

In final analysis, however, therapeutic activities involve skills and insights which are related only indirectly to applied science. Those who deal with the social self require temperamental qualities which cannot be transferred. Compassion, insight, empathy, and the ability to take the role of the other are at least partially genetic, although they may be enhanced by scientific training. These practitioners will need all the help they can get. Ordered scientific knowledge will be increasingly in demand in the decades to come. In his search for self-fulfillment, man is faced with new and baffling social problems of the self and the other.

NOTES

1. Mead, George Herbert, *Mind, Self, and Society* (Chicago: University of Chicago Press, 1943), p. 138.

ADAMSON E. HOEBEL

The Nature
of
Culture

WHAT IS CULTURE?

Human beings are unique among all the creatures of the animal kingdom
in their capacity to create and sustain culture. Each society of men
possesses its own distinctive culture, so that the members of one society
behave differently in some significant respects from the members of every
other society. We observe, for instance, that the Andaman Islander from
the Indian Ocean weeps with ceremonial copiousness when he greets a
friend or relative after a long absence; a Frenchman kisses his comrade on
both cheeks; while we content ourselves with seizing his right hand to
agitate it with a pumping motion.

The situation is the same in each of these instances, as is the social
function of the behavior; namely, to emphasize and reconstitute the
special bond that exists between the two persons. But the cultures of the
Andaman Islander, Frenchman, and American call for and produce
different modes of action.

This is but a single instance of a culture pattern. However, culture is
more than a collection of mere isolated bits of behavior. It is the integrated
sum total of learned behavior traits which are manifest and shared by the
members of a society.

The factor of learned behavior is of crucial importance. It is essential to
the concept of culture that instincts, innate reflexes, and any other
biologically inherited forms of behavior be ruled out. Culture is, therefore,
wholly the result of social invention, and it may be thought of as social
heritage for it is transmitted by precept to each new generation. What is
more, its continuity is safeguarded by punishment of those members of
a society who refuse to follow the patterns for behavior that are laid down
for them in the culture.

Reprinted from *Man, Culture, and Society,* ed. Harry L. Shapiro (New York: Oxford
University Press, 1956), pp. 168-82. Copyright © 1956 by Oxford University Press, Inc.
Reprinted by permission.

Social life as such and cultural processes must not be confused. Many animals in addition to man experience social life and even possess social organization. The complex structure of ant society reveals an intriguing division of labor among queen, workers, fighters, and drones. The ingenious exploitation of captive aphids as food resources by some species of ants adds an auxiliary population to their social organization. Yet for all its complexity the social organization of ant society rests not in culture but upon instinct. There is no transmission, so far as we can tell, of behavior through learning. A set of ant eggs, properly incubated without the presence of any adult ants, will produce a host of ants, who on maturity will re-enact in every detail all of the behavior of the myriad generations of the species before them.

Would the same occur if a collection of human babies were cut off from all adult supervision, care, and training? Assuming that they could survive, which they could not, we would not expect them to manifest any of the special traits of behavior that characterized their parents. They would be devoid of language, complicated tools, utensils, fire, arts, religion, government, and all the other features of life that distinguish man among the animals. They would eat and drink, and they would mate as adults, and they would presumably find themselves shelter, for these would be direct responses to basic biological drives. Their behavior would be instinctive and, in large measure, random. But what they would eat and how they would eat would not be according to the specialized tastes and palates of men as we know them now. Nor would their mating conform to the limiting and channeling rules that give to each human society its present sexual characteristics. Left solely to their own instinctive devices, the children of men would appear as undeveloped brutes, although it is probable that they would soon standardize this behavior as they learned from each other what one or another had discovered. A rudimentary culture would soon take shape. The specific responses to the generalized drives of instinct would quickly become the specific patterns of culture.

The human capacity for culture is a consequence of man's complex and plastic nervous system. It enables man to make adjustments in behavior without going through a biological modification of his organism. As of this moment it is the end product of the whole process of inorganic and organic evolution which has moved in the direction of increasing complexity of the organism, including the nervous system. Only in man has the nervous system reached the stage of complexity and adaptability to make possible the creation *and* sustenance of culture through complex ratiocination, possession of a protracted span of memory for details, and the use of verbal symbols: language.

It would be an error born of self-adulation were we to think that no traces of the culture-creating capacity occur below the level of man. Our near relatives in the primate family are capable of inventing new forms of behavior in the solution of some of the simpler problems that are posed to them by experimental animal psychologists. They apparently can also reason on very elementary levels. The famous experiments of Wolfgang Köhler first demonstrated the ingenuity and intelligence of chimpanzees in joining sticks, piling boxes, and undoing locks in order to gain their goals—usually bananas. Further, it is now thoroughly established that chimpanzees can and do learn from each other the new discoveries and inventions of one of their numbers. The transmission of the discovery spreads by imitation. A new and learned pattern of behavior is temporarily shared by the society of chimpanzees. It is an element of nascent culture.

Yet neither the chimpanzees, nor any other sub-human primates, are capable of more than the most rudimentary discoveries and inventions. What is more important, they are handicapped by their limited memory spans. Unless constantly re-directed by their human masters, they soon drop and forget their new activities which pass away as fads. The accumulation of inventions to build up a permanent body of culture materials is beyond their capacity. Of even more crucial significance, however, is the inability of all sub-human forms to develop speech. The bulk of culture is phrased in thought—sub-vocal speech—and transmitted by word of mouth. It is often said with only slight exaggeration that culture exists in and through communication. The lack of developed communication bars all speechless animals from real culture forever.

In the natural world, culture is a distinct type of phenomenon, which represents the highest level of evolutionary emergence. In the terminology of Herbert Spencer and A.L. Kroeber it is *superorganic*. It rests upon and emerges from the psychic organic mechanism of men, but it is not *in* the organic structure of men. The culture that is acquired by any individual is existent before his birth and persists after his death. Individuals and groups are the carriers and creators of culture, but culture has a quality of anonymity in that it is super-individual.

The levels of natural phenomena and their respective sciences.[1]

LEVEL OF PHENOMENA	TYPE OF PHENOMENA	HIERARCHY OF SCIENCES
IV. Superorganic	Culture	Anthropology, Sociology, Social Psychology, Political Science, Economics (History)
III. Psychic Organic	Sentient animals with highly developed nervous systems	Psychology and Neurology Physical Anthropology
II. Vital Organic	Protozoa, metazoa (plants and animals)	Organic Chemistry, Zoology, Biology, Anatomy, Physiology Biophysics
I. Inorganic	Earth and cosmic matter	Physical Chemistry, Physics, Geology, Astronomy

The relation of culture to society is often left ambiguous, although it is not difficult to distinguish the two. A society may be any animal aggregation, which holds together as an interacting group, and among the members of which exists an awareness of belonging together—the "consciousness of kind." A wild horse herd under the leadership of a dominant stallion is a society. So is the flock of barnyard pigeons wheeling in flight, and organized in nesting pairs.

A human society is also an animal aggregation with just these qualities. In the case of human beings, however, almost all social interrelations are dominated by existing culture. We do not know of any groups of cultureless men. Therefore, a human society is more than a mere aggregation expressing instinctive behavior. A human society is a permanently organized population acting in accordance with its culture. Human society = population + culture.

In its fullest sense, culture is a series of integrated patterns for behavior developed from mass habits. However a group of people may have arrived at their mass habits, and that is a subject for later chapters, habits once established tend to project themselves into future behavior. The habitual way sets the pattern for future action.

Statistically, a mass habit may be called a behavior norm. A norm would be that type of behavior which occurs with the greatest frequency (the mode) among the variable forms, or it may be that type which is closest to the average (the mean) among the variables, or it may represent the mid-point (the median) between the extreme poles of the range of variation.

In social life the norms, which are culture patterns, take on a compulsive, or normative, aspect. Norms as such consist merely of what is done. The normative consists in an additional element of *ought to be.* Patterns *of* behavior becomes patterns *for* behavior. "The folkways," wrote William Graham Sumner, "are the right ways." Deviations are frowned upon and socially discouraged. Conformity is nourished and rewarded. Each new individual as he is born into or enters the group is put through the process of child training or indoctrination now called *enculturation.* Throughout life the deterrent, negative sanctions of society (scorn, ridicule, ostracism, deprivation, and punishment) serve to discourage and check deviation, and the positive sanctions of approbation (rewards and prestige) serve to induce conformity to the norms. Individuals are shaped more or less uniformly to the common mold. A modicum of standardization is the common lot.

Not all norms apply to all of the members of society. Culture does not spread itself evenly over the social loaf. Those norms which do apply to all members of the society and from which there is no permissible deviation are called *universals.* An example would be the prohibition of incest. All persons must refrain from sexual relations with brother, sister, parent, child in most societies. Universals are relatively rare within any given culture.

Much more numerous are the norms that are known as *alternatives*: the patterns that exist where several different norms apply to the same situation. A permissible range of choice and leeway is available. Neckties may be called for, but the choice may be between black, white, or colored four-in-hands or bows. Meat should be cooked, but the individual may choose between baking, boiling, roasting, broiling, rare, medium, well-done, seasoned. or unseasoned.

No society is wholly homogeneous. Differentiation based on sex and age is universal. There are distinct patterns of behavior for male and female, youth and adult, some of which are biologically founded and others not. Social differentiation between married and single persons is world-wide, and all societies have their religious specialists. This means that there are internal sub-groupings in every society. Each of these groups has its own behavior characteristics that are applicable only to its members. Such norms are known as *specialties*.

The specialties of one group may be known to the other members of the society and yet not be used by them, because they are not patterns for their behavior. Many American adult men know the Boy Scout salute, having once been Scouts, but they do not use it as a form of greeting once they have left scouting behind. In a complex society, however, most specialties remain unknown to most of the people. This may be because the specialties require unique aptitudes or a rigorous course of training un-dertaken only by a few. Or, it may be that the specialties are the secret and hidden knowledge of a few, kept within their closed circle for the benefits that may be derived from secretiveness. The result is that no individual can ever acquire or manifest in himself all of the elements of his society's culture. It means, also, that no anthropologist, even the most assiduous, can ever make note of, to say nothing of record, all of the aspects of any culture, even the simplest known to man.

This, then, provides the answer to the oft-asked question, "How can one speak of American culture when there are such divergencies in the cultures of New York City and the Kentucky Highlanders? Between the Italians of Lower Manhattan and the Scandinavians of Minnesota?" The universals and alternatives shared by most Americans are the common binding and integrating elements of American culture and society. The specialties of the different regional groups and socio-economic classes are merely differentiating elements. Even within a quite homogeneous society, however, specialties will occur in connection with subgroup organization. Men have one set of functions to perform, women another. Married men behave differently from the unmarried, fathers from the childless.

Uninitiated adolescents have different norms from those who have passed through to manhood. Medicine men have patterns not available to the laymen.

The cohesiveness of a society is in part an effect of the relative proportion of universals and alternatives to specialties.

To return to our consideration of norms and the normative aspect of norms, note should be taken of the difference between standards for behavior and real behavior. There are always some gaps between what a people say they do, or what they think they ought to do, and what they really do. We must not forget the old admonition, "What you do speaks so loudly that I cannot hear what you say." There is an inevitable conflict between the standards or ideals set up in a culture for control of behavior of persons as members of the social group and errant individual impulses. Cultural standards are selected and tested, on the whole, in terms of group benefit and group well-being. They call for the channeling and suppression of many possible lines of satisfaction of individual impulses.

Since every person is at one and the same time an individual and a group member, he wrestles constantly with the conflict of individual self-interest as against his obligations to the group interests. Thus it is that the members of a society, when thinking and acting as members of the group, express the cultural standards of the group. But when acting in response to dominant individual desires, they may be found consistently to contravene those group standards. They may create in their culture customary norms for violating the cultural standards.

An outstanding example is found in the behavior of the Trobriand Islanders with respect to incest. Clan incest is forbidden and believed to be supernaturally punished through the infliction of loathsome diseases and possibly death. Trobrianders in all seriousness "show horror at the idea of violating the rules of exogamy...when judging the conduct of others or expressing an opinion about conduct in general." Yet to commit clan incest is the great game played by the Trobriand Islanders. It is a custom that gratifies individual desires in defiance of their most highly valued standards. What is most striking is the occurrence of a highly developed body of customary techniques for thwarting the automatic effects of supernatural reaction. The natives possess a system of magic spells and rites performed over water, herbs, and stones, which when properly carried out is said to be completely efficient in undoing the painful supernatural results of clan incest. So strong is the acceptance of such actual behavior, that even when the incestuous activities of a pair are known, there is no social reaction beyond lascivious scandal mongering, unless someone for motives of personal antagonism undertakes to denounce the incestors publicly. Then and only then does the body politic become upset, for this act stimulates a public defense of the group standards. Then is the time for the incestor to commit suicide, blaming the public denouncer for his death—an onus that causes the public benefactor considerable discomfort.

The Comanche Indians of the Plains provide us with another example of such a social incongruity. Their ideal pattern of marriage is one in which a brother bestows his sister upon a man of his, not her, choosing. The groom is usually an older man. The girl is supposed to accept the match and learn to love and respect her husband. All Comanches sagely aver that this is the very best kind of marriage and most satisfactory in its results. Yet it was the regular thing in the old days for a young wife to abscond by joining an enterprising young brave on the war path. The members of the war party never objected to her presence, but aided the couple in their escape. Here was a customary pattern of group assistance in the violation of Comanche cultural standards and tribal law. For law it was, since the offended husband was forced by public opinion to prosecute the male absconder for damages and physically to punish his wife, unless the wife-stealer was powerful enough to protect her.

In these examples we see the existence of "pretend rules": standards that are honored in spoken word, but breeched in customary behavior. Dry Oklahoma gives us a contemporary American example of what was a national exemplification of a similar situation in the days of federal prohibition of alcoholic beverages.

This sets the difference between *real culture*, what people actually do, and *ideal culture*, what they say (and believe) they should do. In awareness of this disparity no well-trained modern anthropologist is willing to take a people's word as full evidence of their real culture. He must observe their activity for himself. He insists on getting down to cases.

There is yet another aspect to this phase of culture that may be phrased in terms of *overt* and *covert* behavior. Overt behavior is that which is manifest in motor activity. It is externalized through movement and muscular action that may be directly observed. Covert behavior is that which goes on internally—thinking, dreaming, and the activity of the internal glands and organs.

The registry of sensory impressions in conscious awareness, is definitely influenced and often determined by culture. The sharp vision of the Indians on the plains is not the result of any superiority in actual visual acuity. It stems from their learned ability to read meaning in the way an animal or rider moves, the kind of dust he raises, and the lay of the land.

The moralistic story of the countryman and the cricket is a case in point. Walking down a busy city street one day, the countryman seized his city-bred friend by the arm, crying, "Listen to the chirp of the cricket!"

The urbanite heard nothing until the bucolic friend led him to a crack in the face of a building where a cricket was proclaiming his presence unheard by the passing throngs.

"How can you hear such a little sound in the midst of all this noise?" the city man wondered.

"Watch!" his friend replied as he tossed a dime upon the sidewalk. Whereupon a dozen people turned at the faint click of the coin. "It depends on the things you are taught to be interested in."

The covert culture of a people forces them to perceive some facts and to fail to perceive others. Trobriand Islanders cannot recognize any physiological similarity between father and sons. We look for and often see similarities that are doubtful at best. We feel that similarities should exist. Trobrianders feel that there should be no similarities, because theirs is a matrilineal society in which the mother's brother rather than the father has the important social position with respect to boys, and in denial of the father's significance the Trobrianders hold to a belief in spirit conception of offspring. To recognize filial similarities might insinuate the falsity of the spirit conception doctrine and work to undermine a sacred Trobriand institution. It would be a subversive implication that the father was biologically connected with his sons' creation. The power of the covert culture is sufficient to blank out the Trobriand perceptive sense at this point.

We are familiar with this phenomenon in our own social life. We know how difficult it is for us to see those facts which would be upsetting to our deep-set beliefs.

Covert culture controls perception, because it sets attitudes and beliefs. These may be translated into overt action, but not necessarily so, or directly. There may be conflicts of standards in the covert culture which permit only one of the standards to be translated into action. Attitudes, too, may be verbalized into overt expression without attaining realization in full behavior.

Anthropologists also make a distinction between *material* and *non-material* culture. Material culture is always the direct product of overt action. It consists of tangible goods: the artifacts and paraphernalia a people possess as products of technology. Non-material culture consists of behavior per se, both overt and covert. Strictly speaking, material culture is really not culture at all. It is the product of culturally determined activity. Behind every artifact are the patterns of culture that give form to the idea for the artifact and the techniques of shaping and using it.

The study of material culture can contribute a good deal toward our knowledge of actual culture, but it is impossible to learn more than a little about the lives of a people from their material culture alone. Archaeology, which deals in a scientific manner with the recovery and study of the objects of material culture buried in the earth, is always limited in the results it can produce. The use and meaning of any object depends almost wholly upon non-material behavior patterns, and the objects derive their true significance from such patterns. A pointed stick may be a dibble, a weapon, a scepter, a stake, or a phallic symbol. This can be determined only through contact with the living culture.

Thus when the archaeologist uncovers a prehistoric culture, it is not really the culture that he unearths but merely the surviving products of that culture, tangible remnants of the intangible reality. The actual culture became extinct when the society that carried it passed out of existence. No culture can exist divorced from living beings.

A culture consists of elements or single traits, but the significance of a culture is less in its inventory of traits than the manner of integration of the traits. It is theoretically possible for two societies to possess identical inventories of culture elements, and yet so to arrange the relationships of these elements to each other that the complexes within the two cultures and the total forms of the two cultures will be quite unlike. By simple analogy, a mason may take two identical piles of bricks and equal quantities of mortar. Yet according to the manner in which he lays his bricks, he may produce a fireplace or a garden wall.

The configuration of a culture is its delineated contours as shaped by the interrelation of all of its parts. It presumes internal integration of all of its parts. It presumes internal integration in accordance with some basic and dominant principles or value systems underlying the whole scheme. These are the *existential postulates* set by the culture: propositions about the nature of things; and *normative postulates:* propositions about the desirability and undesirability of things. A clear and unambiguous configuration reflects the attainment of a high degree of integration through the selection of the numerous elements of the culture in terms of their consonance with the basic postulates.

In the anthropologists' discussion of the configuration of culture the Pueblo Indians of the American Southwest have been shown to possess a culture that stresses restraint and orderliness in behavior, avoidance of emotional excess and display in personal experience and ritual, rigorous suppression of individual initiative and innovation, with quiet co-operation in group endeavor. Pueblo culture presents to the individual the philosophy of a well-ordered universe in which man is but one harmonious part of a delicate balance involving all nature forces. As long as each man plays his ordained roles in the traditional manner, all people will prosper. The rain gods will provide the precious water, the gods of plants and fertility will mature adequate crops, the dancing gods will favor the village. All functions necessary to the good life and survival of the pueblo will be fulfilled. The failure of any person to perform his roles in the traditional and proper way is believed to upset the balance and bring down disaster upon the whole society. This is a cultural code that rests upon a maize-growing subsistence economy as practiced by a sedentary people, who build stone and adobe, multi-storied communal houses in a desert environment.

As a contrasting example we may briefly draw the outlines of configuration for the culture of the people of the island of Alor in Indonesia. Like the Pueblo Indians, the people of Alor are settled gardeners. But in their lives the dynamic principle of culture, which is of outstanding significance, is the continuing exchange of wealth. Striving for personal dominance over fellow tribesmen by means of financial activity, the making and collecting of loans is the chief adult activity, especially of men. It is apparently the consequence of notable individual insecurity caused by the peculiar and unsatisfactory relationships within the family as they affect the growing child. Money, which in Alor consists of pigs, Javanese bronze vessels, and gongs, is lent out as capital on which interest must be paid, so that the debtor is bound by tight bonds of obligation to the creditor. Marriage and death, in particular, call for extensive consumption of pigs in feasts, along with tremendous exchanges and payments in vessels and gongs. The burdens imposed on the participants are immense, for they must usually go into heavy debt to meet the demands of the occasion. Except as it stimulates the growing of pigs, all this heavy economic activity bears little or no relation to economic production or utilitarian needs.

War, until suppressed by the Dutch, did not rest on military interest as such. Rather, it was expressed as a long, drawn out series of feuds marked by cowardly assaults on men and women, and carried out by trickery and stealth.

Illness is marked by a complete collapse of the will to live and an obsessive conviction of hopelessness.

The culture of Alor emphasizes non-utilitarian striving to best one's fellowmen, pushing the ego, to which it denies serenity and security, on to its final collapse in the illness that ultimately brings surcease in death.

In the Pueblos and Alor we have two kinds of culture configurations, which are reasonably clear-cut. This is not always the case, however, for many cultures do not attain concise integration in accord with a consistent set of basic principles. The nomadic buffalo-hunting Indians of the western American Plains had one line of integration of behavior traits that emphasized extravagant sensation seeking. One of the highlights of life was to bring oneself through fasting, thirsting, autosuggestion, and perhaps, self-torture to the phantasy state in which sensational visions would be encountered. Upon these visions, which were interpreted as supernatural visitations through which medicine power was bestowed, depended the successful outcome of any man's career. The purpose of the vision quest was to bring power and glory to the individual. Armed with such powers he could perform reckless deeds in battle. Armed with a record of such deeds, he could boastfully glorify himself, challenging other men to match their records of performance against his. This was but the central core of a whole series of culture traits glorifying rampant individualism and stimulating extreme sensate behavior.

Yet this is not *the* configuration of Plains culture, for equally strong, if not so spectacular, is another web of traits based on a contradictory set of basic principles. The first complex may be called the "egotistical warrior" line. The second would be the "considerate peace chief" line. This emphasized gentleness, generosity, reasonableness, and wisdom. Such virtues called for self-restraint, consideration of others, and a disposition to check the too quarrelsome assertiveness of the aggressive individualism called forth by the other line in the culture. Some men in the Plains tribes followed either one line or the other throughout their lives. In others, the incompatibilities of the two patterns set up an internal conflict for both individual and society. The restrained peace chief concept had its counterpart in important religious ceremonies such as the extremely pious and sober ritual of the Medicine Arrow Renewal of the Cheyenne Indians. For this, all male members of the tribe, except murderers and their close kin, had to be present. When the sacred arrows were unwrapped from their protecting bundle not a cry or sound was permitted to disturb the holy atmosphere. Patroling soldiers clubbed any yelping dog into stunned silence or death.

Consistency in a culture is not, therefore, wholly to be expected. It is probably true, as Sumner maintained, and there is a strain towards consistency in the folkways of any culture: that contradictory elements tend to cancel one or the other out, or else to attain a synthesis in a new form. On the other hand, it is too much to expect a completion of this process in all aspects of any culture. Inconsistencies arise and persist because, in the first place, cultures are never consciously planned or directed in their general growth. In the second place, most cultural traits are acquired through borrowing. Not many human beings are originators. The sources of borrowing for any culture are diverse and unlike. While there is always a certain amount of selection (people do not borrow blindly), new elements may be taken up even though inconsistent with elements or principles already within the culture, because they appear to be desirable in themselves. Finally, there are almost always alternative possibilities among the answers to the problems that culture undertakes to solve. It may be a matter of simple accident that the first solution hit upon and adopted is not wholly consistent with pre-existing forms in the culture. Nevertheless, it may find its way into the cultural whole because it serves a need or interest satisfactorily. If it produces a conflict within the culture, that is a matter to be suffered.

Our discussion of the configuration of culture has indicated that the behavior of each individual is strongly influenced by the patterns of the culture with which he lives. The character of each individual is unique, for one individual's experiences never match those of another, nor is it probable that the constitutional components of any two persons are exactly identical. But the patterns and configurations of the cultures of different societies produce distinctive personality types that are generally characteristic of the members of those societies. In the personality and culture studies that have developed so fruitfully in recent years culturally determined personality configurations have come to be known as national (or tribal) character, ideal personality type, modal personality, and basic personality.

The ideal personality type is the abstract image of the "good" man or the "good" woman that is reflected from the moral standards set in the culture. Much psychopathology is the product of an unmastered conflict within the individual who is unable to assimilate the standards of the cultural ideal to the impulses of the self. It is the Freudian conflict of the super-ego and the id.

The basic personality structure is differently conceived. It exists not as an abstract image but rather as a modal core of attitudes produced in the average individual as a result of the patterns of childtraining characteristic of his culture. How is the infant fed, handled, bathed? What are adult reactions to infant defecation and urination? Does the child receive consistent loving attention? Or is it harshly rejected, or teased, or abused? How and in what way does it suffer deprivation or enjoy gratification of its wants? In so far as the answers to these questions are found in consistent patterns of adult behavior, so will the basic personality structures of the children take form. The basic personality structure tends to persist throughout the life of the individual, coloring adult behavior and completing the cycle by influencing the configuration of adult culture. Thus the grown-up Alorese is "anxious, suspicious, mistrustful, lacking in confidence, with no interest in the outer world. There is no capacity to idealize the parental image or deity. The personality is devoid of enterprise, is filled with repressed hatred and free floating aggression over which constant vigilance must be exercised. The personality is devoid of high aspirations and has no basis for the internalization of discipline." [2] Such is the effect of Alorese infant and childhood experience on the personality of the grown-up native of Alor.

In like manner, each culture puts *its* mark upon the individual who develops under its influence, whose personality is a blend resulting from his unique physical and nervous constitution, the patterns of his culture, and his individual experience in contact with the physical world and other people. Each man is a common type, molded by culture and society, and yet possessed of individuality that culture cannot submerge.

NOTES

1. Adopted and modified from Herbert Spencer, *The Principles of Sociology* (1878), vol. 1, pp. 2-16; A.L. Kroeber, "The Superorganic," *Amer. Anthrop.*, vol. 19, 1917, pp. 163-213.

2. A. Kardiner and associates, *The Psychological Frontiers of Society*, Columbia University Press, New York, 1945, p. 170.

JOHN M. BREWER

Ghetto Children Know
What They're
Talking About

Broken homes are "trees without roots."
Meat markets are "great flesh parlors."
Outsiders looking for thrills are "toys on a fairy lake."
This is the colorful, private speech of the children of America's ghettos, a "hidden language" of haunted phrases and striking subtlety. It is a language little known in the world outside, but for many it is more meaningful, more facile and more developed than the language of standard English.

During the period I was the principal of a large elementary school in the heart of a Negro slum, I became fascinated by this secret language developed by a rough-and-ready group of ghetto children. I found this idiom to be as dazzling as a diamond, invested with the bitter-sweet soulfulness bred by the struggle against poverty's dehumanizing forces.

I discovered that it was developed by the children even before they came to school, passed on from mother to child, and that a quarter of the students came from homes where it is the usual household speech. It is equipment for survival in the black ghetto. Normally it is used only in easy social settings like the home and after-school gatherings, and not in front of outsiders—which helps to explain why the children are often inarticulate when they try to use conventional English in talking to teachers, doctors, the school staff, etc.

As they advance in their schooling, these children also advance their hidden language vocabulary, become infatuated with this kind of verbal play and help it to flower with additions from the standard English they meet in class. They, and their parents, are fully aware of the aliveness of their words and make a serious effort to master the idiom. But, of course, this development conflicts with the formal school pattern and teachers

Reprinted from *The New York Times Magazine,* December 25, 1966, pp. 32-35. © 1966 by The New York Times Company. Reprinted with permission of the publisher and author.

who demand that only conventional English be used, and it often happens that verbally bright children suddenly clam up or become inarticulate in the classroom.

An illustration of the wonderful possibilities of the language of the ghetto helps one to judge how rich and interesting it is.

About 9:45 A.M. one day, Junebug—a small, wiry, shabbily dressed boy with large brown eyes—came into my office. As I looked up, it was obvious that he was hosed down and deep in the mud [embarrassed and had a problem]. Very quickly I got up and asked, "Why are you stretched so thin by joy? Are you flying backwards?" ["Why are you so sad? Are you in trouble?"]

Junebug took a cool view [looked up], cracked up [smiled] and answered, "My special pinetop [favorite teacher] is smoking [angry] and wants to eyeball [see] you fast." I said to him, "I'm stalled [puzzled]. What is this all about?"

He answered, "I wasted [punched] one of the studs [boys] for capping [insulting] me. Teach blasted [yelled] at me and told me to fade away [go] to the hub [office] and fetch you."

I stood up and told Junebug to cool it. "Don't put your head in the bowl and pull the chain" ["Don't do anything rash"]. Hurriedly he grabbed my arm and said: "I hope I don't get a big slap on the rump."

As I headed up the stairs toward his classroom I was deeply concerned. What did he mean by that "slap-on-the-rump" remark? A paddling never fazed him before. Suddenly the message came through loud and clear: He had played the part of an unlikely wrongdoer to tell me something was wrong in his classroom. He was tough and cruel, cunning and ruthless, a master of all the skills needed to survive in his jungle; he was too shrewd to be trapped this way, with so many witnesses, without a motive. He was very fond of his teacher.

I knew his twisted code of honor, which did not allow him to be an informer. He had got in trouble himself so that I would see and uncover something about his class.

Very reluctantly I eased open the classroom door and entered the room. I could sense that the hum of industry was missing. The children—chronologically aged 11-13 but actually precocious young adults—were impenetrable, as though encased in glass, sitting stiffly at their desks. The teacher walked over to me and said, "Whatever has come over this class this morning defies interpretation by anyone—most of all myself."

In a booming voice I said to the class, "Operation Jappin' [teacher harassment] has shot its load [is all over]." Operation Jappin' goes like this:

The tomcat [the sly and ruthless student leading the operation] begins with a stinging hit [first attack] and the sandbaggin' starts—things are thrown, strange noises come out of nowhere, children are unresponsive.

The tomcat tells all his tadpoles [classmates] that it is now time for the chicken to become an eagle [for more aggressive action] and they had better trilly along [join his group] because the sun has fallen on its belly [it's too late to back out].

The first step is to unzip the teacher [make her back down], so the tomcat takes the long dive [openly defies her], hoping she puts him in cold storage [punishes him] so he can then dress her in red tresses [insult her]. He and his friends get bolder, and outflap [out wit] and scramble [gang up on] her daily. All morning they shoot her down with grease [play dirty tricks on her] until finally she is ready for the big sleep [gives in]. They continue the heart-deep kicks [fun] until they are sure she is frozen on the needle [does not know what to do].

The tomcat then decides to wring [exploit] the scene. Now his glasses are on [he's in control], his ashes have been hauled away [his problems are gone]. He sends hotcakes [notes] to some of the children demanding money; the rabbits [timid children] know they will be erased [beat up] unless they pay him. He tells them he is a liberty looter [good crook] who will protect them because he carries a twig [big club]. Five-finger discount [stealing] pays off. The cockroaches crow [gang members are happy].

Poor Tiny Tim [the teacher], her nerve ends are humming [she is overwhelmed], her fleas [nice children] and bust-heads [smart children] have twisted the knob [lost respect for her]. The tomcat doesn't have to waste any more hip bullets on her [continue the harassment]—after all, a cat can't tell a dog what to do [he is the new leader]. He will keep his shoe laces tied [control everything]. Hail the Stinking King.

Quickly I singled out the group I thought was capable of organizing Operation Jappin', and together we went to my office. I told Junebug to go to the outer office and sit down. In spite of the imperturbable look on his face, I knew he was aware that I had captured the scene [found out what was going on]: these cub scouts [amateurs] were bleedin' [exposed].

The climate was a sticky one. I had to converse with them in their hidden language. But since I was a ghetto linguist, they could not victimize me by their idiomatic ambushes so neatly boobytrapped with sudden jolts and dead-end phrases.

I also had to ready them to pay their dues [accept disciplinary action]. I could not offer them two tricks for one until they were ready to turn a somersault [promise them anything until they confessed]. And I had to burn some time [give them time] to talk it over.

Finally, of course, I had to discipline the ringleaders. Operation Jappin' was sandbagged. In the end, I couldn't help but feel sorry for Junebug, and yet how could I tell his teacher how he had sacrificed himself in her behalf? Conceivably all of this might terrify her.

Yet I had to try to provide a bridge between her world and his. It is imperative that teachers see the ways in which the hidden and formal languages cut across, support or collide with each other. In fact, the term "hidden language" is really a misleading one, because in the out-of-school setting it becomes the primary language while the formal language used in the schools is secondary.

I suspect that many teachers are unaware of this inversion. And they are baffled as well by the odd structure of the primary language of the street-corner society. The logic is nonlogic, for instance: "I am full of the joy of being up front" means I am disgusted with my circumstances. The appeal is illusion and fantasy: "It goes to the back of your head and pulls out beautiful things."

If one looks for substance instead of smut, meaning instead of obfuscation, it is possible to harness some of the positive features that lie behind the crust of degradation and depravation explicit in the hidden language. The schools in our urban ghettos are full of children who communicate this way.

It was to make clear the hidden dynamics of the hidden language—realistic, tough, practical, with a broad sweep of understanding—and to explore the inversion process that I began "Operation Capping."

Operation Capping can best be described as a "tug of war" between formal and restrictive language. The long-range goal was systematically to strip away the students' addiction to a hidden language that thwarted their progress with the language of the school and textbook.

I developed a two-pronged approach. One was not to deny the validity of the child's world, his pragmatism, his unwillingness to be deluded, his suspicious nature and his perceptions, his quickness, toughness, and agile imagination. The other was to manipulate and redirect what was already a favorite pastime of the children, called "Capping," which in my youth was called "Playing the Dozens." In it, children try to outdo each other in trading insults and deprecating each other's family. For example: "Your Mama wasn't born, she was trapped"; "Your sisters are side-show bait"; "You ain't got no pappy, you're a S.O.B."; or "So's your Mama."

I decided to borrow this practice and give it a classy academic personality. The technique was simple, because the kids were already highly motivated to surpass each other in verbal intercourse. So I would meet a group for a "buzz session" [dictionary skills and English grammar] and introduce one of their well-known idioms, such as "pad," "crib" or "bread," and the children had to "cap" each other in formal English by providing a synonym.

As time passed we introduced antonyms and moved from simple sentences to complex ones. The kids were so highly competitive that they took up practices to which they previously were indifferent: They used the dictionary, read books, brought samples of word lists and resorted to all the conventional practices of the classroom. They had to win the capping game at any cost.

The spin-off from Operation Capping touched many sensitive and intriguing areas. The students discovered for themselves the built-in disadvantages of their idiomatic phrases; it didn't take them long to determine that these phrases didn't convey the meanings to others that their hidden language did: For example, they were stumped as they tried to find a standard English idiom for such hidden language phrases as: "rising on the wings of power" [a pocketful of money]; "gold is my color" [pay me in advance]; "trailing dark lines" [a hopeless search for something]; "I'm on ice" [in trouble].

The students openly expressed a real concern about their verbal deficit in formal language. But at the end of Operation Capping, they had become less dependent on their hidden language to express themselves, and began to stockpile new standard words and phrases and to wrestle successfully with grammar for the first time.

They also had a purpose for reading, and their ability improved significantly. Learning became fun and exciting because they no longer labored under unfair handicaps. There was a change in their value system, and they had a new sense of identity.

I believe that the operation helped to provide richer opportunities for these children to experience the forces in the tug of war between their two languages and to come to know the language necessary for effective communication in the mainstream of contemporary American society.

HORACE MINER

Body Ritual
Among
the Nacirema

The anthropologist has become so familiar with the diversity of ways in which different peoples behave in similar situations that he is not apt to be surprised by even the most exotic customs. In fact, if all of the logically possible combinations of behavior have not been found somewhere in the world, he is apt to suspect that they must be present in some yet undescribed tribe. This point has, in fact, been expressed with respect to clan organization by Murdock. In this light, the magical beliefs and practices of the Nacirema present such unusual aspects that it seems desirable to describe them as an example of the extremes to which human behavior can go.

Professor Linton first brought the ritual of the Nacirema to the attention of anthropologists twenty years ago, but the culture of this people is still very poorly understood. They are a North American group living in the territory between the Canadian Cree, the Yaqui and Tarahumare of Mexico, and the Carib and Arawak of the Antilles. Little is known of their origin, although tradition states that they came from the east. According to Nacirema mythology, their nation was originated by a culture hero, Notgnihsaw, who is otherwise known for two great feats of strength—the throwing of a piece of wampum across the river Pa-To-Mac and the chopping down of a cherry tree in which the Spirit of Truth resided.

Nacirema culture is characterized by a highly developed market economy which has evolved in a rich natural habitat. While much of the people's time is devoted to economic pursuits, a large part of the fruits of these labors and a considerable portion of the day are spent in ritual activity. The focus of this activity is the human body, the appearance and health of which loom as a dominant concern in the ethos of the people. While such a concern is certainly not unusual, its ceremonial aspects and associated philosophy are unique.

Reproduced by permission of the American Anthropoligical Association and the author from *American Anthropologist* 58 (1956).

The fundamental belief underlying the whole system appears to be that the human body is ugly and that its natural tendency is to debility and disease. Incarcerated in such a body, man's only hope is to avert these characteristics through the use of powerful influences of ritual and ceremony. Every household has one or more shrines devoted to this purpose. The more powerful individuals in the society have several shrines in their houses and, in fact, the opulence of a house is often referred to in terms of the number of such ritual centers it possesses. Most houses are of wattle and daub construction, but the shrine rooms of the more wealthy are walled with stone. Poorer families imitate the rich by applying pottery plaques to their shrine walls.

While each family has at least one such shrine, the rituals associated with it are not family ceremonies but are private and secret. The rites are normally only discussed with children, and then only during the period when they are being initiated into these mysteries. I was able, however, to establish sufficient rapport with the natives to examine these shrines and to have the rituals described to me.

The focal point of the shrine is a box or chest which is built into the wall. In this chest are kept the many charms and magical potions without which no native believes he could live. These preparations are secured from a variety of specialized practitioners. The most powerful of these are the medicine men, whose assistance must be rewarded with substantial gifts. However, the medicine men do not provide the curative potions for their clients, but decide what the ingredients should be and then write them down in an ancient and secret language. This writing is understood only by the medicine men and by the herbalists who, for another gift, provide the required charm.

The charm is not disposed of after it has served its purpose, but is placed in the charm-box of the household shrine. As these magical materials are specific for certain ills, and the real or imagined maladies of the people are many, the charm-box is usually full to overflowing. The magical packets are so numerous that people forget what their purposes were and fear to use them again. While the natives are very vague on this point, we can only assume that the idea in retaining all the old magical materials is that their presence in the charm-box, before which the body rituals are conducted, will in some way protect the worshipper.

Beneath the charm-box is a small font. Each day every member of the family, in succession, enters the shrine room, bows his head before the charm-box, mingles different sorts of holy water in the font, and proceeds with a brief rite of ablution. The holy waters are secured from the Water Temple of the community, where the priests conduct elaborate ceremonies to make the liquid ritually pure.

In the hierarchy of magical practitioners, and below the medicine men in prestige, are specialists whose designation is best translated "holy-mouth-men." The Nacirema have an almost pathological horror of and fascination with the mouth, the condition of which is believed to have a supernatural influence on all social relationships. Were it not for the rituals of the mouth, they believe that their teeth would fall out, their gums bleed, their jaws shrink, their friends desert them, and their lovers reject them. They also believe that a strong relationship exists between oral and moral characteristics. For example, there is a ritual ablution of the mouth for children which is supposed to improve their moral fiber.

The daily body ritual performed by everyone includes a mouth-rite. Despite the fact that these people are so punctilious about care of the mouth, this rite involves a practice which strikes the uninitiated stranger as revolting. It was reported to me that the ritual consists of inserting a small bundle of hog hairs into the mouth, along with certain magical powders, and then moving the bundle in a highly formalized series of gestures.

In addition to the private mouth-rite, the people seek out a holy-mouth-man once or twice a year. These practitioners have an impressive set of paraphernalia, consisting of a variety of augers, awls, probes, and prods. The use of these objects in the exorcism of the evils of the mouth involves almost unbelievable ritual torture of the client. The holy-mouth-man opens the client's mouth and using the above mentioned tools, enlarges any holes which decay may have created in the teeth. Magical materials are put into these holes. If there are no naturally occurring holes in the teeth, large sections of one or more teeth are gouged out so that the supernatural substance can be applied. In the client's view, the purpose of these ministrations is to arrest decay and to draw friends. The extremely sacred and traditional character of the rite is evident in the fact that the natives return to the holy-mouth-men year after year, despite the fact that their teeth continue to decay.

It is to be hoped that, when a thorough study of the Nacirema is made, there will be careful inquiry into the personality structure of these people. One has but to watch the gleam in the eye of a holy-mouth-man, as he jabs an awl into an exposed nerve, to suspect that a certain amount of sadism is involved. If this can be established, a very interesting pattern emerges, for most of the population shows definite masochistic tendencies. It was to these that Professor Linton referred in discussing a distinctive part of the daily body ritual which is performed only by men. This part of the rite involves scraping and lacerating the surface of the face with a sharp instrument. Special women's rites are performed only four times during each lunar month, but what they lack in frequency is made up in barbarity. As part of this ceremony, women bake their heads in small ovens for about an hour. The theoretically interesting point is that what seems to be a preponderantly masochistic people have developed sadistic specialists.

The medicine men have an imposing temple, or *latipso*, in every community of any size. The more elaborate ceremonies required to treat very sick patients can only be performed at this temple. These ceremonies involve not only the thaumaturge but a permanent group of vestal maidens who move sedately about the temple chambers in distinctive costume and headdress.

The *latipso* ceremonies are so harsh that it is phenomenal that a fair proportion of the really sick natives who enter the temple ever recover. Small children whose indoctrination is still incomplete have been known to resist attempts to take them to the temple because "that is where you go to die." Despite this fact, sick adults are not only willing but eager to undergo the protracted ritual purification, if they can afford to do so. No matter how ill the supplicant or how grave the emergency, the guardians of many temples will not admit a client if he cannot give a rich gift to the custodian. Even after one has gained admission and survived the ceremonies, the guardians will not permit the neophyte to leave until he makes still another gift.

The supplicant entering the temple is first stripped of all his or her clothes. In every-day life the Nacirema avoids exposure of his body and its natural functions. Bathing and excretory acts are performed only in the secrecy of the household shrine, where they are ritualized as part of the body-rites. Psychological shock results from the fact that body secrecy is suddenly lost upon entry into the *latipso*. A man, whose own wife has never seen him in an excretory act, suddenly finds himself naked and assisted by a vestal maiden while he performs his natural functions into a sacred vessel. This sort of ceremonial treatment is necessitated by the fact that the excreta are used by a diviner to ascertain the course and nature of the client's sickness. Female clients, on the other hand, find their naked bodies are subjected to the scrutiny, manipulation and prodding of the medicine men.

Few supplicants in the temple are well enough to do anything but lie on their hard beds. The daily ceremonies, like the rites of the holy-mouth-men, involve discomfort and torture. With ritual precision, the vestals awaken their miserable charges each dawn and roll them about on their beds of pain while performing ablutions, in the formal movements of which the maidens are highly trained. At other times they insert magic wands in the supplicant's mouth or force him to eat substances which are supposed to be healing. From time to time the medicine men come to their clients and jab magically treated needles into their flesh. The fact that these temple ceremonies may not cure, and may even kill the neophyte, in no way decreases the people's faith in the medicine men.

There remains one other kind of practitioner, known as a "listener." This witch-doctor has the power to exorcise the devils that lodge in the heads of people who have been bewitched. The Nacirema believe that parents bewitch their own children. Mothers are particularly suspected of putting a curse on children while teaching them the secret body rituals. The counter-magic of the witch-doctor is unusual in its lack of ritual. The patient simply tells the "listener" all his troubles and fears, beginning with the earliest difficulties he can remember. The memory displayed by the Nacirema in these exorcism sessions is truly remarkable. It is not uncommon for the patient to bemoan the rejection he felt upon being weaned as a babe, and a few individuals even see their troubles going back to the traumatic effects of their own birth.

In conclusion, mention must be made of certain practices which have their base in native esthetics but which depend upon the pervasive aversion to the natural body and its functions. There are ritual fasts to make fat people thin and ceremonial feasts to make thin people fat. Still other rites are used to make women's breasts larger if they are small, and smaller if they are large. General dissatisfaction with breast shape is symbolized in the fact that the ideal form is virtually outside the range of human variation. A few women afflicted with almost inhuman hyper-mammary development are so idolized that they make a handsome living by simply going from village to village and permitting the natives to stare at them for a fee.

Reference has already been made to the fact that excretory functions are ritualized, routinized, and relegated to secrecy. Natural reproductive functions are similarly distorted. Intercourse is taboo as a topic and scheduled as an act. Efforts are made to avoid pregnancy by the use of magical materials or by limiting intercourse to certain phases of the moon. Conception is actually very infrequent. When pregnant, women dress so as to hide their condition. Parturition takes place in secret, without friends or relatives to assist, and the majority of women do not nurse their infants.

Our review of the ritual life of the Nacirema has certainly shown them to be a magic-ridden people. It is hard to understand how they have managed to exist so long under the burdens which they have imposed upon themselves. But even such exotic customs as these take on real meaning when they are viewed with the insight provided by Malinowski when he wrote:

> Looking from far and above, from our high places of safety in the developed civilization, it is easy to see all the crudity and irrelevance of magic. But without its power and guidance early man could not have mastered his practical difficulties as he has done, nor could man have advanced to the higher stages of civilization.

PART IV

The
Organization
of
People

THE FINAL SET OF SELECTIONS IN THIS VOLUME IS CONCERNED
with the central concept of sociology—social organization.
Very early sociologists noted numerous regularities and
patterns in human interaction. Certain sets of behaviors were
observed to be performed by different individuals and these
sets of behaviors were named *roles*. Waitress, cook,
policeman, teacher, and secretary are examples of roles with
which we associate certain routine behaviors. Further, there
appeared to be routine ways that the people in these roles
related to each other, giving another dimension to the appearance of orderliness in many human relationships. On a
larger scale, orderliness can be observed in community life.
Organizations, such as banks, stores, transportation companies, churches, and governmental bureaucracies, perform
certain known functions routinely and often relate to each
other in routine, orderly ways. A part of the concept of social
organization refers to this ordered behavior that people often
exhibit. Their behavior is constrained so that rather than
behaving in random, unpredictable ways, people usually
behave in orderly, predictable ways.

Two of the articles in this volume illustrate this characteristic of orderliness in human groups. The first of these was
Sudnow's article in Part II on the public defender (role) and
the court system (social organization) in which he works. The
content of his role—his behaviors—and the differences between his role and that of a private lawyer practicing in the
same courts are described. The way he relates to prosecuting
attorneys and how it differs from the ways private lawyers
relate to them is also noted. The author also shows that there
are predictable and orderly ways in which the public defender
relates to his clients.

The second article is William F. Whyte's classic study of
the social organization of the restaurant. This article is instructive in many ways. It illustrates clearly the concepts of
role, status, patterns of interaction, and division of labor—all
of the basic concepts of the more orderly side of social
organization. It shows how different patterns of interaction
can have unintended consequences for the people involved:
i.e., the tearful waitresses. Whyte's study also describes what
can happen to the structure of an organization as it increases
in size and some of the new problems that arise when such
increases occur.

Earlier in this volume Horton argued that an emphasis on
the ordered aspect of human organization gives a rather
narrow view of what is happening in human groups. People
modify their roles or others modify them for them. The fact
that they are individuals is reflected in that while there may be
fifty people performing the same role, there will be differences, large or small, in how they perform them. Intelligence, personality, and the social situation are among the
factors that give rise to these differences.

Further, over time human organizations discard some
patterns of interaction among the participants and create new
ones. Organizations are not unchanging or static, but instead
are rather dynamic affairs. These elements of change, flux,

and improvisation are essential to any model of human organization that bears a verisimilitude to life.

Even in the seemingly most monolithic and orderly of organizations—the totalitarian society—there is an undercurrent of resistance, deviance, pressures for change, and other "de-organizing" forces. This is the major thrust of David Riesman's essay on the totalitarian state. He suggests that the appearance of order may mask these contrapuntal forces and the individual is more capable of retaining non-totalitarian values and attitudes than many people give him credit for. Since this essay was published, these opposing forces have become more apparent in Soviet society and have had marked effects on the organization of that society. If this type of organization can exhibit change, improvisation, and deviance from the formal rules, then what can we say about more open societies?

Above we noted that changing circumstances can evoke changes in organizations. Economic and political changes can also cause organizational adjustments. New technologies can have profound effects. Disasters—events that are so irregular in their occurrence that they cannot be predicted in advance—can produce an organizational trauma which often results in rapid changes in what people do and how they relate to each other. Fritz's article describes some community reactions to disasters. He shows that different styles and types of leadership are required in these situations as well as different patterns of interaction among the people coping with the disaster. The concepts of role, status, and patterns of interaction used in the order model need to be modified to account for the considerations that Riesman and Fritz suggest.

WILLIAM FOOTE WHYTE

The Social Structure
of
the Restaurant

While research has provided a large and rapidly growing fund of knowledge concerning the social organization of a factory, studies of other industrial and business structures are only beginning. Sociologists who are concerned with working out the comparative structures of economic organizations must therefore look beyond as well as into the factory. This paper represents one effort in that direction. It grows out of a fourteen-month study of restaurants.[1] We do not claim to have studied a representative sample of restaurants. In an industry having so many types of operations and sizes of units, such a task would have taken years. We did aim to find out, at least in a general way, what sort of structure a restaurant is and what human problems are found within it.

Here I shall present a schematic picture of the findings as they bear upon problems of social structure. I am also using the discussion of research findings to illustrate certain points of theory and methodology in studies of social structures. Discussions of theory and methodology, divorced from the research data upon which the theory and methods are to be used, are generally fruitless. In a brief paper, discussion of our research findings must necessarily be sketchy, but that will provide a basis for at least tentative conclusions.

CHARACTERISTICS OF THE RESTAURANT

The restaurant is a combination production and service unit. It differs from the factory, which is solely a production unit, and also from the retail store, which is solely a service unit.

The restaurant operator produces a perishable product for immediate sale. Success requires a delicate adjustment of supply to demand and skilful co-ordination of production with service. The production and service tie-up not only makes for difficult human problems of co-

---

Reprinted by permission of The University of Chicago Press from *The American Journal of Sociology* 54 (January 1949): 302-10. Copyright 1949, The University of Chicago.

ordinating action but adds a new dimension to the structure of the organization: the customer-employee relationship.

The contrast between factory and restaurant can be illustrated by this simple diagram, representing the direction of orders in the two structures:[2]

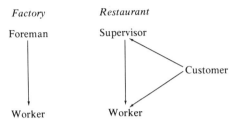

The problems of co-ordination and customer relations are relatively simple in the small restaurant, but they become much more difficult as the organization grows. This may be illustrated structurally in terms of five stages of growth.[3]

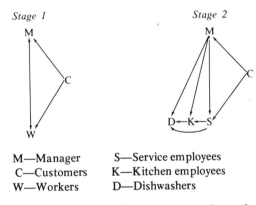

M—Manager	S—Service employees
C—Customers	K—Kitchen employees
W—Workers	D—Dishwashers

In the first stage, we have a small restaurant where the owner and several other employees dispense short orders over the counter. There is little division of labor. The owner and employees serve together as cooks, countermen, and dishwashers.

In the second stage, the business is still characterized by the informality and flexibility of its relationships. The boss knows most customers and all his employees on a personal basis. There is no need for formal controls and elaborate paper work. Still, the organization has grown in complexity as it has grown in size. The volume of business is such that it becomes necessary to divide the work, and we have dishwashers and kitchen employees, as well as those who wait on the customers. Now the problems of co-ordination begin to grow also, but the organization is still small enough so that the owner-manager can observe directly a large part of its activities and step in to straighten out friction or inefficiency.

As the business continues to expand, it requires a still more complex organization as well as larger quarters. No longer able to supervise all activities directly, the owner-manager hires a service supervisor, a food production supervisor, and places one of his employees in charge of the dishroom as a working supervisor. He also employs a checker to total checks for his waitresses and see that the food is served in correct portions and style.

Stage 3

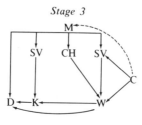

M—Manager	W—Waitress
SV—Supervisor	K—Kitchen worker
CH—Checker	D—Dishwasher
C—Customer	

In time, the owner-manager finds that he can accommodate a larger number of customers if he takes one more step in the division of labor. Up to now the cooks have been serving the food to the waitresses. When these functions are divided, both cooking and serving can proceed more efficiently.

Stage 4

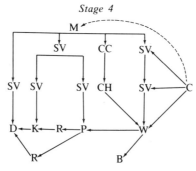

M—Manager	W—Waitress
SV—Supervisor	B—Bartender
CH—Checker	P—Pantry worker
CC—Cost control	K—Kitchen worker
supervisor	R—Runner
C—Customer	D—Dishwasher

Therefore, he sets up a service pantry apart from the kitchen. The cooks now concentrate on cooking, the runners carry food from kitchen to pantry and carry orders from pantry to kitchen, and the pantry girls serve the waitresses over the counter. This adds two more groups (pantry girls and runners) to be supervised, and, to cope with this and the larger scale of operation, the owner adds another level of supervision, so that there are two supervisors between himself and the workers. Somewhere along the line of development, perhaps he begins serving drinks and adds bartenders to his organization.

Stage 5 need not be diagrammed here, for it does not necessarily involve any structural changes in the individual unit. Here several units are tied together into a chain, and one or more levels of authority are set up in a main office above the individual unit structures.[4]

This expansion process magnifies old problems and gives rise to new ones. They may be considered under three headings: administration, the customer relationship, and the flow of work. Whenever we lengthen the hierarchy, adding new levels of authority to separate top executive from workers, the problem of administration becomes more complex. However, this is true for any organization, and therefore these problems of hierarchy need not be given special attention in an article on restaurants.

The particular problem of the large restaurant is to tie together its line of authority with the relations that arise along the flow of work. In the first instance, this involves the customer relationship, for here is where the flow of work begins. The handling of the customer relationship is crucial for the adjustment of the restaurant personnel, and a large part of that problem can be stated in strictly quantitative interaction terms: Who originates action for whom and how often? In a large and busy restaurant a waitress may take orders from fifty to one hundred customers a day (and perhaps several times for each meal) in addition to the orders (much less frequent) she receives from her supervisor. When we add to this the problem of adjusting to service pantry workers, bartenders, and perhaps checkers, we can readily see the possibilities of emotional tension—and, in our study, we did see a number of girls break down and cry under the strain.

Our findings suggested that emotional tension could be related directly to this quantitative interaction picture. The skilful waitress, who maintained her emotional equilibrium, did not simply respond to the initiative of customers. In various obvious and subtle ways she took the play away from customers, got them responding to her, and fitted them into the pattern of her work. She was also more aggressive than the emotionally insecure in originating action for other waitresses, service pantry people, and supervisor.

While in the rush hour the waitress works under a good deal of tension at best, the supervisor can either add to or relieve it. Here again we can speak in quantitative terms. In one restaurant we observed a change in dining-room management when a supervisor who was skilful in originating action for customers (thus taking pressure off waitresses) and who responded frequently to the initiation of waitresses was replaced by a supervisor who had less skill in controlling customers and who originated for the girls much more frequently and seldom responded to them. (Of the new supervisor, the waitresses would say, "She's always finding something to criticize"; "She's never around when we need her"; "She's always telling you; she doesn't care what you have to say"; etc.) This change was followed by evidences of increased nervous tension, especially among the less experienced waitresses, and finally by a series of waitress resignations.

Here we see that the customer-waitress, waitress-supervisor, waitress-service-pantry-worker relationships are interdependent parts of a social system. Changes in one part of the system will necessarily lead to changes in other parts. Furthermore, if the people involved in the system are to maintain their emotional balance, there must be some sort of compensatory activity to meet large interactional changes. For example, when waitresses are subject to a large increase in the originations of customers (at the peak of rush hours), the supervisor allows them to originate action for her with increasing frequency and diminishes the frequency with which she gives them orders. This is, in fact, the sort of behavior we have observed among supervisors who enjoy the closest co-operation with waitresses, as reported by the waitresses.

The customer relationship is, of course, only one point along the flow of work which brings orders from dining-room to kitchen and food from kitchen to dining-room. In a large restaurant operating on several floors, this is a long chain which may break down at any point, thus leading to emotional explosions in all quarters. The orders may go from waitress to pantry girl and then, as the pantry girl runs low in supplies, from pantry girl to pantry supplyman, from pantry supplyman to kitchen supplyman, and from kitchen supplyman to cook. And the food comes back along the same route in the opposite direction. Where drinks are served, the bar must be tied in with this flow of work, but there the chain is short and the problem less complex.

We have here a social system whose parts are interdependent in a highly sensitive manner. Thus the emotional tension experienced by waitresses is readily transmitted, link by link, all the way to the kitchen.

I have already noted how a skilful dining room supervisor may help to relieve the tension on the entire system at its point of origin. Here we may consider other factors which affect the relations among employees along the flow of work: status, sex relations, and layout and equipment.

I would propose the hypothesis that relations among individuals along the flow of work will run more smoothly when those of higher status are in a position to originate for those of lower status in the organization and, conversely, that frictions will be observed more often when lower-status individuals seek to originate for those of higher status. (This is, of course, by no means a complete explanation of the friction or adjustment we observe.)

While more data are needed on this point, we made certain observations which tend to bear out the hypothesis. For example, in one kitchen we observed supplymen seeking to originate action (in getting food supplies) for cooks who were older, of greater seniority, more highly skilled, and much higher paid. This relationship was one of the sore points of the organization. Still, we discovered that there had been one supplyman who got along well with the cooks. When we got his story, we found that he had related himself to the cooks quite differently from the other supplymen. He sought to avoid calling orders to the cooks and instead just asked them to call him when a certain item was ready. In this way, he allowed them to increase the frequency of their origination for him, and, according to all accounts, he got better co-operation and service from the cooks than any other supplyman.

Much the same point is involved in the relations between the sexes. In our society most men grow up to be comfortable in a relationship in which they originate for women and to be uneasy, if not more seriously disturbed, when the originations go in the other direction. It is therefore a matter of some consequence how the sexes are distributed along the flow of work. On this question we gave particular attention to the dining-room-service pantry and dining-room-bar relationships.

In the dining-room-pantry situation there are four possible types of relationship by sex: waiter-counterman, waiter-pantry girl, waitress-pantry girl, and waitress-counterman. We were not able to give much attention to the first two types, but we did make intensive studies of two restaurants illustrating the third and fourth types. Ideally, for scientific purposes, we would want to hold everything else constant except for these sex differences. We had no such laboratory, but the two restaurants were nevertheless closely comparable. They were both large, busy establishments, operating on several floors, and serving the same price range of food in the same section of the city.

Perhaps the chief differences were found in the dining-room-pantry relationship itself. In restaurant A, waitresses gave their orders orally to the pantry girls. On the main serving floor of restaurant B, waitresses wrote out slips which they placed on spindles on top of a warming compartment separating them from the countermen. The men picked off the order slips, filled them, and put the plates in the compartment where the waitresses picked them up. In most cases there was no direct face-to-face interaction between waitresses and countermen, and, indeed, the warming compartment was so high that only the taller waitresses could see over its top.

These differences were not unrelated to the problems of sex in the flow of work. One of the countermen in restaurant B told us that, in all his years' experience, he had never before worked in such a wonderful place. Most workers who express such sentiments talk about their relations with their superiors or with fellow-employees on the same job or perhaps about wages, but this man had nothing to say about any of those subjects. He would discuss only the barrier that protected him from the waitresses. He described earlier experiences in other restaurants where there had been no such barrier and let us know that to be left out in the open where all the girls call their orders in was an ordeal to which no man should be subjected. In such places, he said, there was constant wrangling.

This seems to check with experience in the industry. While we observed frictions arising between waitresses and pantry girls, such a relationship can at least be maintained with relative stability. On the other hand, it is difficult to prevent blowups between countermen and waitresses when the girls call their orders in. Most restaurants consciously or unconsciously interpose certain barriers to cut down waitress origination of action for countermen. It may be a warming compartment as in this case, or, as we observed in another restaurant, there was a man pantry supervisor who collected the order slips from the waitresses as they came in and passed them out to the countermen. There are a variety of ways of meeting the problem, but they all seem to involve this principle of social insulation.

The rule that all orders must be written also serves to cut down on interaction between waitresses and countermen, but this in itself is not always enough to eliminate friction. Where there is no physical barrier, there can be trouble unless the men who are on the receiving end of the orders work out their own system of getting out from under. Such systems we observed at one bar and at one of the serving counters in restaurant B. The counter in this case was only waist high. While the girls wrote out their orders, they were also able to try to spur the men on orally, and there was much pulling and hauling on this point both at the bar and at the pantry counter.

The men who did not get along in this relationship played a waiting game. That is, when the girls seemed to be putting on special pressure for speed, they would very obviously slow down or else even turn away from the bar or counter and not go back to work until the offending waitresses just left their order slips and stepped away themselves. Thus they originated action for the waitresses. While this defensive maneuver provided the men with some emotional satisfaction, it slowed down the service, increased the frustrations of the waitresses, and thus built up tensions, to be released in larger explosions later.

One bartender and one counterman not only enjoyed their work but were considered by waitresses to be highly efficient and pleasant to deal with. Both of them had independently worked out the same system of handling the job when the rush hour got under way. Instead of handling each order slip in turn as it was handed to them (thus responding to each individual waitress), they would collect several slips that came in at about the same time, lay them out on the counter before them, and fill the orders in whatever order seemed most efficient. For example, the bartender would go through the slips to see how many "Martinis," "Old Fashions," and so on were required. Then he would make up all the "Martinis" at once before he went on to the next drink.

When the work was done this way, the girl first in was not necessarily first out with her tray, but the system was so efficient that it speeded up the work on the average, and the girls were content to profit this way in the long run. The men described the system to us simply in terms of efficiency; but note that, in organizing their jobs, they had changed quantitatively the relations they had with the waitresses. Instead of responding to each waitress, they were originating action for the girls (filling their orders as the men saw fit and sending them out when the men were ready).

Along with our consideration of layout and equipment in the flow of work, we should give attention to the communication system. Where the restaurant operates on one floor, the relations at each step in the flow can be worked out on a face-to-face basis. There may be friction, but there is also the possibility of working out many problems on a friendly, informal basis.

When a restaurant operates on two or more floors, as many large ones do, face-to-face interaction must be supplemented by mechanical means of communication. We saw three such mechanical means substituted for direct interaction, and each one had its difficulties.

People can try to co-ordinate their activities through the house telephone. Without facial expressions and gestures, there is a real loss of understanding, for we do not generally respond solely to people's voices. Still, this might serve reasonably well, if the connection between kitchen and pantry could be kept constantly open. At least in the one restaurant where we gave this subject special attention, that solution was out of the question, as one call from kitchen to pantry tied up the whole house phone system and nobody could call the manager, the cashier, or anybody else on this system as long as another call was being made. Consequently, the telephone could be used only to supplement other mechanical aids (in this case, the telautograph).

The public address system has the advantage over the telephone that it can be used all the time, but it has the great disadvantage of being a very noisy instrument. Busy kitchens and service pantries are noisy places at best, so that the addition of a public address system might be most un-welcome. We do not yet know enough of the effect of noise upon the human nervous system to evaluate the instrument from this point of view, but we should recognize the obvious fact that surrounding noise affects the ability of people to communicate with each other and becomes therefore a problem in human relations.

The telautograph makes no noise and can be used at all times, yet it has its own disadvantages. Here we have an instrument in the service pantry and one in the kitchen. As the pantry supplyman writes his order, it appears simultaneously on the kitchen telautograph. The kitchen's replies are transmitted upstairs in the same way. The machine records faithfully, but it does not solve the problem of meaning in interaction. We may pass over the problem of illegibility of handwriting, although we have seen that cause serious difficulties. The more interesting problem is this: How urgent is an order?

When the rush hour comes along, with customers pushing waitresses, waitresses pushing pantry girls, and pantry girls pushing supplymen, the supplyman is on the end of the line so far as face-to-face interaction is concerned, and he is likely to get nervous and excited. He may then put in a larger order than he will actually use or write "Rush" above many of his orders. If he overorders, the leftovers come back to the kitchen at the end of the meal, and the kitchen supplymen and cooks learn thus that the pantry supplyman did not really know how much he needed. They take this into account in interpreting his future orders. And, when everything is marked "Rush," the kitchen supplymen cannot tell the difference between the urgent and not so urgent ones. Thus the word becomes meaningless, and communication deteriorates. Stuck in this impasse, the pantry supplyman may abandon his machine and dash down to the kitchen to try to snatch the order himself. The kitchen people will block this move whenever they can, so, more often, the pantry supplyman appeals to his supervisor. In the heat of the rush hour, we have seen pantry supervisors running up and down stairs, trying to get orders, trying to find out what is holding up things in the kitchen. Since they have supervisor status, the kitchen workers do not resist them openly, but the invasion of an upstairs supervisor tends to disrupt relations in the kitchen. It adds to the pressures there, for it comes as an emergency that lets everybody know that the organization is not functioning smoothly.

It is not the function of this article to work out possible solutions to this problem of communication. I am concerned here with pointing out a significant new area for sociological investigation: the effects on human relations of various mechanical systems of communication. It is difficult enough to coordinate an organization in which the key people in the supervisory hierarchy are in direct face-to-face relations. It is a much more difficult problem (and one as yet little understood) when the co-ordination must be achieved in large measure through mechanical communication systems.

IMPLICATIONS FOR THEORY AND METHODOLOGY

In presenting our observations on the restaurant industry, I have discussed formal structure, quantitative measures of interaction, symbols in relations to interaction, attitudes and interaction, and layout and equipment (including mechanical systems of communication). Data of these categories must be fitted together. The uses of each type of data may be summarized here.

1. *Formal structure.*—We have ample data to show that the formal structure (the official allocation of positions) does not *determine* the pattern of human relations in an organization. Nevertheless, it does set certain limits upon the shape of that pattern. Thus, to analyze the human problems of a restaurant, it is necessary to outline its structure in terms of length of hierarchy, divisions into departments, and flow of work (as done in the five stages above).

2. *Quantitative measures of interaction.*—Within the limits set by the formal structure, the relations among members of the organization may fall into a variety of patterns, each of which is subject to change.

The pattern we observe we call the *social system.* A social system is made up of *interdependent* parts. The parts are the *relations* of individuals in their various positions to each other. This is simply a first description of a social system, but there are important theoretical and practical conclusions which flow from it.

The relations of individuals to one another are subject to *measurement,* sufficient to allow them to be compared and classified. We can, for example, count the number of times that a waitress originates action for her customers compared with the number of times they originate it for her in a given period and observe how often she originates action for her supervisor and how often the supervisor does so for her, and so on, through the other relations in the system. So far, mathematically precise measurements of interaction have only been made in laboratory situations involving interviewer and interviewee.[5] Nevertheless, in the present state of our knowledge, we can get, through interviewing and observation, quantitative data which, though only approximate, are sufficiently accurate to allow us to predict the course of developments or explain how certain problems have arisen and point the way to their possible solution.

As the terms are used here, *interaction, origination,* and *response* are abstractions without content. That is, they are indices which have no reference to either the symbols used or the subjective reactions felt by the interacting individuals. Such measures do not, of course, tell us all it is useful to know of human relations. Indeed, many students will think it absurd to believe that any useful data can come from abstractions which leave out the "content" of human relations. To them I can only say that science is, in part, a process of abstraction, which always seems to take us away from the "real world." The value of such abstractions can be determined only by testing them in research to see whether they enable us better to control and predict social events.

Since the social system is made up of *interdependent relations,* it follows that a change in one part of the system necessarily has repercussions in other parts of the system. For example, a change in origin-response ratio between waitresses and supervisor necessarily affects the waitress-customer and waitress-service-pantry-girl relations, and changes in those parts lead to other changes in the system. Therefore, in order to study the social system or to deal with it effectively, it is necessary to discover the *pattern* of relations existing at a given time and to observe changes within that pattern. The nature of the interdependence of the parts of the system can be discovered only through observing how a change in Part A is followed by change in Part B, is followed by change in Part C, etc. Therefore, social systems must be studied *through time*. A static picture of the social structure of an organization is of little value. Science requires that we develop methods of study and tools of analysis to deal with constantly changing relations.

3. *Symbols in relation to interaction.*—We cannot be content simply with quantitative descriptions of interaction. We need to know why A responds to B in one situation and not in another or why A responds to B and not to C. In part, this is a matter of habituation, for we respond to the people we are accustomed to responding to and in the sorts of situations to which we are accustomed. But we must go beyond that to explain the development of new patterns and changes in old patterns of interaction.

We observe that individuals respond to certain symbols in interaction. I have discussed here status and sex as symbols affecting interaction (the problems of the originating from below of action for high status individual or by woman for man).

I have noted some problems in language symbols in the discussion of mechanical means of communication. That leaves the whole field of symbols in face-to-face interaction untouched, so that it represents only the barest beginning of an attempted formulation of the relations between symbols of communication and interaction.

Especially in economic institutions, it is important to examine the bearing of *economic symbols*[6] on interaction, but this is a large subject and can only be mentioned here.

As we analyze social systems, symbols should always be seen in terms of their effects upon interaction. They are *incentives* or *inhibitors* to interaction with specific people in certain social situations. Thus, to put it in practical terms, the manager of an organization will find it useful to know both the pattern of interaction which will bring about harmonious relations and also how to use symbols so as to achieve that pattern.

4. *Attitudes and interaction.*—Changes in relations of individuals to one another are accompanied by changes in their *attitudes* toward one another and toward their organizations. In recent years we have developed excellent methods for attitude measurement, but the measurement in itself never tells us how the attitudes came about. The whole experience of our research program leads us to believe that the dynamics of attitude formation and change can best be worked out as we correlate attitudes with human relations in the organizations we study.

5. *Layout and equipment.*—Here the sociologist is not directly concerned with the problems of the mechanical or industrial engineer. He does not undertake to say which machine or which arrangement of work space and machines will be most productively efficient. However, he cannot help but observe that, for example, the height of the barrier between waitresses and countermen or the nature of the mechanical communication system have important effects upon human relations. Only as these effects are observed do the physical conditions come in for sociological analysis. (Of course, human relations have a bearing upon efficiency, but the sociologist, if he tackles the problem of efficiency, uses types of data and schemes of analysis quite different from those used by the engineer.)

A few years ago there was a great debate raging: statistics versus the case study. That debate is no longer waged publicly, but it still troubles many of us. On the one hand, we see that an individual case study, skilfully analyzed, yields interesting insights—but not scientific knowledge. On the other hand, we find that nearly all statistical work in sociology has dealt with the characteristics of aggregates: How much of a given phenomenon is to be found in a given population? Such an approach does not tell us anything about the relations among the individuals making up that population. And yet, if we are to believe the textbooks, the relations among individuals, the *group* life they lead, are the very heart of sociology.

So let us have more individual case studies, but let us also place the individual in the social systems in which he participates and note how his attitudes and goals change with changes in the relations he experiences. And let us have more quantitative work, but let us at least bring it to bear upon the heart of sociology, measuring the relations among individuals in their organizations.

NOTES

1. The research was financed by the National Restaurant Association. The field work was done by Margaret Chandler, Edith Lentz, John Schaefer, and William Whyte. We made interview or participant-observation studies of twelve restaurants in Chicago and did some brief interviewing outside Chicago. From one to four months was spent upon each Chicago restaurant. In *Human Relations in the Restaurant Industry* (New York: McGraw-Hill Book Co., 1948), I report the study in detail. Since the book is primarily addressed to restaurant operators and supervisors, the sociological frame of reference given here does not duplicate the more detailed publication.

2. This is, of course, an oversimplified picture, for many factory workers interact also with inspectors, engineers, time-study men, etc., but the frequency of such interaction does not

compare with that which we observe between customers and waiters or waitresses in a restaurant.

3. I am indebted to Donald Wray for the particular structural approach presented here.

4. The structural changes arising with union organization are beyond the scope of this article. They are discussed in the book, *op. cit.*, in the chapter, "The Role of Union Organization."

5. Eliot D. Chapple, with the collaboration of Conrad M. Arensberg, *Measuring Human Relations: An Introduction to the Study of the Interaction of Individuals* ("Genetic Psychology Monographs," No. 22 [Provincetown, Mass.: Journal Press, 1940]); Eliot D. Chapple and Carleton S. Coon, *Principles of Anthropology* (New York: Henry Holt & Co., 1941), esp. first four chapters; Eliot D. Chapple and Erich Lindemann, "Clinical Implications of Measurement of Interaction Rates in Psychiatric Interviews," *Applied Anthropology,* I, No. 2 (January-March, 1942), 1-12.

6. See Whyte's "Economics and Human Relations in Industry" to be published in *Industrial and Labor Relations Review.*

DAVID RIESMAN

Some Observations on
the Limits of
Totalitarian Power

PREFACE (1964)

There was a time not so long ago when intelligent people sought to interpret totalitarianism either in terms of the ideological smoke screens of Communists or Nazis, or in terms of some conspiracy theory of history. As against such largely extrapolative interpretations, it was an intellectual advance to insist (as Hannah Arendt did in her brilliant and evocative *The Origins of Totalitarianism*) that modern totalitarianism brought something new into the world, not simply a new version of an older despotism or lust for power and destruction. Historians, to be sure, can find precursors for anything which exists now, and scholars have emphasized totalistic elements in the French Revolution, or for that matter, in the work of the Puritan reformers. Still, these earlier efforts at "permanent revolution" did not have quite the built-in psychological and political dynamism attained by specifically modern totalitarianism.

"Some Observations on the Limits of Totalitarian Power," was presented in 1951 at a meeting arranged by the American Committee for Cultural Freedom to discuss totalitarianism. I chose to emphasize not the savage, mysterious, terrifying aspects of totalitarianism (all of which we can find in some measure in ourselves) but the ordinary aspects that connect with our own more routine experience of human frailty, caprice, and jurisdictional dispute. I was emphasizing that the real world puts limits—not enough, to be sure—on the wishes of even the most powerful and cruel tyrants. I could safely do so without encouraging complacency toward the Communist countries, since I was on the program with such

The article "Some Observations on the Limits of Totalitarian Power" is reprinted with the permission of the Macmillan Company from *Individualism Reconsidered* by David Riesman. Copyright 1954 by the Free Press, a Corporation. The preface was taken from a different and later work by the author: *Abundance for What? And Other Essays* (pp.6-8). Copyright © 1964 by David Riesman. Reprinted and abridged by permission of the author, Doubleday and Company, Inc., and Chatto and Windus, Ltd.

experienced antitotalitarians as Hannah Arendt, Bruno Bettelheim, and Nathan Leites. But in the discussion it became clear, as it often has since, that many experts on the Soviet Union believe that no move is made anywhere in the Soviet sphere without Politburo planning and approval—doubtless the leaders wish it were so! Certainly, totalitarianism does make an effort to politicize all of life (just as both antifascism and anticommunism do when pushed to fanatical extremes); but it is a mistake to assume that such a movement, no matter how terrible its aims or clever its methods, can step outside of history entirely and cut all connections with social structures of an ordinarily inefficient sort.

I have no doubt that there has been created, in the phrase employed by Raymond Bauer, a "new Soviet man": dogmatic, puritanical, mechanical, and exploitative of his own and others' best human qualities. Even so, what the essay suggested was that the Soviet regime could not completely cut the bonds of human solidarity, extirpate weakness, and restructure human personality—yet. Many of my listeners and readers resented this idea; they seemed to feel that I, an unhurt outsider, was necessarily innocent, unable in my rationalistic liberalism to grasp the terrible monolithic quality of "the system." Because too many Americans had been inert in earlier decades when first faced with the challenge of totalitarian domination, the idea that there were elements of inertia and tradition even under Soviet communism seemed to many a kind of willful blindness.[1]

It is still common in Europe and elsewhere to regard Americans as inherently innocent, unable to grasp what communism is *really* like (and, increasingly, what poverty is *really* like). The charge has often been accurate. But with respect to communism, an overreaction may have occurred, so that Americans often show a greater and less controlled fear (and perhaps concealed admiration) of communism than do people who have lived more closely under its shadow. Americans on the whole were not prepared for the Hungarian Revolution, or for the riots that broke out in East Berlin in 1953, or later in Poland. The reminder that totalitarianism can kill men and silence them, but not permanently crush them, was a salutary one, even though the outcome was tragic for those who were trapped.

My paper was also criticized at the symposium by those who suggested that social science, in its effort to probe and understand our times, must necessarily miss the basic evils and deeper irrationalities of totalitarianism and remove our indignation and will to fight. I think I recognize these dangers. When I have made myself read some of the literature on concentration (and labor) camps, I have been aware of my wish for mechanisms to put this terrible material at a distance. Science can serve many concurrent aims; it can both disclose the truth and give a safe-conduct pass to the scientist—an asbestos coating in hell. But at the present time there are many thinkers to warn us that their tragic sense of life is more tragic than other people's tragic sense of life. In this atmosphere, people can plead rank on the basis of more intense suffering; and a refusal to use all available techniques for examination can appear as a noble disdain for evil and, at the same time, a recognition of its depth. We need both satire and sermon, both psychology and theology.

SOME OBSERVATIONS ON THE LIMITS OF TOTALITARIAN POWER   (1952)

Twenty and even ten years ago, it was an important intellectual task (and one in which, in a small way, I participated) to point out to Americans of good will that the Soviet and Nazi systems were not simply transitory stages, nor a kind of throwback to the South American way—that they were, in fact, new forms of social organization, more omnivorous than even the most brutal of earlier dictatorships. At that time, there were many influential people who were willing to see the Nazis as a menace but insisted that the Bolsheviks were a hope. And even today one can find individuals who have no inkling of the terror state—people who, for instance, blame "the" Germans for not throwing Hitler out or for compromising themselves by joining Nazi party or other organizations, or who attribute Soviet behavior to the alleged submissiveness of the Russian character or trace it back to Czarist despotism and expansionism and whatnot. Yet it seems to me that now the task of intellectual and moral awakening has been pretty well performed, and stands even in danger of being overperformed; in pursuit of the few remaining "liberals who haven't learned," groups such as this [the American Committee on Cultural Freedom] may mistake the temper of the country at large, misdeploy their energies, and, paradoxically, serve complacency in the very act of trying to destroy complacency.

Intellectual communication, in this as in other cases, cannot avoid the ambiguities arising from the differing attitudes in the American audience at large. I know that I will be misunderstood. For one thing, those who have suffered directly at the hands of the totalitarians, and who can undoubtedly find many audiences where complacency still rules—where, for example, the Soviet Union is still sneakingly regarded as somehow on the right track as against "capitalist exploitation"—such people may feel that I take too lightly the domestic well-wishers of the Soviet Union, or the lethargic. No one likes being robbed of a well-earned agenda.

Yet I cannot help but feel that the telling of atrocity stories—undoubtedly true stories—may have ambivalent consequences and, after a time, may harm the very cause in hand. Let me give as an illustration the way in which many liberals today, in government service or in academic life, repeat tales of loyalty-probe incompetence or injustice, of school-board and trustee confusion between liberals and "Reds," of stupid FBI questions, and so on. Such tales are meant to arouse us against the dangers of domestic reaction, but they have frequently the consequence of leading a government employee to burn back issues of *The New Masses,* of a faculty to drop *The Communist Manifesto* from its reading list, of a student to fear getting involved with even Americans for Democratic Action lest it prejudice his possibilities for employment. Then such tales are in turn spread, to justify still further concessions to an alleged need to conform to the prevailing climate of opinion...

Now I want to suggest that something of the same sort may occur if we begin, after greatly underestimating, greatly to overestimate the capacity of totalitarianism to restructure human personality. During the last war, I talked with people who were concerned with the plans for occupying Germany at war's end. Most assumed that there would be not only physical but organizational chaos and that it was necessary to have skilled civil affairs officers to take over tasks that the Germans, broken by Hitler and the war, could not assume for themselves. I felt that this was unduly patronizing of a great and gifted people, capable of spontaneous organization and of settling affairs with the Nazis if the occupying powers merely held the ring and supplied some necessities of life. I think we can make the same mistake—for I believe it was a mistake—about the Soviet Union and its satellites, and fail to see that even the terror is not omnipotent to destroy all bonds of organization among its victims.

Similarly, I think we can become so fascinated with the malevolence of Stalinism that we may tend to overestimate its efficiency in achieving its horrible ends; and we may mistake blundering compulsions or even accidents of "the system" for conspiratorial genius. Overinterpretation is the besetting sin of intellectuals anyway, and even when, with Hannah Arendt, we rightly point to the need to cast traditional rationalities aside in comprehending totalitarianism, we may subtly succumb to the appeal of an evil mystery; there is a long tradition of making Satan attractive in spite of ourselves. And the more practical danger of this is that we may, again reacting from underestimation,[2] misjudge not so much the aims as the power of the enemy and be unduly cowed or unduly aggressive as a result.

Consequently, I want to open up a discussion of some of the defenses people have against totalitarianism. Not that these defenses—I shall discuss apathy, corruption, free enterprise, crime, and so on—threaten the security system of the Soviets; that system is a new social invention and there are as few defenses against annihilation by it as against annihilation by atom bombs. Indeed, in some ways totalitarianism is actually strengthened by these partial defenses people are able to raise against it, which make it possible for many people to compromise with the system as a whole. But at least a few European thinkers may be perplexed by the readiness of Americans, lacking firsthand experience of people's capacity to resist, to assume that totalitarianism possesses the kind of psychological pressure system pictured by Orwell in that sadistic but symptomatic book *1984*: here is a fantasy of omnipotent totalitarian impressiveness which I think may itself, among those who admire efficiency and have little faith in man, be an appeal of totalitarianism for those outside its present reach.

For we must distinguish, first of all, between the appeals of totalitarianism when it is out of power and its appeals when in power; my concern here is mainly with the latter. Out of power, totalitarianism competes like any other party, only more so: it can be all things to all men, attracting the idealist by its promise to reform society, to clean out the swindlers; attracting the disoriented and bewildered by its simplistic "explanations" of their misery and of their world, and by promising to get rid of seeming anarchy by enforcing social co-operation; and attracting the sadist in the way the Berkeley study of the "Authoritarian Personality" has documented. (In the Moslem countries and the Far East, the Communists do not need even this much of an armory: a promise to drive out the foreign devils while promising Western-style commodities to everyone may be almost enough.) Most large-scale societies will offer a spectrum of people available for the high-minded, middle-minded, and low-minded aspects of totalitarian politics, though probably a crisis is necessary to convert their organization into a fighting revolutionary party with a real hope of capturing power. That is, the fact that totalitarianism has captured a country doesn't tell us as much as some observers have supposed about the character of its total population; the mass base necessary can be far less than a majority and it can include people of profoundly nontotalitarian personalities who have been fooled—to whom the appeal has not been a very deep-going one.[3]

When the latter wake up to the fact that the God they followed has failed them, it is of course too late to change deities. For many years it seemed to me that the Soviet Union was more dangerous in this respect than the Nazis, let alone the Fascists in Spain and Italy, because the latter were so clearly corrupt that they could not help but disillusion their idealists rapidly. Thus, during the Nazi regime, while the concentration camps were more or less hidden, the power and pelf struggles within the Nazi echelons were not: Hitler might remain for some unsullied, but hardly the party bums and barons of lesser magnitude, struggling to build up private empires of business and espionage. The ideological trappings fell away speedily enough. To be sure, there remained some fanatics, especially perhaps in the SS, savagely incorruptible. But many Germans who were drawn to the Nazis precisely by their claim to eliminate corruption were quickly enlightened when they saw the even greater corruption introduced. As against this, the Communists have seemed more incorruptible—a kind of Cromwellian type, hard-bitten and ascetic—thus perhaps retaining ideological impressiveness as well as gaining physical oppressiveness even after being installed in power. And certainly that impressiveness remains even today for many of those outside the system. Inside, however, there is some evidence—and of course only tantalizingly little—that corruption, blackmarketing, crime, and juggling of figures are widespread; presumably this makes it hard for the idealistic young to be overimpressed with the system's ethical rightness. To be sure, we have had such "training" in contempt for bourgeois comfort-seeking and the dangers of the desire for wealth, that if a Communist is desirous not of wealth but of power he can more readily appear idealistic; perhaps we should learn that the *auri sacra fames*, the cursed hunger for gold, is not half so dangerous to the human race as the ascetic drive for power—a point recently remade by Eric Hoffer in *The True Believer*. Indeed, anyone who claims he wishes to eliminate vice utterly is declaring a very dangerous and antihuman heresy—one all too prevalent, I might add, in today's municipal and national politics in this country. We must teach ourselves, and the young, to distinguish between genuine idealism and arrogant, curdled indignation against behavior which falls short of some monastic image of virtue.

More generally, I have long thought that we need to re-evaluate the role of corruption in a society, with less emphasis on its obviously malign features and more on its power as an antidote to fanaticism. Barrington Moore in *Soviet Politics,* and Margaret Mead in *Soviet Attitudes toward Authority* present materials documenting the Soviet campaign against the corrupting tendencies introduced into the system by friendship and family feeling—some of Mead's quotations could have come from Bishop Baxter or other Puritan divines, and others from American civil service reformers. While Kravchenko shows how one must at once betray friends in the Soviet regime when they fall under state suspicion—and here, too, the Soviets are more tyrannous than the Nazis who expected friends to intercede with the Gestapo—it would appear that such human ties have never been completely fragmented, whether by Puritanism,[4] industrialism, or their savagely sudden combination in Bolshevism. Actually, people have had to defend themselves against the Soviet system's high demands for performance by building personal cliques, by favoritism, by cultivating cronies; thus, an informal network has continued to operate alongside the formal one, whose extraordinary expectations can in fact be met only in this way. (Similarly, Petrov points out that no amount of indoctrination has persuaded the Russian people to like and admire spies and informers, or to extirpate from their own reactions the profoundly human emotion of pity.)

To be sure, corruption does not always and inevitably work as a solvent for ideological claims. Hannah Arendt, returning from Germany last year, described the way in which many middle-class, educated Germans, in order to justify to themselves within their rigid code the compromises they made with the Nazi system, had to exalt that system ideologically; they were trapped by complicity as they would not have been had they been more cynical. Incidentally, their wives, who had to hunt for subsistence on the black market, were probably better off in this respect—they did the needful things to keep going, while allowing their husbands to remain deceived in their older morality. And it could at least be argued that women—as the Bachofen-Fromm interpretation of the Oedipus trilogy would indicate—are more immune than men to impersonal and abstract ideals; they are more conservative in the good and in the bad sense—more "realistic."

I am not, it should be clear, discussing what are called resistance movements, but rather what might be called resistance quiescences. I am talking about the quieter modes of resistance to totalitarianism, not so much in practical life as in mental obeisance, in refusal to internalize the system's ethical norms. I am, moreover, quite unable to say what *proportion* of people, either under the Nazi regime or the Soviet, succumbed or managed to defend themselves in this way; I cannot assign quantitative weights to one mode or the other. It is one of our difficulties as intellectuals that we cannot easily assign such weights. We are likely to overestimate symbolic behavior that appears to give deference to totalitarian power. And the testimony of intellectuals who once believed in totalitarianism and have now fled it is further indication as to the dangers of a totalitarian regime for the emotional life of people like ourselves: ours is in many ways the most exposed position since overt obedience to mere power is least habitual, and since we need—whatever our rational beliefs about men's irrationality—to justify and integrate our behavior in some fashion, perhaps especially so when we ourselves are wholesalers or retailers of ideology.

Gunnar Myrdal, when he visited this country, commented on the "protective community" of the Negroes and of lower-class people generally who, vis-à-vis the whites and the authorities, "ain't seen nothing or nobody"; long training has made them adept in duplicity, evasion, and sly sabotage. (A similar phenomenon exists in Italian peasant communities, under the name of *"la omertà."*) True, this kind of protective community breaks down on occasion, even under the relatively mild pressures and promises of white or official society; the Soviets have much more violent and fearsome methods. Moreover, the Soviet secret police are facing a population most of which is new to urban life, ways and byways:

industrialization always stirs the melting pot and throws strange peoples together who have little understanding of or sympathy for each other, or whose suspicion of each other can be easily aroused. Whereas the workers of Hamburg were already accustomed to the industrial revolution and its problems and prospects of social interaction, the Soviet Union is in a sense one vast labor camp where social organization has to start pretty much from scratch.[5] Even so, I think it likely that there are protective communities in Russian farms and factories, which punish Stakhanovites and cope with spies.

In a brilliant article in *The Reporter*, Lionel Trilling has delineated the antisocial, antisocietal bent of a great deal of American literature: Huck Finn escaping the well-meant civilizing clutches of the Widow Douglas is a good illustration of his theme. But we may raise the question whether such escapes—if not to the open spaces then to a protective community or an underground institution like a blind pig or a whorehouse—are not to be found in all the major cultures which have any complex institutions at all, and possibly even in the simplest cultures if we only knew where to look for them. We must never underestimate the ability of human beings to dramatize, to play roles, to behave in ways that seem contradictory only if we do not appreciate the changes in scene and audience. A friend of mine, Mark Benney, riding a train with peasants in Nazi Germany, was struck by their impassivity of feature. When he and another stranger, a Nazi, got off the train, he could feel behind him a sudden relaxation of facial and postural tensions, and looking back he saw people who were, in a sense, not at all the same people.[6]

By the block system and the other machinery of a police terror, the Soviets can cut off many of the traditional underground institutions, and make others too hazardous for all but a few heroes. But even in such a case, human ingenuity is not completely helpless. Overfulfillment—literal obedience to extravagant Soviet demands—can be another form of sabotage; I have heard tell of one group of Moscow cynics who would go to meetings and joyfully accuse all and sundry of deviationism as a sure way to break up the party. All fanatical movements, I would suggest, are as threatened by the real or pretended deviations in the direction of perfect obedience as by the underground. Beyond all this, there remains the escape into the self, the escape of withdrawal, of what Kris and Leites have termed "privatization." The Soviet press, by its attacks on the practice, gives evidence that depoliticization tendencies are strong, and one would expect people to develop ritualized ways of responding to political exhortations without inner conviction.

In my 1931 visit to the Soviet Union, I talked with students who had decided to go into medicine or engineering, rather than journalism or writing, as more protected, less polemical and sensitive areas; doubtless, many of them were sadly fooled when, in the purges, they found themselves accused of sabotage and wrecking, or even theoretical deviations based on their seemingly unideological decisions. Ever since then, I have sought to find out whether young people were able to choose army careers, or skilled labor, as ways of avoiding such dangers; I have found some evidence that such escapes are extremely unlikely, since bright boys are already spotted in high school and compelled as well as bribed to develop their talents and deploy them; they cannot hide their light under a bushel.

One of the reasons why young people are willing to assume dangerous responsibilities is of course that the rewards of success in managerial posts are very great. It has become obvious that Soviet managers are no longer held, as in the earlier years of the regime, to ascetic standards of living. It is possible that, among the abler cadres, an entrepreneurial risk-taking attitude toward life is encouraged, which makes the prospect of becoming a factory manager with access to women, *dachas*, power, and glory worth taking the risk that it won't last, and may even be succeeded by exile and still grimmer fates—a psychology which bears some resemblance to that occasionally found among professional soldiers for whom battles mean promotions as well as deadly dangers.

But monetary rewards have their own logic. The loose change in people's pockets tends to encourage free enterprise or, as it is known in the Soviet Union, the black market. The black market also enters when managers scrounge for goods in order to fulfill production quotas and so remain managers. And business as usual, like other forms of corruption, is a wonderful "charm" against ideologies, useful particularly because of its own ordinarily unideological character. Under the Nazis, both in Germany and in the occupied countries, business was often almost an unconscious sabotage of the regime: people in pursuit of their private ends violated the public rules without, so to speak, intending any resistance. They did not have to be heroes, any more than the scofflaws were who drank under American prohibition, or the fellow who wants to make a fast buck in the Western war economies. Guenter Reimann, in his book *The Vampire Economy*, tells as a characteristic story the answer to a question as to what a permit from a Party member for a certain commodity would cost: "Well, it all depends on what kind of a Party member you have to deal with. If he no longer believes in National Socialism, it will cost you a hundred marks. If he still does, five hundred marks. But if he is a fanatic, you will have to pay a thousand marks."[7]

In the past, we have tended to interpret such signs of passive resistance in terms of our hope for an eventual overthrow of the system from within; we have been like the Marxists who thought contradictions would bring capitalism down. Now we know that it takes more to destroy a system than its own contradictions, and we have been apt to go to the other extreme and assume that the system, therefore, since it didn't collapse, was all-seeing and all-powerful over the minds of men. Two errors common to the social sciences have worked together to this end. The first error, as just indicated, is to imagine social systems as monolithic, and as needing to be relatively efficient to remain in power. Actually, systems roll on, as people do, despite glaring defects and "impossible" behavior. We have created an imaginary image of what it takes for an institution to keep going; in fact, it can go on with little support and less efficiency. One reason for this mirage we have is that when a revolution does occur, we explain it as a matter of course by pointing to the defects of the previous system—and we fall here into the error of supposing that what happened *had* to happen. Barring relatively accidental factors, the system might well have gone on for a long while. (Incidentally, this same historicist error is an element in the overestimation of the power of totalitarian appeals; we assume, for example, that these appeals were responsible for Hitler's victory in Germany as if that victory were a foregone conclusion and not a series of reversible choice-points.) Social scientists, having logical minds and being efficient themselves—even when they sing the praises of irrationality— seldom take a sufficiently perspectivistic view of a society to see it as rolling along in spite of all the things which should bring it to a stop. In this error, of course, they do not stand alone; most of us tend to overinterpret the behavior of others, especially perhaps when we are menaced by them.

The second error, which is perhaps historically older, is more formidable. It assumes that men can be readily manipulated and controlled, either as the earlier Utopians thought in pursuit of some greatly uplifted state, or as the more recent anti-Utopians such as Huxley and Orwell have thought, in pursuit of vulgarity and beastliness. (Orwell, to be sure, exempts his proles from the ravages of ideology.) Social science is concerned with prediction, with categorizing human beings and social systems. So it has perhaps a professional bias toward cutting men down to the size of the categories, and not allowing them to play the multiplicity of roles, with the multiplicity of emotional responses, that we constantly show ourselves capable of. Thus we run into a paradox. On the one hand, we think men can be adjusted into some Brave New World because of fundamental human plasticity and flexibility, while on the other hand we do not see that men's ability precisely to fit, part-time, into such a world is what saves them from having to fit into it as total personalities. We have assumed—and in this of course we reflect our own cultural attitudes—that people must be co-operative in order to co-operate, whereas throughout history people have co-operated because to do so made realistic sense, because certain conditions were met, and not because of the psychological appeal of co-operation per se. We have, under the pressure of recent events, reacted against the older view of writers like Sumner that people and cultures can hardly be changed at all toward the view that they can not only be changed but can be easily destroyed.

Ever since the rise of the bourgeoisie and of public opinion and mass politics, people have been afraid of the seeming chaos created by the open fight of special interest groups. The fight is open because there is a press and because each group tries both to solidify its own members and to recruit others by universalizing its appeals. In the contemporary world, there are many influential men who believe that this war of vested interests, occurring within the framework of a democratic society, will endanger consensus and disrupt the entire social fabric. Totalitarianism, in fact, makes an appeal, less to people's special interests as, let us say, workers, than to their fear of all competing interests, including even their own as these are organized by lobbies and pressure groups. Having an image of society as it ought to be, as orderly and co-operative, they tend to welcome, especially of course when the going gets rough, a system which promises to eliminate all social classes and other vested interests which impede co-operation. Thus, on the one hand they are frightened by the ideal of a pluralistic, somewhat disorderly, and highly competitive society—still the best ideal in the business, in my opinion—while on the other hand, their view of men as plastic allows them to suppose that the totalitarians will change all that and transform men into automatically socialized creatures like the ants. When we put matters this way, we can see that there may be grandiose fantasies at the bottom of the fears of people like Orwell, deeply repressed fantasies of human omnipotence such as Hannah Arendt has traced in the totalitarians themselves.

For me, the most striking conclusion to be drawn from the state of Germany today, from the stories of the refugees from behind the Iron Curtain, even from the present behavior of former concentration camp inmates, is precisely how hard it is permanently to destroy most people psychologically. Once the terror is removed, they appear to snap back, ravaged as in any illness, but capable of extraordinary recuperative efforts. In extreme situations such as Dr. Bettelheim has described, people sink to almost incredible abysses or more rarely rise to incredible heights; but if they survive at all, they exhibit an astonishing capacity to wipe away those nightmares.

As the concept of social harmony and integration has misled us as to the amount of disorganization a going society can stand, so I believe that the concept of psychological integration has misled us as to the amount of disintegration and inconsistency of response that an individual can stand. Even in our society, we tell lies to ourselves and others all day long; we are split personalities; yet, with a minimum amount of support from the system, we manage to keep going. All our days we give hostages to history and fortune, and yet are able to call on self-renewing aspects of the ever filled cup of life.

A certain immunity to ideologies seems to me to be spreading in the world, if not as fast as totalitarianism, at least in its wake. This immunity is far from perfect, even in its own terms. Totalitarianism can appeal to cynics in their cynicism just as much as to idealists in their idealism. An ideology can be fashioned out of anti-ideology, as totalitarian parties have been fashioned out of an anti-party program. And a world is certainly ill-omened in which we must fear the enthusiasm of the young, and prefer their apathy, because we have learned (a hundred and fifty years after Burke) to fear ideas in politics.

We simply do not know whether, over a series of generations, it is possible to rob people even of the freedom of their apathy. Very likely people need at least some ability to communicate disaffection if they are not to conclude that only they alone are out of step. And privatization implies accepting the given regime as part of the order of nature, not to be fought by the likes of oneself—only in that way can terrible guilt feelings be avoided.[8] There comes to mind the story of a German anti-Nazi who, shortly after Hitler's coming, had taken a job as stenographer to an SS committee. Everything went well for a while; his convictions remained unshaken, and he continued old Socialist associations. But then one day he had a paralysis of his right arm; he could not move it at all. He went to a psychiatrist, who came quickly to the source of the paralysis, namely that the stenographer could not resign himself to the constant Heil Hitler salutes.

And, indeed, many of the defenses I have discussed are little better than forms of paralysis which, by their presence, evidence the resistance men put up against seemingly implacable destinies. I would prefer to see men fighting back through paralysis than succumbing through active incorporation of the enemy. But this is hardly an optimum way to live one's life, and we cannot be—even apart from the danger to ourselves—unmoved by the plight of those now living and dying under Communist regimes. All we can do while we seek ways to bring those regimes down without war is to find our way to a more robust view of man's potentialities, not only for evil, about which we have heard and learned so much, not only for heroism, about which we have also learned, but also for sheer unheroic cussed resistance to totalitarian efforts to make a new man of him.

NOTES

1. Many anti-Nazis have contributed, I think, to wrong evaluations of Hitler's aims and accomplishments. When I was briefly in Germany in 1931, my colloquial German (learned from a nurse "just off the boat" who knew no English) was just enough to allow me to talk with students and other young men who were Nazis. Many of them were very idealistic—indeed, it was their ideals, as well as their unconscious aggressions, that were betraying them. I then thought it likely that Germany would fall to Hitler, and wondered at the complacency of the older people who felt, with the wisdom of experience, that if Hitler did reach power the responsibility would sober him—as it had sobered the Social Democrats. To be sure, when Hitler took power in 1933, he was in many ways quite inhibited and cautious; he was less confident of the outcome in the early years, both before and after 1933, than many who now retroactively see a malign logic in all that he did. Without tacit or open support from the Western democracies before 1939 and from the Soviet Union after that, he might neither have stayed in power nor brought on the war, and but for the war it is unlikely that he would have achieved his aim of totalitarian domination (or his extermination of the Jews); even at the height of the war scholars now believe, his industry was less geared to war production than that of the United States.

2. I have had some fairly extended experience of this. I remember in 1931 talking with American engineers in the Soviet Union who thought the Russians too incompetent in the mechanical arts ever to build tractors, let alone planes; they failed, as it seemed to me, to realize how the huge friction of Soviet incompetence could be partly overcome by the even huger burning up of human resources if one cared not at all about them. Likewise, when some seemed complacent about the Chinese Communists on the ground that "you could never organize the unbelligerent Chinese for aggressive war," I felt that this left out of account the awful weapon of systematic terror and utter ruthlessness about killing one's "own" people that is Moscow's first export to its satellites and "national" Communist parties.

3. What I have said here needs to be qualified by an understanding of the less conscious motives which attract people to a totalitarian party. The Nazis, for example, were not really all things to all men; they gave the wink to some men that, for instance, their legality was merely window dressing, and the latter could use the window dressing to satisfy their conscious inhibitions against what at bottom drew them to the party. See, for example, Erik H. Erikson's discussion of "Hitler's Imagery and German Youth," in *Childhood and Society* (Norton, 1950), pp. 284-315.

4. While I think that there are many revealing analogies between theocratic Calvinism in its heyday and Stalinism, I do not think the similarities should be pressed too far; among many other differences, the Puritans—in any case, far less powerful—believed in law.

5. There is no space here to go into the analogous problem of the concentration camps themselves. Kogon's and David Rousset's accounts would seem to indicate that in these camps some prisoner rule developed, and much corruption (reminiscent of the kangaroo courts in the worst American jails), with various groups of prisoners fighting among themselves, and with guard allies, for hegemony. When I raised this problem in the Committee's meeting, Hannah Arendt insisted that the camps described by Kogon and Rousset were exceptions, and that in most no such prisoner ingenuities and defenses developed. Reliable evidence is hard to come by; see, however, Theodore Abel, "The Sociology of Concentration Camps" in December, 1951, *Social Forces,* vol. 30, pp. 150-55, which offers some support for my own position; and see, also, David P. Boder, *I Did Not Interview the Dead* (University of Illinois Press, 1949).

6. In a letter, Norman Birnbaum has suggested that the peasants' uneasiness was prepolitical—due to their natural reserve with urban people (city slickers) not of their kind. But he also points out that if this were the case it would not change the fundamental fact; the ability of people to be "two-faced" and to practice social concealment on the basis of minimal cues.

7. Dr. Arendt in her rebuttal criticized the relevance of this and similar incidents on the ground that they occurred prior to Germany's entry into World War II—prior, that is, to the descent of the iron curtain which protected and facilitated complete totalitarianism. Without the slightest doubt, the Nazis grew ever more ferocious as the war progressed—thus, mass

genocide did not really get under way until then; nevertheless, just because of the iron curtain, it is all the more necessary to examine whether the system did ever become efficiently monolithic even when all possible restraints of a humanitarian or public-relations sort disappeared. Cf. Trevor-Roper's *The Last Days of Hitler* (2nd ed., The Macmillan Company, 1950).

8. We must be careful in evaluating evidence here. A group of people near Frankfurt remarked to Everett Hughes, when he had won their confidence, *"Unter Hitler war Es doch besser."* This did not mean they had been or were still Nazis, but just the opposite, namely that they were making an unideological judgment, immune as well to Occupation, to democracy, as to Nazism.

CHARLES E. FRITZ

Disasters Compared in
Six American
Communities

INTRODUCTION

Before reporting on our findings, I would like to describe the nature and purposes of the National Opinion Research Center Disaster Project. Since 1950, the Center has maintained a specially-trained disaster team to conduct field investigations of domestic disasters. The maintenance of rapid re-establishment of effective social organization in community disasters, either wartime or peacetime, is the central problem with which the project is concerned. Subsumed under this more general problem are many specific problems concerning human behavior in disasters—e.g., the nature of fear and panic reactions, crowd behavior, leadership, rumor and other forms of communication, the effectiveness of various rescue, relief, control, information and rehabilitation measures, and the changes in personality and social structure which are produced by disasters. The practical aim of the project is to develop findings which will aid the development of effective disaster preparedness and control measures.

The project has been designed to cover disasters varying in scope, type of disaster, and type of groups or population affected—with a view to deriving a systematic body of knowledge concerning human behavior under conditions of stress. Altogether, we have interviewed nearly 1,000 persons who have been involved in over 70 different major or minor crises—ranging from large-scale tornadoes, explosions, and earthquakes to airplane crashes, industrial fires and accidents, building collapses, train wrecks, and so on. However, the majority of our interviews were obtained in 8 field trips to the following community disasters:

1) An airplane crash into a crowd of air show spectators in the small farming community of Flagler, Colorado, September 15, 1951. The crash killed 20 persons and injured approximately 30.

Reprinted with the permission of the Society for Applied Anthropology and the author from "Disasters Compared in Six American Communities," *Human Organization* 16 (Summer 1957): 6-9.

2) A series of house explosions and fires occurring over a period of about two hours in Brighton, New York, September 21, 1951. Despite heavy property damage—16 houses completely demolished, and about 25 heavily to slightly damaged—only 2 persons were killed and 24 injured.

3) The West Frankfort, Illinois coal mine explosion, December 21, 1951, which killed 119 miners.

4) Three separate airplane crashes in Elizabeth, New Jersey which took place within a period of two months. The first occurred on December 16, 1951; the second, on January 22, 1952, and the third on February 11, 1952. Each of the crashes involved passenger planes and each occurred in different residential areas of the city. Total death toll for the three crashes was 106 passengers, and 10 residents of Elizabeth; approximately 50 passengers and residents suffered injuries.

5) The Bakersfield, California earthquake of August 22, 1952. Damage extended over 98 city blocks, with the central business district sustaining the heaviest destruction. The earthquake occurred during business hours; however, only 2 persons were killed and 32 injured.

6) A tornado in White County, Arkansas, March 21, 1952. Part of a widespread series of devastating tornadoes covering 6 states, the tornado in White County was particularly severe. At least 49 persons were killed, and 675 injured. Over 400 houses were demolished and nearly 600 damaged.

The design of each field investigation has been varied to suit the particular problems and events studied. In general, however, the various studies have had a number of features in common. First, although our studies have covered a very large range of problems, we have put primary emphasis upon the reactions and problems occurring during the immediate emergency and post-emergency period. This is the period in which the greatest stress and disorganization occur. In order to obtain valid data on the immediate behavior of the community being studied, we have attempted to get into the field as rapidly as possible. Most of our field investigations have begun within a period of a few hours to three days following the occurrence of the event. Length of time in the field has ranged from one to three weeks, depending upon the scope of the study.

The persons selected for interviewing are divided into two groups: 1) those representing the general population of the community; 2) those persons who were in a special position to observe the work of the various formal and informal rescue, relief, information, medical, control, and rehabilitation groups or agencies. For convenience, we label these the "general" sample and the "special" sample respectively.

In the general sample, the purpose has been to determine differences in the behavior of persons in relation to their spatial, physical, and social psychological involvement in the situation. In practice, this means that we select persons ranging from those most directly and intimately affected (e.g., those who were themselves directly in impact; seriously injured or incapacitated; persons who had family members or other intimates killed or injured; or whose house or other personal property was destroyed or damaged) to those indirectly or remotely affected (e.g., had acquaintances injured, experienced the disruption of community services; and persons who suffered no deprivations but learned of the event indirectly through rumor or the mass media of communication). The methods used in selecting this general sample have varied somewhat, depending upon the nature of the problems focused upon. In the smaller scale investigations, a combination of purposive and random area sampling have been used; in the large-scale study of the Arkansas tornado (over 400 interviews), five separate communities having differing types and degrees of involvement were selected and respondents from these communities were chosen by probability methods.

The major purpose of the special sample is to derive information concerning the behavioral and logistic problems faced by the various formal and informal groups who assume responsibility for the various relief, rehabilitation, and control functions. These "special informants" include representatives of the local, state, and national government, Red Cross, Salvation Army, Civil Defense, police and fire departments, hospitals, mortuaries, utilities companies, radio stations, newspapers, etc., and informal and emergent leaders of various types. In this sample, we attempt to obtain a complete coverage of the formal and informal groups who performed the various functions already mentioned.

A disaster, by its very nature, tends to individuate behavior because it initially confronts persons with unpredictable and highly divergent situations. The same disaster means many different things to the affected populace, depending largely upon the nature of their involvement and their previous experience. If you try to superimpose a rigid, preformulated structure upon the event, you are likely to be misled.

For this reason, we have used an almost completely unstructured, non-directive type of interviewing in all of our investigations.[1] The major goal of the interview is to determine how the actor structured or defined the situation and to obtain an exhaustive account of the meaning of the event for him and his immediate associates. Using minimal probing activity and neutral questions whenever needed, the interviewer tries to obtain a complete account of the person's objective and subjective behavior during the pre-impact, impact, and post-impact period; how his behavior influenced and was influenced by interaction with others; his observations and evaluations of the behavior of other persons, groups, and agencies; and his previous experience in disasters and other crises. The final report on this series of studies will take the form of both descriptive and statistical analysis.

In this paper some of the general findings of our studies are presented.

The detailed and carefully tested findings of these investigations will not be available until the completion of the present analysis.[2] However, our experience during the past four years indicates that there is substantial evidence to support these general findings.

SOCIAL PSYCHOLOGICAL EFFECTS OF DISASTER

A few general observations of the nature of disaster behavior in relation to the *type of disaster* follow. Several factors should be taken into account in comparing disasters: 1) the speed of the precipitating agent and length of forewarning to the population; 2) the nature of the destructive agent; 3) the physical scope and destructiveness of the disaster; and 4) the length of the threat.

Our data indicate that an instantaneous disaster—i.e., one in which there is no forewarning—tends to produce the maximum in social and psychological disruption. If persons are given sufficient forewarning to prepare psychological and social defenses, the traumatic effects of the disaster will be minimized. Similarly, if the nature of the destructive agent is clearly perceivable and is well known to the affected populace, it is less likely to be psychologically disturbing than if the agent cannot be directly perceived and its effects are unknown. With reference to the physical scope and destructiveness of the disaster, the evidence suggests that the larger the number of persons killed or injured and the greater the amount of property destroyed, the greater the intensity and scope of the psychological impact. However, the types of persons affected and the nature of the deaths, injuries, and property destruction may introduce important qualifications to this generalization. To cite only one example: Men who successfully withstood active combat and witnessed considerable bloodshed during World War II frequently report that the sight of "helpless" women and children being killed or injured is much more disruptive psychologically than any wartime experience. A further important feature in studying the social psychological effect of disasters concerns the length of the threat. If the threat is over quickly, the affective reactions and social disorganization are likely to be less intense and briefer in duration than if the population is subjected to prolonged or intermittent stress.

At least two general social features should be taken into account when making social psychological comparisons of disasters: 1) the nature of the social situation at the time of impact; and 2) the previous degree of social solidarity among the affected populace. The first is of paramount importance in determining the initial responses to the disaster. The maximum in disruption of the population is likely to occur if the disaster takes place when families and other primary group members are separated. The anxiety and concern over missing family members and intimates usually leads to desperate seeking and searching activity and considerable social disruption. Contrarily, the fear and anxiety engendered by the impact tend to be minimized when primary group members are together at the time of impact or their whereabouts can be quickly ascertained immediately following impact.

With regard to the influence of the pre-existent solidarity, the comparison of our disaster cases suggests that a socially cohesive community is likely to recover more quickly from the impact than a community characterized by lack of social solidarity. In the former, spontaneous mutual assistance and emotional support tend to minimize the psychological impact. However, close social relationships among an affected population also have a negative aspect—namely, that the secondary shock of the loss of members of the community and communal property is more widely shared than in a community where the social relationships are more constricted.

COMMON PERCEPTIONS IN DISASTER

In presenting a few of the more specific findings of our study, I would like to indicate some which seem to parallel those reported by Dr. Spiegel. He indicated that the initial disaster cues were interpreted within a normal frame of reference. This tendency to assimilate disaster cues to a normal definition is particularly common in an instantaneous disaster or in a disaster where the precipitating agent is unknown or undetectable. In the Arkansas tornado, for example, many persons initially interpreted the "roaring" sound of the tornado as a train passing on the railroad tracks nearby. In a carbon monoxide asphyxiation incident occurring in an industrial plant, we found that most of the workers initially assimilated their physical symptoms to such "normal" definitions as excessive eating or drinking, staying up too late the night before, chronic illnesses from which they normally suffered, and so forth. In some cases, this process of assimilation went on for so long that they inhaled nearly fatal doses of the gas before they became aware of the danger in their immediate surroundings.

This is closely related to another common feature of disaster perceptions—i.e., the tendency for persons to assess the nature and extent of the disaster in terms of their immediate surroundings. For example, when a sudden increase in the gas main pressure set off the widespread series of house explosions in Brighton, New York, each housewife initially tended to interpret the situation in terms of her own household. "I thought it was *my* gas in *my* house," was a typical expression of this tendency. This tendency for individuation of interpretation is understandable, of course, in terms of the limited spatial perspective of any given actor or set of actors. However, it is precisely this tendency, together with the nature of the person's ego-involvement, which helps account for the heterogeneity of behavior in relation to the threat. Each person or group tends to act initially on the basis of a definition that is somewhat private, in the sense that it is formulated on the basis of the immediate situation which he perceives. The highly variegated nature of the situations in any large-scale disaster makes for considerable heterogeneity in the behavior of the populace.

INITIAL BEHAVIOR IN DISASTER

Another observation concerning the initial forms of behavior occurring in disasters can be made. The imagery of disaster behavior that is often fostered by the popular literature is one which pictures the population engaging in bizarre, irrational, uncontrolled, and maladaptive types of behavior. This is a grossly distorted and inaccurate picture. It seems to arise from the failure to differentiate between social disorganization and individual disorganization. It is true that the initial behavior frequently violates the usual social expectations and is often socially disorganized. However, as Thomas and Znaniecki pointed out, social disorganization and individual disorganization are not necessarily coextensive, and nowhere is this better exemplified than in the initial responses of a disaster struck population. From the point of view of the actor, the usual norms are no longer appropriate to the changed situation which he can perceive. In view of his immediate situation, the behavior may be quite rational, controlled, and adaptive. The "total picture" frequently distorts this essential fact.

As a matter of fact, the evidence from our studies is overwhelming in indicating that the non-rational and uncontrolled forms of behavior are much rarer and much briefer in duration than is commonly supposed. Panic, for example, is a relatively infrequent form of behavior on the part of persons in an impact area. Defined as an acute fear reaction followed by flight behavior, it tends to occur only under fairly specific conditions: 1) when a person or group is immediately and directly threatened by danger (e.g., when an explosion or fire occurs in his immediate vicinity); and 2) the person or group defines the situation as one in which escape is possible at the moment but may become impossible in the immediate future. Moreover, when it does occur, panic tends to be short-lived, lasting only until the person escapes from the immediate source of danger. Controlled withdrawal—i.e., where the withdrawal is not only oriented in terms of *escape from* the danger but *movement toward* a goal—is a much more common form of behavior than panic. In general, the goal-oriented forms of behavior are much more common than the uncontrolled, non-rational types, even on the part of persons who are in the epicenter of a disaster. Persons on the periphery or outside the impact area most frequently engage in anxiety motivated behaviors—e.g., attempting to locate, rescue, or retrieve intimates or other cherished objects in the impact area. It is not the irrationality or maladaptiveness of individual behavior that raises logistic and control problems in disasters; rather it is the lack of coordination among the large number of actors who are acting on the basis of relatively private definitions. This is why the reestablishment of the channels of communication becomes so crucial in disasters. In order to restore concerted behavior, it is necessary to substitute a common or collective definition for the multitude of private definitions.

LEADERSHIP IN DISASTER

It has already been indicated that the assurance of the safety of intimates and a high degree of previous solidarity are positively related to self-control and organized response to disaster. Additional positive factors include the possession of specific, well-defined role responsibilities; previous experience in disasters; pre-rehearsed plans of action; the possession of disaster-related skills; and the absence of strong ego-involvements in the disaster.

Generally speaking, we have found that persons who take an organizing, initiating, or leadership role in disasters have one or more of the above characteristics, and I believe that it is reasonable to hypothesize that the greater the number of these characteristics or relationships, the greater the likelihood of a person taking a leadership role. We have found that emergent disaster leaders tend to fall into two major categories: 1) those whose usual occupational or social roles have inured them to danger and prepared them for the types of problems which are found in disasters, and 2) those who have no strong ego-involvements in the disaster. Preeminent among the first group are the "disaster role functionaries"—e.g., firemen, policemen, physicians, nurses, utilities workers, priests, morticians, etc. Since they are prepared for the types of problems which arise in disaster, the event usually does not constitute as shattering an experience for them as it does for the general populace. Hence, they can maintain self-control or regain their self-control more quickly. These persons, of course, do not necessarily take an organizing or leadership role with reference to the large community. Oftentimes, they experience a definite role conflict. The physician, for example, may be faced with the choice of assuring the safety and care of his wife and child or playing his professional role as physician. Unless these persons are assured of the relative safety of persons with whom they are highly ego-involved, the conflict is initially resolved in favor of concern for primary group attachments.

Strangers and other persons who have no strong emotional involvement in the disaster also appear more likely to take an initial leadership role. Having no strong ego-involvements, they can maintain greater detachment and critical control over their behavior than residents who have such involvements. All of this suggests that, ideally, disaster leadership should be composed of persons who have a great deal of training and empirical experience in disasters and who have minimal involvement in the community struck by the disaster.

I do not wish to imply by the latter statement that a disaster-struck community becomes completely helpless and dependent. On the contrary, we have found that the greater share of the immediate rescue and relief work is undertaken by persons or agencies in the stricken community, often before the arrival of outside aid. This informal relief work usually consists of thousands of small, spontaneous acts which, in summation, are of major importance in coping with the emergency. However, for the most part, these efforts are uncoordinated and unsystematic in nature. The community-oriented, coordinating, organizing type of leadership is most frequently performed by persons with special training and lack of strong ego-involvement.

CONCLUSION

In conclusion, I would like to comment briefly on a problem mentioned by Dr. Spiegel—i.e., the problem of blame, resentments, hostility, and aggressions in disasters. Much of the literature suggests the notion that scape-goating or the assessment of blame is a sort of automatic by-product of disasters or crises. Furthermore, there is a rather widespread belief that the expression of hostility is a matter of aggressive reaction to the deprivations posed by a disaster and is capable of being discharged against any target. The choice of a target, according to this conception, is an irrational, fortuitous process.

Our data do not support these contentions. We have not found widespread or intense hostile feelings or aggressive actions in any of the disasters that we have investigated, including the "man-made" ones. Persons who experience the most intense losses and deprivations frequently exhibit no feelings of resentment or aggression. Of course, people do speculate on the cause or reasons for the disaster. However, this is usually a fairly rational process, aimed at understanding the event and control over possible future occurrences. It does not necessarily indicate that the objects singled out will be the object of aggressive orientation or action. Our evidence suggests that feelings of resentment or hostility are unlikely to be generated, or will be of little consequence, unless the following conditions apply: 1) the persons or groups singled out for responsibility have been grossly negligent in the performance of their expected roles or the actions or inaction of these persons or groups blatantly violates the general social norms or established values; and 2) there was widespread dissatisfaction or antagonism toward these persons or groups prior to the disaster. Admittedly, this problem needs further study, particularly by periodic re-sampling of the same disaster-struck population over a long time span. Some of the feelings of resentment are likely to arise in the later stages of relief and rehabilitation, when discriminations are made in terms of "who gets what and why."

NOTES

1. Tape recorders are used to obtain a complete transcript of the interview. In their tape recorded form, the interviews range in length from approximately 15 minutes to four hours with an average length of about one and one-half hours. The typewritten manuscripts of the interviews obtained in the eight field trips mentioned average 29 pages per interview; yielding a total of over 15,000 typewritten pages.

Systematic codes are currently being built for the interviews obtained in the 8 field investigations. When the final code structure is completed, each case will be coded and later transferred to IBM cards for statistical tabulation.

2. (Editor's Note:) The final, three-volume report on the NORC Studies was completed in 1954. See Eli S. Marks, Charles E. Fritz, *et al.*, "Human Reactions in Disaster Situations" (Unpublished report, National Opinion Research Center, University of Chicago, Report No. 52, June 1954). (Available to qualified Armed Services Technical Information Agency users as ASTIA document No. AD-107594.) A review of some of the salient findings of these studies is contained in Charles E. Fritz and Eli S. Marks, "The NORC Studies of Human Behavior in Disaster," *Journal of Social Issues*, X, No. 3 (1954), pp. 26-41.